EX LEBRES

PREACHING VALUES
in the
EPISTLES OF PAUL

Halford E. Luccock

PREACHING VALUES
in the
EPISTLES
OF PAUL

Volume I

ROMANS AND FIRST CORINTHIANS

HARPER & BROTHERS   NEW YORK

CONTENTS

6 CONTENTS

FOREWORD

In the life of Dean Stanley there is a story of a visit which Merle d'Aubigne, the historian of the Reformation, once paid to a prominent Roman Catholic ecclesiastic. The dignitary, not knowing his visitor, spoke to him of the advantages the Roman Church enjoyed in possessing the bones of St. Paul.

D'Aubigne answered modestly, "We, too, have some relics of St. Paul."

"Indeed," said the priest. "What are they?"

"We have some letters," replied D'Aubigne.

The letters are indeed "relics of St. Paul"! They are part of the great heritage of the Church and of the world. They are amazingly alive, for a great soul has poured his life into them. The words of St. Paul in his letters are like a searchlight on a ship that throws light on the immediate landing spot and also throws a shaft of light on distant hills. So Paul's words light up the immediate foreground, whether it be the conflict in Corinth or the legalism of Galatia. They also throw light on the scene far beyond in time, on the issues of today, and to the hills of eternity.

Among other things Paul's letters bear on a tremendous subject—the conversion of Greece and Rome. Gilbert Highet has put this subject vividly before the imagination in *A Clerk of Oxenford*:

One of the greatest subjects in the world is still waiting for a gifted writer to make into a book. It could hardly be converted into a play, unless by a stupendous genius.

It would make the theme of a magnificent novel on the lines of *War and Peace*. A historian could devote his life to it. There have been some operas dealing with it, some spectacular but superficial films, and not enough poetry, although it could become the basis of a dramatic poem like *The Dynasts*.

It is a superb subject, one of the most important that ever emerged; it combines horror with beauty; hard fact and the loftiest mysticism, violent physical action and difficult philosophical discussion. This subject is the conversion of the Greek and Roman world to Christianity.

Paul's letters come from the very center of that great drama.

The comments in this book on passages in the Epistles of Paul are not a commentary. Some of the greatest texts are not even mentioned. They are not studies in exegesis, although effort has been made to convey Paul's actual meaning. The attempt follows the program pictured by one of Paul's great interpreters, C. H. Dodd. He writes that "first of all the effort should be to find out what Paul meant, and second, to try to indicate the bearing of what Paul meant upon our own experience, our own questions, and our own thought."

Here are what is hoped will prove suggestive starting points for thought. The paragraphs in this book are not sermons; they are not sermon outlines. They are starting points, not arrivals, attempts to lay an arresting hand on the shoulder of the reader. They follow the general scheme of the author's previous books, *Preaching Values in the New Translations of the New Testament*, 1928, and *Preaching Values in the Old Testament in the New Translations*, 1933. They are indications of possible ways in which fresh and vivid rendering of the words of the New Testament into the daily speech of our time may be put to the service of winning an eager hearing for New Testament truth.

The text used, unless otherwise indicated, is that of the *Revised Standard Version* of the Bible. Frequent use is made of the very suggestive and often exciting translation of the New Testament by J. B. Phillips.

Grateful acknowledgment is made to The National Council of the Churches of Christ in the United States of America for permission to quote from the *Revised Standard Version*, copyright 1946 and 1952 by the Division of Christian Education, the National Council of Churches.

My hearty thanks are given to The Macmillan Company for permission to quote from *Letters to Young Churches* by J. B. Phillips, and to Harper & Brothers for permission to quote from James Moffatt's translation of the New Testament.

My thanks are given to publishers and authors who have permitted the use of poetry and prose quotations as acknowledged in the Notes.

Halford E. Luccock

Hamden, Connecticut

*The Epistle of Paul
to the Romans*

1. CALLED TO BE SAINTS

Called to be saints. ROM. 1:7

These words do not describe the vocation of being a stained-glass window. That is what the word means to many people. A saint has been thought of and pictured as a figure in a robe long enough to trip up a queen, with a halo swinging above the head at a precarious angle.

The word "saint" has fallen on evil days. There are many men who would resent being called a "saint" as vehemently as they resent being called a liar. They associate the role of a saint with the protest of Bunthorne in *Patience* by Gilbert and Sullivan:

> *I am not fond of uttering platitudes*
> *In stained glass attitudes.*

Paul was not thinking of any canonized beatific figure. The official canonization of saints came much later than the first century A.D.

For Paul the saints were the faithful Christian men and women, not perfect people but separated and consecrated to the service of God. The best and shortest description is that in J. B. Phillips' translation, "called to be Christ's men and women." A few of the sixty references to saints in the New Testament denote supernatural living souls, but the overwhelming majority are to "Christ's men and women." The New Testament saints were not figures found in legends. They were people found in the streets, in workshops, in homes, and in "the church which is in thy house." The word "saint" was not a rigidly limited aristocratic word; it was a gloriously democratic word. F. W. H. Myers has drawn the portrait of the saint as "Christ's man":

> *Christ, I am Christ's and let that name suffice you;*
> *Aye, and for me, too, it greatly hath sufficed.*
> *Lo, with no winning words would I entice you,*
> *Paul hath no honor and no friend but Christ.*
>
> *Yea, through life, death, through sorrow and through sinning,*
> *Christ shall suffice me, for he hath sufficed;*

Christ was the end, for Christ was the beginning
Christ the beginning, for the end is Christ.

The great danger is that when men and women give up any desire
or ambition to become saints who get into stained-glass windows,
they also often give up the true vocation to become dedicated Christ's
men and women. We are called to be belligerents in the moral battle.
We betray our calling when we haul down the belligerent flag and
run up the white flag of indifference or surrender.

Richard Burton has drawn a partial picture in his poem, "The
Modern Saint":

> *No monkish garb he wears, no beads he tells,*
> *Nor is immured in walls remote from strife.*
> *But from his heart deep mercy ever wells;*
> *He looks humanely forth on human life.*
>
> *In place of missals or of altar dreams*
> *He cons the passioned book of deeds and days,*
> *Striving to cast the comforting sweet beams*
> *Of charity on dark and noisome ways.*
>
> *Not hedged about by sacerdotal rule,*
> *He yearns to make the world a sunnier clime*
> *To live in; and his mission everywhere*
> *Is strangely like to Christ in olden time.*
>
> *No medieval mystery, no crowned*
> *Dim figure, halo-rimmed, uncanny bright,*
> *A modern saint; a man who treads earth's ground*
> *And ministers to men with all his might.*

Sainthood in the New Testament sense is a vocation, not of rest
but of motion. Saints are those who have responded and are respond-
ing to a call from God, and are in motion toward the high goal of
their calling.

2. TWO-WAY TRAFFIC

That we may be mutually encouraged by each other's faith.   ROM. 1:12

The Christian churches of the West have waited at least fifteen hundred years to discover the far reach of these words. Paul simply indicated his eagerness for two-way traffic in spiritual gifts with the

Christians of Rome. He wished that he could *give* to them some spiritual gifts, and he hoped to *receive* gifts from their experience and faith. He showed a marvelous humility, to get from them as well as to give.

But if we turn our imagination loose, we can see beyond the literal meaning the long, long reach of this mutual sharing among present-day Christian thinkers. For a long time the older churches have been eager to *give* to "the heathen in his blindness" the spiritual light they have. At the most they have felt,

> *Can we, whose souls are lighted*
> *With wisdom from on high,*
> *Can we to men benighted*
> *The lamp of life deny?*

And, unconsciously, that attitude of complacent generosity has been transferred to the young Christian churches in overseas lands. Missions have been thought of as "giving." Today, the churches of the West are overtaking Paul; spiritual traffic is going both ways. The older churches are receiving tremendously from the "younger churches," the very name marking a new era in Christian thinking. No longer "mission churches," they are younger sisters literally endowed with immeasurable gifts they are gloriously conferring, to the encouragement of the older churches. One reason is that the younger churches reproduce the experience of the early church, in facing a pagan world at close and deadly grip.

Sholem Asch, the novelist, says that in preparation for background for the novels dealing with the New Testament, he spent a long time in Palestine to "get the feel of New Testament." He went from the below sea level of the Dead Sea to the top of the Mount of Transfiguration. But in a deeper and larger sense, the only way in which people today can "get the feel" of the New Testament church is to take part in the New Testament task of evangelizing a non-Christian world. There is a great truth in the statement that no one can really understand the New Testament who has not been on the mission field. There we have the original situation of a desperately small Christian group facing a world of paganism, beginning to make converts. That plunges them right back into the book of Acts as nothing else could. If we want to make the Bible times real, we can take part in facing the paganism in our own time and environment. When we engage in that, we realize we are part of the company of the first heralds of the Cross.

Two other related gifts which the younger churches give are priceless. One is a fresh faith, the gift of youth. The younger churches are God's springtime in Asia. They bring a gift of renewal. They also bring wisdom for a common battle. For in so many ways, the churches of the West are facing a non-Christian world. Toynbee calls it an "ex-Christian world." To the task of faith at home, the West can be encouraged by that faith.

3.   LIKE TO SEE RESULTS

I should like to see some results among you.   ROM. 1:11 (Phillips)

This is a characteristic word of a pastor, and Paul was emphatically a pastor. Again and again his heart is enlarged for his converts. He puts this yearning into violent figures of speech, telling Christians in Galatia, "My little children, with whom I am again in travail until Christ be formed in you" (Gal. 4:19). We can almost overhear his deep sigh of disappointment, "I am afraid I have labored over you in vain" (Gal. 4:11). He always wanted to see results.

This is also the desire of a practical age, such as ours boasts itself to be. Everyone wants results. The sales manager barks out, "We want results, not excuses!" This desire for the tangible "result" sometimes gets over into the life of a church. Those results are tabulated in an array of columns, increased attendance, increased salary, increased market place prestige. But Paul made constantly clear the kind of results he wished to see, "grace and peace." Christ formed in a life. Nothing less ever satisfied him.

Often the "results" in a life are so meager, compared to the investment made. The results are so tawdry, when measured by personality and inner spiritual possession.

> *The prince of commerce spent his days*
> *In crafty calm and busy strife.*
> *He thus amassed a million pounds*
> *And bought a penny's worth of life.*

He got results, all right. But look at him!

A keen analysis of two men, whose lives were full of shabby results, has been made by Kate O'Brien in her *Romance of English Literature*. The two men were contemporaries much of their lives, among the best-known diarists of all time. Of Samuel Pepys, she wrote:

For my part I have never liked Pepys' diary . . . to have dared so much for so tiny a result To empty out breast, brain and entrails, and to have so wretchedly little to show for the awful violence; and to be, after all, with all said, nothing better nor worse than a fussy, kindly, nervous, lecherous, dirty, self-pitying and respectable. . . . It bears about it an insect quality.

"So tiny a result . . . an insect quality"!

The other man is John Evelyn. Several cuts above Pepys, he had talents, quickness of mind. Rich, free, and honorable, his positive endowments might have done wonders. Yet, the verdict is:

Yet, the contagion of the world, and of his own concern for the world and for getting the best of it did somehow blight his life, making it neatly perfect, like the gardens he cherished, instead of free and incalculable, as it might have been. . . . He might have been a leader of his age; instead he was one of its most fixed and tarnished decorations.

He might have been a leader. He became a decoration.

God desires to see better results in us.

4. LIVING IN THE RED

I am debtor both to the Greeks, and to the Barbarians.   ROM. 1:14 (AV)

This means living in the red.

Most of us know what that means financially. Shakespeare speaks of "seas incarnardine." Those are the seas most of us have navigated —a sea of red ink. The breaking waves dash high the first of every month, and keep dashing.

We hear a great deal about "a deficit economy." Here is a man who lives in a deficit economy and boasts about it. He says, "I am under obligation" to all. It is a high way to live, for it gives to life the dignity and lift of a great obligation. We hear much good advice about keeping out of debt. Paul offers different and better advice: "Get in debt." That is a Christian economy.

Paul had cried, "I must see Rome." He must be on his way to those who belonged to the Greek-speaking world. But he acknowledges an obligation to preach the gospel to those outside the world to which he belongs. The barbarians were beyond the boundaries, those with a strange tongue and a strange culture. He recognizes that God's invitation knows no fences.

As we think of those words set in our own time and place, it can be said in general that a church does far better saying "I am debtor" to the Greeks than to the barbarians. A church's great danger is that of ministering to its own kind, those within the circle of like-minded-ness, of mutual educational range, of like financial and social stand-ing, and neglecting its obligation to those outside that world, often a snug little world. Its danger is neglect of those of a different class, color, and bank account, in other words, the barbarian. In relation to those outside the forbidding fence, the church begins to live in the black. It is in little debt to "the barbarians."

Paul's list of accepted obligations comes as a sharp challenge, sometimes a rebuke to the minister. Consider the words "Debtor to the unwise," that is, to the uneducated, to those who do not know the language of the theological scribes, and who must receive the Word in plain English. There is a tendency often in the minister to be a debtor to the educated. There is an intellectual glamor and rep-utation in that "our pastor is such a deep thinker."

The plea of the repentant thief on the cross, taken entirely out of its context, still has true appeal, regarded as the plea of the unedu-cated to whom the preacher speaks. The thief said, "When thou comest into thy kingdom, remember me" (AV). So the preacher may carry in his hand and heart this plea: "When you come into any king-dom, and you come into many, of learning, of eloquence, of language, remember the person who has missed all those advantages." Be a debtor to the "unwise" as well as to "the wise"!

The words are an urgent plea for the church to escape from the prison of ministering only to the like-minded, of one class, of one color. Debtor to the barbarian. One aspect of this danger to a denom-ination is that of pulling away from the group which made up its original constituency.

5. PRIDE IN AN AGE OF POWER

I am not ashamed . . . : it is the power of God for salvation. ROM.
1:16

What a word for an age of power! We can say, above the hum of the dynamos, "I am not ashamed of our time, for it is power." We can lift our eyes, keeping far enough away, of course, to the hydrogen bomb and sing, "Ten thousand times ten thousand . . . times the power of a ton of dynamite." We are proud of power. A current mood of complacency is reflected in a cartoon published in the spring of 1957, concerning the voyage across the Atlantic of the second *Mayflower*. Two avaitors who had just crossed the Atlantic in a few hours are talking. One says, "How'd you like to be on the *Mayflower* just loafing along at five knots?" The inference is, of course, that anything less than our superspeed is contemptible, and our time is far superior in every way to any former time for "it is power." We can travel three times the speed of sound. Our planes can reach the Pacific Coast from New York half an hour before they start!

The dominant impression made on a traveler by train across the continent is the transmission of power. Up hill and down dale, from the tops of the Rockies to the flat desert, towers for transmitting power dominate the landscape. The most vivid illustration of physical power in our world would be obsolete by the time the words could be printed.

Yet along with this mood of complacent pride in power is a deep and growing skepticism. More and more people are not proud but *ashamed* of power. Ashamed of power which already has made of so much of the world a mass of rubble. More deeply ashamed of the power that can make a shambles of the world. In sensitive minds and hearts there is a feeling of shame over such power as intercontinental missiles, which are skyrockets raised to the billionth power. Only the deaf, dumb, and blind can say, "I am proud of irresponsible power." As J. B. Priestley has put this feeling, "It is good for man to open his mind to awe and wonder. Without science we are helpless children. But without a deep religion, we are blundering fools, reeling in our new and terrible cocksureness into one disaster after another." This power in men's hands makes the naïve confidence of two generations ago not only look ridiculous, but tragically blind. Here is one paean of praise to power by Berton Braley, typical of a widespread feeling:

> This is a song of the men who master
>   Motor, dynamo, fuse and switch,
> Who lift our life to a pace that's faster,
>   Who move the world—by a finger twitch.
> Men in office and laboratory,
>   Men who work with the thunder bolts
> Who outmatch even Aladdin's story
>   With a magic lamp—of a million volts.
>
> This is the song of the singing wires
>   That throb responsive to serve our will,
> The song of a Genie that never tires
>   But toils for greater enchantments still;

The song of NOW—and the days before us
With vaster marvels for us to scan
A song whose jubilant, lifting chorus
Rings with the hopes and the dreams of man!

It sounds like a Hallelujah Chorus, but stand in our devastated, bankrupt world today and try to sing that jubilant song! It turns to ashes in our mouths! There is no salvation or survival for men in sheer power.

Far more fitting to our thunderbolts is the impassioned word of Dr. Harold C. Urey, the atomic scientist: "I am a frightened man."

Our pride rests on other power. Dr. Moffatt puts this verse positively: "I am *proud* of the gospel; it is . . . power."

In the London of the seventeenth century, tradesmen sat in front of their shops and cried out to passers-by, "What lack ye? What lack ye?" So, in imagination, we can hear the call going to our world, "What do you lack?" Paul went up and down the Mediterranean world, asking, "What do you lack?" The answer, then and now, was *power*. "For I do not do the good I want" (Rom. 7:19). To meet that need, Paul does not propose Operation Bootstrap. There is no salvation for the world today in a bootstrap lift, no matter how ingenious the straps. We need power to become the sons of God. Man needs spiritual power to control the powers in his hands. The horsepower has outrun the man power. For one man or two and a half billion men, we need the power of God for salvation.

6. HINDERERS

But God's anger is revealed from heaven against all the impiety and wickedness of those who hinder the Truth. ROM. 1:18 (Moffatt)

How that word "hinder" steals into our imagination and even seems to be pointing the finger of accusation at us! The phrase "wrath of God" is a key word in Romans, and calls for study and clear understanding. It does not convey the human emotion of anger. God is not "mad" at man. It portrays, rather, the inevitable consequences of sin. There is the righteous quality in the nature of God which condemns unrighteousness, done in defiance of God. It is inevitable, yet it is not automatic. Sin does not encounter the automatic action of the universe. It is the wrath of *God* which is revealed.

The word translated by Moffatt as "hinder" is actually a more violent word. Indeed, it suggests a wrestling match, certainly a display of violence, and it is so translated in the British Revised Version, "Hold down." The wicked are wrestlers who pin the shoulders of truth down to the floor and never let it get up and walk.

That word "suppress" (RSV and Goodspeed) vividly pictures many current actions, and lack of actions, in a church's dealing with the truth. How effectively "suppressed" has been, in many places, the truth about race and God's demand for justice and love to all races. Some churches and preachers do not need to oppose it. Nothing so crude! They can, and do, just suppress it, smother it.

So also with the embarrassing condemnation of the lust for profits in the gospel. Just hold it down—suppress it. This has been done so well that many people have gone to church for a lifetime and never heard it mentioned! So also, God's truths have been made "dumb and inoperative" (Phillips). We render a truth "dumb" when we do not give it voice. So much of our gospel has laryngitis, often it cannot speak above a whisper. Sometimes the word of God becomes as dumb as a bronze Buddha, or it is inoperative in the way in which a bill in Congress is passed, and then very simply the operating clause is removed!

But that word "hinder"—"those who hinder God's truth"—has a wide range and comes terribly close to us. We can hinder while we are proclaiming the word. We can hinder by an austere manner, grim and forbidding. Some such hinderers seem to be dressed in granite. "You have," says one, "such a February face, so full of frost and storm and cloudiness."

The fact that there is a joy of the Lord which we may have is kept as highly "classified information," and kept a secret.

Powerful hinderers of the word of God are those in whom the word does not make any difference, or does not seem to.

And what hindrance has been erected by the human invertebrates who never stand up to anything. They make a high stone wall around the truth. Zoologists have told us that there are nearly a million kinds of animal invertebrates, from amoebas to bees. No one can tell how many kinds of human invertebrates there are, entirely without backbone, particularly in a crisis. So do the Christians hinder the truth who always manage to get their religion in the *negative*. They never sing a Hallelujah Chorus of "He shall reign forever and ever." They are so busy scolding about some negative "don't do this" that they never see the glorious blazing positives of their gospel. And how about leaders who never lead?

7. WISE FOOLS

Claiming to be wise, they became fools. ROM. 1:22

Prodded by these words, our mind drifts off to the description of King James I of England as "the wisest fool in Christendom." There have been a lot of dumb ones if James I was the wisest! He was a pedant, a master of the irreverent and the unimportant, and an illiterate in all that really counted in life.

That phrase, "wise fools," meant to Paul those who had given up the worship of "the glory of the eternal God" for the worship of idols. A fool's trade!

There are so many varieties of wise fools in every age, and our own is heavily populated with them. Medicine has a name for its own brand of "wise fools." They are "unfortunates who have been known in medical circles as the Idiot Savants, i.e. the imbecile, devoid of conflict, who can use his small segment of brain with greater economy and efficiency than a Ph.D from M.I.T. can use his whole one.

One particular variety of erudite savants of limited vision, quite vocal in recent months, is that of the people who, in a spell of hysteria, would junk the whole glorious tradition of liberal arts in education, and turn to science education exclusively. As a salute to such shortsightedness, Ellen Glasgow wrote:

Science, the promised savior, may become, in the end, the destroyer of man—and of the awkward pattern Western man has agreed to call civilization. It is a civilization built on science, that has discarded philosophy. Yet fewer scientists and more philosophers, less knowledge and more wisdom, might, whether we are saved or not, at least make us worth saving.

In general the erudite fools are those who have no sharp sense of values. They shop for cheap bargains. Those who take pride in the name "sophisticates" are very wise fools. They are wise with the assorted wisdoms of the world. But their minds are a blank to any high or eternal meaning in life. G. K. Chesterton has given a memorable description of one large group of these current wise fools, saying that "they know the last word about everything and the first word about nothing." They may know all the varied lore of the latest crazes, they may be perfect encyclopedias of the last words about life among the night clubs or cafés, but know the *first* word about nothing! The last word about glamor, but not the first word about the true grace of living! The last word about getting, often even to getting all four feet in the financial trough, but not the first word about the joy of giving! The last word about lust, but not the first word about love. The last word about the glittering idols of the market place but not the first word about the splendor of God.

8. HIGH AND MIGHTY

They considered themselves too high and mighty to acknowledge God.
ROM. 1:28 (Phillips)

It is a common phrase and denotes a person who, in his manner, and often in his walk and stance, is a parading ramrod. He has no joints in his back or neck. He cannot bow. He is "a solemn processional of one." Such a "high and mighty" person is usually a comic figure. But "the high and mighty," as Paul saw them, were not comics. They were tragic figures. Such men put God out of their lives. They cannot bow in humility; that is a word for slaves. But the next four verses, Rom. 1:29–32, form the most frightening look into the lower depths of human nature which have ever been portrayed. When God is shoved out of life, these are some of the things which rush in to fill the empty space.

One of the top "high and mighty" of our generation was certainly Hitler. He did not bow God out of the universe, as has been the manner with the more genteel. He shoved Him. He put his disdain for God into picturesque speech. He said, "Leave the sky to the sparrows." But the world discovered that when God's sky is abolished, what fills the sky is not sparrows but *vultures,* the carrion birds of death.

Some people are far, far distant from the disdain of a Hitler. They are just too busy to allow the intrusion of God into an already overcrowded schedule. They do not subscribe to atheism. That is not good form in our day. They just try to create a spiritual vacuum, and spiritual nature abhors a vacuum as violently as does physical nature. One of the strangest exhibits on earth is that of the substitutes for God, to fill the vacuum. These idols vary all the way from a stock ticker, or a bottle, to a picket fence of exclusion.

There is the high and mighty intellect which "does not see fit to acknowledge God." That is for children! Yet many of the mighty who reject the "superstitions of Christianity," will cheerfully swallow some prodigious legends of unbelief. They are precisely like the people of whom Jesus said, "They strain at a gnat and swallow a camel."

Here is a declaration by a prominent scientist, and a very able one, too. Professor George Gaylord Simpson, Professor of Fossil Mammals and Birds in the American Museum of Natural History, writes in his book, *Life of the Past:* "Man belongs to no plan and fulfills no supernal purpose. He stands alone in the universe, a unique product of a long unconscious, impersonal, material process, with unique understanding and potentialities. These he owes to no one but himself and it is to himself that he is responsible." So, man did it all himself. To which we can say with gusto, "A nice trick if you can do it." Is there any match anywhere for the dogmatic sweep of the statement, "Man owes nothing to anyone but himself"?

A notable philosopher, Professor W. T. Stace of Princeton University, has given voice to a statement which many people will call, surely, a superstition and legend of a quality which defies belief. It, too, is a sweeping affirmation that man is really nothing but "matter in motion." Swallow this, if we can. Most of us can't, no matter how hard we try. It takes a mightier brain than most of us have. He writes:

For my part, I believe in no religion at all. Since the world is not ruled by a spiritual being, but rather by blind forces, there cannot be any ideals, moral or otherwise, in the universe outside us. Our ideals, therefore, must [notice that little word, "must." They "must" because Professor Stace says so] proceed from our own minds; they are our own inventions. Thus the world that surrounds us is nothing but an immense spiritual emptiness, it is a dead universe . . . purposeless, senseless, meaningless. Nature is nothing but matter in motion.

Roll that around in the mind for a while! We must not imagine any meaning in the world, because Professor Stace says there is none. Augustine, Sir Isaac Newton, John Milton, Louis Pasteur, and a thousand others of the world's finest minds, should apologize to Professor Stace for believing in the superstition of a personal God.

Or, can it be that a poet, Alfred Noyes, has a truer logic and a more compelling reason when he writes his own faith:

Was the eye contrived by blindly moving atoms,
Or the still, listening ear fulfilled with music
By forces without knowledge of sweet sound?
Are nerves and brain so sensitively fashioned
While that for which we came, the power that made us
Is drowned in blank unconsciousness of it all?

9.   EYELIDS SEWN TOGETHER

Full of envy.   ROM. 1:29

The title above is from Dante's *Divine Comedy*. It represents one of the many insights which help to make Dante one of the world's greatest poets, and the *Divine Comedy* one of the world's greatest poems. It is an imaginative picture which has much to say to our present age. Dante pictures the eyes of the envious in Purgatory as being sewn together. The idea is that envy closes the vision to worth, loveliness, mutuality, and brotherhood. It locks people in the dark poverty of their meager resources.

Thus, in the poet's thinking, envy ranks as one of the great sins. It is often disregarded, but it can be fatal to the Christian life. It stirs up the unchristian feeling of desire and ill will toward the one who has what we want, and it induces a disregard for the finer qualities of spirit which are the fruits of the spirit of Christ in a life.

This picture from Dante has close relevance to many of the conditions under which we live today. Envy lies in wait for everyone. Let him that thinketh he standeth, take heed lest he fall. Envy is the sharp sting of discontent or ill will at seeing another's superiority, advantages, or success. A portrait of the envious is etched in the words of old Thomas Fuller: "An envious man is a squint-eyed fool." Francis Bacon was impressed by the eternal wakefulness of envy. "Envy", he wrote, "has no holidays. It walketh the streets and doth not keep at home." We might say that it never even takes a "coffee break," once it gets inside of the heart and mind.

One point to remember with watching and prayer is that to a degree never approached in our day, people are bombarded by enticements to envy. So much of our economic structure seems to be kept standing by envy. The devil whispers between the leaves, "Don't you wish it were yours?" Envy must be cultivated, or we will have a "recession." The immense development of the arts of advertising and display do much to create the feeling of envy in many people. In a modern city there is a deliberate rush at all of the five senses. From morning to night in newspapers, store windows, television, and radio there is an incessant screaming, "Get this! Get that!" It leaves one with the impression that unless you purchase the articles which the salesman is displaying and shouting his lungs out about, life is hardly worth living. Dissatisfaction is stirred up in thoughtless minds. The enticement to envy runs something like this: "Don't you wish you could drive a high-powered, this year's model car? Aren't you ashamed to be driving that old crate of yours, four years old?" So the pangs of envy are on their way! To many a woman the seduction to envy comes like this: "You would look marvelous in a mink coat. Don't you envy Mrs. Millions that lovely coat of hers? You would set it off much better than she does." So the eyelids are getting sewn together so that the real worth is not visible.

Note that envy comes first on the detailed list which Paul draws up (Rom. 1:29-30) of the evil things which can come in when God goes out of life. The dictionary tells us that envy is a feeling of "mortification" over something we wish we had. It is a fitting word, "mortification," for it means that something dies. In the cause and effect which Paul is tracing, God has died. When a mind is "steeped in envy," a person cannot look at a thing objectively. It is always in relation to "me, me, me."

The escape from envy is by the great liberator, God. We read that Jesus, quoting from Isaiah, declares that he was sent to proclaim release to the captives. He does release men and women from the dreary captivity of envy, for the man who looks at life with the eyes of envy is like a man who looks on a landscape while he has an agonizing toothache.

He has the great preoccupation with "me and my ache!" The riches which a Christian relationship opens up within a person save life from becoming our envious "squint."

10. THE SIN OF APPLAUSE

They not only do it themselves but they applaud those who practise it.
ROM. 1:32 (Moffatt)

There is a double condemnation here, against the doing of vice, and the applause of others. Applause of evil as well as the evil act is sin.

That sin of applause brings a sharp indictment against a generation and a culture such as ours in which applause plays such a large and noisy part. The entertainment world lives on applause or dies from the lack of it. We have machines to measure it to the last decibel. We "dub" it in to a performance on a screen, trying to create the illusion that a scene played to a dead studio is being given thunderous applause by a live audience. Promoters make large use of applause cards, telling docile audiences to clap their hands. The nation applauds winners, Miss America, the heavyweight champion, the homerun king. Our whole culture is partly shaped by applause.

We had better note that applause may be a sin. We may say with Marguerite Wilkinson:

> *I never cut my neighbor's throat*
> *I never stole my neighbor's wife.*

But we may be guilty of sin by augmenting the power of evil through our approval and applause. We give new power to the pressures squeezing people into conformity. We do it for many reasons. Thoughtless irresponsibility is one. Also, we hate to be a "killjoy" or a "sour ball." We are afraid to withhold our applause from what is evidently popular. We dare not risk being called a "back number," our most feared invective.

So, to be safe, men and women applaud sheer inanity, vulgarity, or immorality.

Such lack of discrimination is a contribution to more confusion. Untold harm was done in the political international world by the prewar applause of Mussolini by one of the leading advertising pundits of America. He said, in 1930, "How can we develop the love of country, the respect for courts and law, the sense of national obligation which Mussolini has recreated in the soul of Italy? Must we abolish the Senate and have a dictatorship to do it? I sometimes think it would be worth the cost." The sin of applause!

This sin of indiscriminate applause has been a cause of that sad feature of American life, the disappearance of the hero. He has gone out of fashion, to the great debasing of literature and debasing of taste, and hence, eventually, the character of the young.

Van Wyck Brooks ascribes the tendency of young American writers to join the clique applauding the shoddy and the vulgar to their lack of "memories." Many of them have, he says, "no knowledge of the American tradition. They have no doubts with which to criticize the spectacle of the modern world."

There is a parallel cause of the sin of applause which so easily besets a great multitude of people. They have no knowledge or, at best, small secondhand knowledge of high Christian moral and spiritual values. Few standards of criticism of life, or none at all. When we lose the power and instruments of criticism we are like many audiences at television shows, who will violently applaud anything, even the tired commercials which they have heard to a nauseating degree.

We might bring back into circulation the words of Queen Victoria, usually repeated as something to laugh at: "We are not amused." In addition, as an evidence of repentance of the sin of indiscriminate applause, we might revive the power of positive appreciation. "Let us now praise famous men."

11.   WHEN JUDGMENTS BOOMERANG

For in judging another you condemn yourself.   ROM. 2:1 (Moffatt)

One of life's most common confusions is to imagine we are in the judge's bench, when we are really the prisoner being judged. Our judgments often come back on us, like a boomerang, and judge us. There is the familiar painting by Munkácsy, "Christ before Pilate." Pilate, in purple, looks sternly at the prisoner, garbed in white. But it should be entitled "Pilate before Christ," for that is what it really is. Pilate's judgment of Christ merely judged himself. Paul's point in these words is that the Jew condemns idolatry, but when he is unfaithful to the truth, he has, in so condemning the idolater, really condemned himself.

The reason that we condemn ourselves often in our severe judgments is that in them we *reveal* ourselves. When a person tells us, for instance, that Beethoven's music is just a tiresome noise, that is not a fact about Beethoven, but just a fact about the man who passes the judgment. When the critic in *Blackwood's Magazine* wrote scornfully of John Keats, in a review of his poetry, "It is a better and a wiser thing to be a starved apothecary than a starved poet. Go back to the shop, Mr. John Keats, back to the 'plasters, pills and ointment boxes,' . . . but for heaven's sake, young Sangrado, be a little more sparing of extenuatives, and soporifics in your practice than you have been in your poetry," that was not a fact about Keats, or poetry. It was just an advertisement of the ignorance and malice of the writer. Look at the boomerang quality of Samuel Pepys about Shakespeare. He wrote in his journal: "Up and to Depford, by water, reading *Othello, Moor of Venice,* which I had hitherto esteemed a mighty good play, but having so lately read *The Adventures of Five Hours,* it seems a mean thing." And so does Pepys! So, a popular novelist in the United States in the early nineteenth century, one who received much adulation, wrote that *The House of Seven Gables* was "an affliction," and *Wuthering Heights* a "waste of time." Look out, there comes the boomerang!

Here is the godlike Daniel Webster, supposedly giving a sweeping exposure of the idiocy of expecting anything of good to come from the wild desert Pacific Coast. He spoke thus eloquently to the United States Senate in 1840:

What do we want with this region of savages and wild beasts, of deserts of shifting sands and whirlwinds of dust, of cactus and prairie dogs? . . . What could we do with the Western Coast of three thousand miles, rockbound, cheerless and uninviting?

We refer that last query to the Chamber of Commerce of Los Angeles! His judgment merely judged his remarkable limitations. Alexander Hamilton summed up Thomas Jefferson as "a man of profound ambition and violent passions." About that judgment, Dumas Malone wrote that "he must have been looking in the glass."

So in our own judgments of Christ and of what he taught, we put ourselves in the dock and are judged by our own judgments. Judge not, that you be not judged, by your own judgments.

12. A GOD OF WRATH

You are storing up wrath for yourself on the day of wrath when God's righteous judgment will be revealed. ROM. 2:5
when, in his holy anger against evil (Phillips)

The word "anger" as applied to God badly needs restoration in much Christian thinking. And in all Christian not-thinking! The wrath of God, in the New Testament, is not the burst of human anger often found in the Old Testament, leading to cruelty. There are in many instances a petulance and irritation and vengeful vindictiveness which will not fit into the God and Father of our Lord Jesus Christ. We have renounced the God of Jonathan Edwards' "Sinners in the Hands of an angry God." But in leaving that out, many have left out of their thinking and acting a God of righteousness with a holy anger against sin and indifference to conduct.

With many people, the idea of God has been obscured by a theological and moral blur. The Christian religion has become a journey into fog. God has been dissolved into a smile. He has been removed from the Bible, and taken over to the tent of Omar Khayyám:

> There are those who tell
> Of a God who flings to hell
> The reckless pots he marred in making.
> Pshaw! He's a good fellow,
> And 'twill all be well.

So, on with the dance! The highest being of the Christian faith is transformed into a "good fellow." That is surely trading a birthright of high heritage for a mess of pottage.

God is not a God of vengeance but a God of righteousness. Paul writes that the man of indifference who has rejected God's law and has made no repentance is storing up wrath *for himself*. For the God of righteousness is implacably against sin. Wrath is the effect of sin, not the personal resentment of God, not of his getting "mad." In the moral and spiritual world cause and effect operate.

When we lose the God of wrath against evil, we drop into the moral and spiritual collapse of "It doesn't make any great difference what we do. It will all be the same in a hundred years." To Paul, sin won't be the same in a hundred years or a billion years.

When we have an easygoing, or an indifferent God, we become easygoing and indifferent in our attitude to conduct ourselves. Old Thomas Fuller declared, "Anger is one of the sinews of the soul. He that lacks it hath a maimed mind." True, when we do not care enough about sin and evil to be angry, when they strut through the earth, we have a maimed mind; we have a badly maimed mind. Someone has written about a biography of Thoreau, "the sanest biography ever written," that it was so "sane" that "all the real passion of the man, all the anger, all the ardor simply evaporate." That is what is the matter with us often, our anger against evil has evaporated. God's cause is not close enough to our hearts to make us angry at the evil which opposes Him. The Son of God Goes Forth to War. But many do not get excited about it. *Ye that love the Lord, hate evil* (Psa. 97:10, AV).

13. THE CINDERELLA VIRTUE

To those who by patience in well-doing seek for glory and honor and immortality, he will give eternal life. ROM. 2:7

Patience is a Cinderella among the virtues. At least it is so, very often in the opinion of the sophisticated. Patience sits at home among the ashes, while her more glamorous sisters, such as courage, energy, and daring, go off to the ball, gorgeously arrayed. Patience is rated a very minor virtue, finishing in life's race about fifth place, if that high. Patience is viewed with a complacent "ho hum." Kingsley's lines seem to fit, telling the dull story:

Be good, sweet maid, and let who will be clever.
Do noble things, not dream them all day long.
And so make life, death and that vast forever,
One grand sweet song.

Incidentally, those who look down on the sweet maid's program as boring forget that life and the happiness of life depend very little on cleverness. They depend absolutely on goodness. But a very common feeling is that if you haven't got the animation to make a smashing drive in life, you can be satisfied with patient plodding. "That's about all you're good for."

There is this much excuse for the ignorant sneer at patience. Very often patience is made a mask for laziness, and for indifference. The person who says loftily, "I am a patient man," may be only an indifferent clod.

Also, patience is often joined to another unjustly despised word, "routine." A "patient routine" suggests a mule in a coal mine, rather than a spirited race horse. But real patience is power under control for a high end. And what God hath joined together let not man put asunder. In this passage patience is joined to "glory, honor and immortality." The sequence seems strange to those who do not place patience high. But life demonstrates patience as a way unto glory and honor. Think of the tremendous achievements in history's domain, made possible by the invincible power of patience. By patience discoveries have been made by watchers of the skies; inventors have wrought their wonders by experiments done over and over again. By patience Pasteur reached the glory of lifting a sure bondage to the human race; by patience Anne Sullivan Macy achieved the honor of bringing the soul of Helen Keller out of a dark prison.

The race is not to the swift, nor the battle to the strong. The deepest prayer that can be made for any of us is this: "May the Lord direct your hearts towards . . . Christ's patience" (2 Thess. 3:5, Moffatt).

14. HEARERS AND DOERS

For it is not the hearers of the law who are righteous before God, but the doers of the law who will be justified. ROM. 2:13

Two men met on a bus. They exchanged familiar questions, ones we hear everyday.

One asked, "What do you know?" The other asked, "How are you doing?"

Two questions, both important. The first, "What do you know," has always been extremely important since the dawn of time. The whole history of science lies in the answer to that question. It will always be important.

But the second question, "How are you doing?" is a completion of the first question and is vastly more important.

In our world today we have overestimated the values of hearing. In our common life, of course, up until a little over thirty years ago, the ear was rapidly passing out of the picture, compared to the importance of the eye as a means of communication. It was emphatically a case of "the eyes have it." But with the advent of radio, television, sound movies, the ear has gained in importance. And along with it there comes a curious elevation of the importance of hearing. In church life, for instance, people "sit under" a minister, until merely hearing becomes an end in itself. We are always beset by one of the persistent delusions of life, the comfortable feeling, which is a constant boost to our complacency, that by hearing about a situation or a need, we have actually done something about it.

For this reason, the word of Paul's that only the *doers* of the law, not the *hearers,* are justified, comes as a needed and arresting reminder to us all. It is tremendously needed in our religious life, for it cuts the importance of merely hearing down to size. A small size!

Kierkegaard wrote one of his vivid parables on the danger of becoming a specialized hearer of religion, an occupation so absorbing that it left no inclination to *do* anything about it. He imagined that near the cross of Christ had stood a man who beheld the terrible scene, and then became a professor of what he saw. He explained it all. Later he witnessed the persecution and imprisonment and cruel beating of the apostles, and became a professor of what he had witnessed. He studied the drama of the cross, but he was never crucified with Christ in his own life. He studied apostolic history, but he did not live apostolically. He was a hearer, not a doer.

That is a sin that does so easily beset us. We see its infection in the words of a minister who said testily, when a bothersome call came over the telephone, "I am writing a great sermon on sympathy, and do not have time for individuals."

> *Give us to build above the deep intent,*
> *The deed, the deed.*

15. THE MALIGNED GOD

The name of God is maligned among the Gentiles because of you.
ROM. 2:24

Maligned is a strong word. It means "to slander, to speak ill, to heap shame." The word has an even stronger meaning, as Phillips translates it here—"The name of God is *cursed*." Paul is telling the renegade Jews that they dishonor, blaspheme, malign God by disobedience to His laws.

How that word "malign" has traveled down the years! Not that God has been maligned by Jews, but by Christians! The organized church itself has maligned God among the non-Christians by committing, ostensibly in His name and for His honor, every crime known to degenerate man. Murder, cruelty, slaughter, have all masqueraded as saintliness. The Inquisition, in the name of Christ, could have taught lessons to Attila. God, through the centuries, has been thoroughly maligned.

The worst enemies of God and Christianity have not been the savage attacks of blasphemers, but the failures of His followers to believe His word and command. As Kipling puts it acutely:

> But His own disciple
> Shall wound Him worst of all.

Consider the long agony of war and how Christians have merited the bitter satire of Thomas Hardy:

> After two thousand years of mass,
> We've got as far as poison gas.

That was forty years ago. We have made a big improvement on that record. We have provided far bigger and better wars. As Phyllis McGinley brings us up to date in satirical verse more fitting to today:

> It seems vainglorious and proud
> Of Atom-man to boast so loud
>   His prowess homicidical
> When one remembers how for years,
> With their rude stones and humble spears,
> Our sires, at wiping out their peers,
>   Were almost never idle.

Though doubtless now our shrewd machines
Can blow the world to smithereens
*   More tidily and so on,*
Let's give our ancestors their due
Their ways were coarse, their weapons few.
But ah!, how wondrously they slew
*   With what they had to go on.*

How even the cross of Christ has been shamefully maligned! We
sing of the cross, with great unction:

All the wealth of sacred story
Gathers round its head sublime.

But we forget that during the centuries, other things beyond the
wealth of sacred story have gathered round the head of the cross. It
has been for millions in pogroms in Russia and elsewhere the terrifying symbol of slaughter and torture.

In other ways, other great blessings are maligned before the
world. Think of how democracy in the United States has been and
is violently maligned before the world by racial injustice and the
denial of democratic rights in some parts of the United States.
Among the billion and more of colored peoples of the world, such
actions win nothing but jeers. A missionary in India reported a few
years ago that the best-known places in the United States were
Scottsboro, Alabama, and Cicero, Illinois, both scenes of violent
treatments of Negroes.

May Paul's forthright indictment never drop from our memory.
Unless we obey the law of love, the name of God is maligned by us.

16.   THE DISORDER OF GRACE

Justified by his grace as a gift.   ROM. 3:24

God's bookkeeping would be the despair of a certified public ac-
countant. It is all so disorderly. It never ends up in a neat balance,
debits balanced by credits. A few verses before this sentence, in
Rom. 3:10–18, there is the most sweeping indictment ever drawn up
against the human race. "None is righteous . . . the throat is an
open grave, full of venomous lies . . . shedders of blood . . . no
fear of God." That is a terrific true bill. Sin here set forth is not
merely breaking an ethical code of conduct. It is a state of mind
against God. Man has not a prop to stand on.

Now for the sentence . . . "Justified by his grace as a gift"! All indictments set aside! All debts canceled!

As a matter of history, such bookkeeping *was* the despair of the certified accountants of the Jews. The double-entry experts, the Pharisees, believed in orderly thinking, so much punishment for so much evil-doing. But in the Christian gospel, there is one page, full of all the crimes which humanity can imagine or commit, and the other side has the entry, "paid in full." It doesn't make sense. It makes "grace," the free gift of God, unexpected, unmerited, the unearned increment of God's free gift of forgiveness and restoration.

It is a world of disorder, according to man's thinking. At the first assembly of the World Council of Churches at Amsterdam in 1948, the theme of the discussions was "Man's Disorder and God's design." A great theme. But much of the Christian revelation might be discussed under the head, "God's Disorder." We have a saying which affirms that "order is heaven's first law." But deeper than that is the disorder of grace—"While we were yet sinners, Christ died for us." God took the initiative.

That is the soul of the Epistle to the Romans and of the Christian gospel. Unless we are overwhelmed by this gift of God, we are still outside of the household of God. That is chiefly what is the matter with Christ's church. Too few of its members are completely overwhelmed by the measure of God's grace. There is only one entrance into the fullness of Christian experience:

> *Were the whole realm of nature mine,*
> *That were a present far too small.*
> *Love so amazing, so divine*
> *Demands my soul, my life, my all.*

17. ARE WE MONOTHEISTS?

Since God is one. ROM. 3:30

In these verses there is a strong overtone of the consequences of belief in one God, which is disturbing and challenging. It is not explicitly stated, but strongly implied. It is this: that since God is one, man is one. If in our actions we fail to treat men as one family, we do not really believe in one God. If we have not thought of the matter in that way, we had better begin in a hurry. God treats all men, Jew or Gentile, in the same way, says Paul, on the ground of their faith. God is color blind. He has no favorites. He despises picket fences which put some peoples off in a herd as inferior. If we hold them as untouchable, we are not believers in one God, no matter how loudly we intone the Nicene Creed. If we deny by our actions, often thoughtless, the oneness of man, equal before God and with equal civil rights before man, we are really polytheists. There are many polytheists in our churches. Canon Edward West of the Cathedral of St. John the Divine, in New York, has satirized this attitude in regard to anti-Semitism:

> There was once a man of Judea
> Whom everyone said I should hear.
> In front of another
> He called me his brother,
> With his mother a Jewess, my dear!

St. Theresa has written:

Our Lord asks but two things of us: love for Him and for our neighbor. . . . We cannot know whether we love God, although there may be strong reason for thinking so, but there can be no doubt about whether we love our neighbor or no.

St. Theresa argues justly and acutely. Our love for men as members of one family, our family, is the test of our love for God. And if we do not love God, we do not really believe in Him. We have no real faith in Him.

True theism supplies power for justice and brotherhood in deed. We had better face it. Do we believe in one God? Before we answer with an easy "yes," we might reflect that our treatment of our brothers' rights in our society is the measure of our faith in one God.

18.   BELIEVING AGAINST HOPE

In hope he believed against hope.   ROM. 4:18

These words have a close relevance and timeliness to our day. For if we are to believe at all, it will have to be against hope. That is, we shall have to believe against the findings and forebodings of many of the stern clear-eyed realists of our time.

There are two reasons why hope has fallen from its high estate as one of the chief Christian virtues.

One is that we live against hope. Hope is out. The sad knell sounded by Cyril Connolly, "It is closing time in the garden of the earth," has fallen on the ears of a great multitude. This is particularly true of the intellectuals. Thomas Hardy, even a generation ago, was spokesman for many when he asked why the church keeps up the farce of hope. He asked, "Why not throw in the sponge?" The sponges are already in the hands of many in the world today. And sponges seem reasonable, in the face of many estimates. Thus, the chances in the next war, on its way, are assessed by one scientist: "The people who are on the various ground zeros (when the bombs fall and where they fall) will probably be the most fortunate." That is, those who instantly die. About that, Gilbert Seldes writes: "I cannot follow the feeling that it would be worth-while to survive in a world so monstrously stupid as to let the bombings occur." Closing time!

A second reason for the dwindling of hope is that to many it seems banished from the Christian faith. During two generations Christian thinking has realized the empty and unchristian character of the immoral optimism which prevailed rather vigorously up to World War I, and, in some quarters, even beyond. But this illusion of automatic progress has been seen for what it was, paganism, the trust in pagan gods. Christian thinkers, thank God, have had the insight to recognize the non-Christian quality of this muddled optimism. They have known that this paen of thanksgiving to an unknown god is not Christian. "How excellent is thy name in all the earth, thou hast set thy glory among the steel mills and cyclotrons."

But among many very vocal thinkers, there has been an overcompensation. In the reaction against an immoral optimism, hope has been regarded as a juvenile illusion. It is all right for retarded minds, but not for full-grown men facing reality. What we need, it is assumed, is not the milk of hope, but the strong meat of a realism that takes hold on pessimism.

In Paul's words in this chapter, Abraham was hopeful for an impossible miracle. That is, impossible to common view. Today, we look for the same thing, an "impossible" miracle as hope moves up to faith in a Christian expectation. For the banishment of "the God of hope" from our minds and hearts is the surrender of Christian faith.

How that word "hope" sings all the way through the New Testament! There was no naïve optimism, but there was the God of hope. You can no more miss it than you could miss the Atlantic Ocean while crossing it in a ship. "The God of hope fill you with all joy and peace in believing." "The Lord will be the hope of his people."

It is a great and timely word spoken by the atomic scientist, Leo Szilard. He said to some downcast people, "Maybe God will work a miracle, if we don't make it too hard for him."

Hope says, "Maybe He will, if we don't make it too hard."

19.   PEACE, PERFECT PEACE

Peace with God through our Lord Jesus Christ.   ROM. 5:1

These are big days for peace. The pursuit of peace, peace of mind, peace of soul, peace of feelings, has become for many a major occupation. The theme song of a great host has become "Peace, Perfect Peace," although it often turns out to be, in practice, "Peace, Imperfect Peace." A popular motto is, "Seek peace and pursue it," though it is often in a very different manner than that prescribed in the 34th Psalm. This runs all the way from Father Divine's "Peace, it's wonderful," to Liebman's "Peace of mind," which did much to start the pursuit, to all the other psychological prescriptions. No blanket criticism of the whole movement would be fair, for various segments of it differ widely. One would be blind who ignored the exorcism of devils of anxiety, fear, and turbulence brought about by search for peace of mind.

Yet, this phrase, "peace of God through our Lord Jesus Christ," a phrase reiterated by Paul, reveals the true source of peace. It is the peace of *God* which brings an end to devastating war of mind. There is something vulgar in seeking peace in itself. The direct head-on assault on peace of mind, seeking to win it by dint of frontal attack, is not according to New Testament direction.

Here is a sharp-pointed criticism of this attack by a great psychiatrist, who knows the truths of Jesus as well as those of Freud and other pychological pundits. Dr. Karl Menninger writes:

Unrest of spirit is a mark of life; one problem after another presents itself and in the continuous solving of them we find our greatest pleasure. The continuous encounter with continually changing conditions is the very substance of living. From the acute awareness of the surging effort we have the periodic relief of seeing one task finished and another begun, and the comfort of momentary rest and nightly sleep. . . . This magnificent drama of conflict sets us our highest ideal—spiritual nobility and social achievement. . . . To seek after peace of mind is to forsake this truth for an illusion. It is the *search* to which I object, because striving for personal peace means turning one's back on humanity and its suffering, losing one's life in trying to save it.

Peace is a by-product, an effect of something else. It is never captured by an onslaught. Notice the word "through" in the sentence, "peace of God *through* our Lord Jesus Christ." Peace comes by an agency—"through."

So the true coming of peace is not pictured by the subjective whining plea, "I want to be happy," of which there are so many varieties extant. That is only the selfish cry of "gimme, gimme" masquerading as prayer. Peace means more than "How do I feel?" It is a matter of our relationship to the will of God, which alone gives peace. So the true source of peace appears in the glorious, outgoing objective worship of the hymn:

> *Immortal, invisible, God only wise,*
> *In light inaccessible, hid from our eyes,*
> *Most blessed, most glorious, the Ancient of Days,*
> *Almighty, victorious, Thy great name we praise.*

God himself intervenes. We have peace through the grace wherein we stand.

20.   SHARING THE GLORY OF GOD

We rejoice in our hope of sharing the glory of God.   ROM. 5:2

Audacious words, so audacious they are shocking. Sharing the glory of God? We ascribe glory to God, we praise God's glory, we wonder at it. But to *share* it? Hardly. That seems to call for the prayer, "Hold back thy servant from presumptuous sins."

We see God's glory in the sky, "Who hast set thy glory above the heavens" (Ps. 8, AV). We are accustomed to see God's glory in a cathedral, which, as the cornerstone proclaims, was erected to the glory of God. Its vaulted arches, high altar, and rose window show His glory. *Share* is the right word. We have such a perverted and inadequate sense of the glory of God. In fact, the idea of glory is one of the most corrupting ideas in all human life. Men have sought glory with a fiercer lust than that of gain. They have sought with frenzy some of the glory that was Napoleon.

The true glory of God is, in the words of C. H. Dodd, "the divine likeness which man is intended to bear." Jesus saw the glory of God in human life. He saw it in the widow who, in outgoing love, gave her whole living to those in need. The glory of God is the glory of love, of giving, the glory of service. Wherever genuine love is, wherever the spirit of sacrifice lights up a life with radiance, there is the sharing of the glory of God.

21. CALCULATED RISK

While we were yet sinners Christ died for us.   ROM. 5:8

During the years of World War II, we heard much about "calculated risk." Often the discussion seemed so callous that it made the
blood run cold. Thus, for instance, it was roughly calculated that to
secure a beachhead would cost five hundred lives, but be worth it.
Human life was "expendable." It was a calculated risk. The expression spread over into other areas of life. These words of Paul, "while
we were yet sinners," show a "calculated risk" spreading over into
the area of divine grace. The words make a sharp and vivid picture
of the hazard of grace. We can even say truly, "while we were yet
sinners" God takes a chance. We are saved by the divine initiative.

These words picture the surpassing quality of the love of God.
James Moffatt has an inspired exclamation point in this passage. He
translates, "for the ungodly!" Exclamation point! Absolutely! It calls
for a huge exclamation point, that God should hazard so much. He
takes the initiative—He does not wait till we approach in humble
repentance, "While we were yet sinners Christ died for us," taking
the risk of failure. He took the risk. In an old song we no longer
sing, wonder was expressed at the amazing grace that Christ should
die for "such a worm as I." We eliminated the word "worm" from our
thinking. We have not eliminated the amazing grace.

This is a quality which should go into our daily living. We hear
much of "games of chance." Many, many people frown on them and
abstain from them. But there is a glorious game of chance. We should
make life a game of chance, in that we take the initiative, that we
take a calculated risk, doing the loving, generous act, before there is
any proof that it will pay. That is what the grace of God did, "while
we were yet sinners." That is what the grace of God should effect in
us. We should "get the jump" in extending forgiveness, in investing
strength and effort, in good causes for which there seems only a
forlorn hope. A game of chance for high stakes, for God's cause and
man's benefit, is a great thrill.

22. SLAVES OF GOD

Now that you . . . have become slaves of God.   ROM. 6:22

It has been pointed out by many Biblical scholars that there is a sharp division of the Epistle to the Romans at the end of Chapter 5. It is asserted that up to Chapter 6 the stress is chiefly on salvation on its negative side—on the plight of men without salvation in Christ. But in Chapters 6 to 8, the positive idea of salvation is set forth in which power is given for a higher life.

Here we have an exchange of slavery pictured, from "slaves of sin" (Rom. 6:17) to become "slaves of righteousness" (Rom. 6:18) and "slaves of God" (Rom. 6:22). "Slave" is a strong word. But slavery to God is a strong thing. No lesser word can portray the undivided allegiance that Christ demands.

The obedience pictured in the word "slave" brings a timely warning and reminder to a time where the idea of discipline has dropped out of the religious life of so many people. The idea of a firm discipline has dropped out of the lives of so many people in so many different areas of thinking and acting. The very word is distasteful to multitudes, regarded as obsolete. In the bright lexicon of a large section of youth there is no such word as "discipline." As for slavery to anything, it is unthinkable. The word "freedom" has degenerated, until it means freedom to indulge any desire, and freedom to "try anything once," even if it is freedom to jump off a cliff.

Paul's ideal of slavery to God is later elevated to sonship. But if this word "slave" and the idea of undivided allegiance drops out of the idea of sonship, there is nothing much left but mawkish sentimentalism.

One stern truth of life, from which we cannot escape, is that we will be slaves of *something*. If we deny this, and say "I am free to do anything I want to," we have been shackled with the most galling slavery in the world, which is servitude to the whim of the moment. One person is a slave to appetite. It is not always what is called "vicious appetite." It may be just appetite for food, but it can be a worse slave driver than Simon Legree.

Here is a bit from the biography of Diamond Jim Brady:

His stomach was six times the normal size. His breakfast consisted of beefsteak, chops, pancakes, eggs, fried potatoes, hominy, corn bread. For luncheon he had oysters, lobster, roast beef, salad, and pie. At dinner, more oysters, more lobsters, more steaks smothered in chops, five or six vegetables, more salad and dessert. At midnight, a snack consisting of two or three warm birds and a quart of orange juice.

That was an abject slavery.

From the same slave quarters is the weary remark of a widow, who was asked for a suggestion for a small carving to be put on her husband's tombstone. "I would suggest," she said, "after the name and dates, a carving of a two-inch porterhouse steak. That is all he ever got excited about."

We can be slaves of instincts. The potentials are within us. Carl Sandburg gives a humorous, but realistic, catalogue of the zoological park we carry within us, in his poem "Wilderness":

> *There is a wolf in me*
> *Fangs pointed for tearing gashes,*
> *A red tongue for raw meat . . .*
> *I keep this wolf because the wilderness gave it to me,*
> *And the wilderness will not let it go.*
> *There is a fox in me, . . .*
> *Oh, I got a zoo,*
> *I got a menagerie inside my ribs*
> *Under the bony head.*

But when a person becomes a slave of God, there is a new power. He is no longer just a man fighting serpents, as in the Laocoön, but a man endowed with a new order of life. For in his service is perfect freedom—and power.

23. THE CIVIL WAR

I can will what is right, but I cannot do it. ROM. 7:18

These words paint a panorama of the Great Civil War which has been going on in man ever since he graduated from the subhuman class, and went on to the first grade in the education and progress of the race. The key passage in describing this inner conflict between desire and power is here: "I can will but not do."

The recognition of this civil war has become clearer in our day than ever before. Some of that increasing high visibility we owe to Freud. He has been called by some students, in extravagant phrase, the most profound interpreter of Paul. Much of St. Paul has been a blank to Freud, but in this recognition of the divided self—"I see in my members another law at war with the law of my mind" (Rom. 7:23)—Freud did analyze and picture for our time the plight of man, which is set forth in religious language in the seventh chapter of Romans.

Another picture, and a vivid one, of this same plight is found in the judgment which John Stuart Mill gave on his education under the stern regime of his father: "I had a rudder, but no sail." The same civil war in the members—that is our biography.

A humorous description of the lack of a sail, the lack of power to do, in minor matters, is given in verse by Agnes Rogers Allen:

> I should be better, brighter, thinner,
> And more intelligent at dinner.
> I should reform and take some pains,
> Improve my person, use my brains,
> There's lots that I could do about it,
> But will I? . . . Honestly, I doubt it.

But what Freud and many psychological interpreters of this inner civil war miss is the whole eighth chapter of Romans, the whole empowering of man's will by the gift of God in Christ. The exhortation to get out of the seventh chapter of Romans and to overcome man's lack of power by our own efforts is futile. The positive power for a "sail" to go with the "rudder" is expressed in a song used in other days in Sunday schools:

> I feel the winds of God today,
> Today my sail I lift.

It is the wind of God, which is needed and provided.

H. G. Wells first coined the oft-quoted phrase which describes this inner war. He said of his character, Mr. Polly, that "he was a walking civil war." Aren't we all? But there is no end of that civil war in Mr. Wells' philosophy. He complained once of the slowness of progress. Until the bitter despair of his last days he was a worshiper at the altar of "Progress." He conceded that we do make progress slowly, we do get on. But he said, "O God, we need a gale out of heaven." That is exactly what man needs and exactly what Wells never had to offer, "a gale out of heaven," the "wind" of God, the spirit of God. We should note well that in quite a bit of recent theological thinking there has been more emphasis on the negative plight of man than in his deliverance through Christ. There has been more specific and vivid treatment of Rom. 7:19, "the evil that

I would not, that I do," than of 2 Cor. 5:17, "If any one is in Christ, he is a new creature."

Turn the page from the seventh chapter of Romans to the eighth.

24.   CHRIST THE DELIVERER

Who will deliver me from this body of death? Thanks be to God through Jesus Christ our Lord!   ROM. 7:24–25

This is the key passage in Paul, in many ways. It is the axis on which the whole Epistle to the Romans turns. Man is pictured truly as reaching complete despair: "Who will deliver me," he cries, "from this body of death?" The answer in Moffatt's translation is brief, and exultant—"God will!"

The Christian gospel of deliverance is a thrilling thing. It is incredible and unpardonable that we ever make it seem, in our telling, a dull, lifeless affair.

The deliverance of man by Christ is the greatest of all the stories of escape. Some of the world's greatest stories have been stories of escape. Homer's *Odyssey* is a collection of thrilling stories of escape and deliverance, stories which have held the world's attention for centuries. There have been gripping stories of escape from jails, sometimes by tunneling as done by prisoners in Libby Prison, Richmond, during the Civil War, and from one of the Nazi murder camps in World War II. But in all the literature of escape there is nothing like the deliverance from the bondage of sin through Jesus Christ. Dorothy Sayers puts the truth without any exaggeration: "The Christian faith is the most exciting drama that ever staggered the imagination of man." Dorothy Sayers is an expert in excitement. When the author of *Gaudy Night* and *The Nine Tailors* says a drama "staggers the imagination," that is what it does! She affirms rightly that the drama is in the act itself, the deed of God in Christ. She grieves deeply that in many places "a kind of pageant of sentiments and pale emotions has been substituted for the drama that is the Christian way. And the dogma is the drama."

The condition of man, without the deliverer in Christ, is etched sharply in Stephen Vincent Benét's "Minor Litany":

> *This being a time confused and with few fixed stars,*
> *Either private or public,*
> *Out of its darkness I make a litany*
> *For the lost, for the half lost,*
> *For the desperate.*

Chloral have mercy upon us,
Luminol have mercy upon us,
Nembutol have mercy upon us.

Freud have mercy upon us.
Life have mercy upon us.

Set against that desperate prayer to idols is the revelation in Romans that God has mercy upon us, delivers from sin and desperation in Jesus Christ. This does not mean that Christ makes life easy for us. In all truth, Christ makes life harder. If one wishes only to sail through life easily, with as little burden as possible, then he should keep a long distance from Christ. He adds to the loads to be lifted, the concerns that weigh upon the heart, the costly sacrifices of time, strength, and money demanded by him who said, "Take up a cross and follow me."

Christ brings not ease but deliverance, deliverance from sin, from fear, from self.

25. TO SET THE MIND

Those who live according to the Spirit set their minds on the things of the Spirit. ROM. 8:5

This phrase "set the mind" occurs three times in three sentences. Evidently, it is important, indeed a dominant factor in life. It is well worth noting that this exhortation to "set the mind" on the Spirit, a truly severe intellectual exercise, comes in the midst of a rejoicing in the gift of God in Christ, freeing us from the law of sin and death. To receive the gift is not a passive affair. It demands a major operation in life—to set the mind.

Some people never set the mind at all. Their mental steering gear is all loose. Their minds are like ships in which the wheel has no connection with the rudder. They never truly and painfully set the course. No grip of mind to hold the rudder. They are like the famous land lubber who was taken on to steer a fishing boat and told simply to keep it pointed to the North Star. After a while, he called out gaily, "Give me another star to steer by, I've sailed past that one!"

Now, of course, the mind can be set with too much rigidity. The life of the spirit, the emotions, the imagination, the individuality may be squeezed out for the sake of a narrow and inflexible orthodoxy.

But the mind can be set, so that movement is provided for, as the steering wheel of an automobile provides direction, flexibility, and stability. The mental and moral danger to which so many in this generation have succumbed is a distaste for nearly everything that represents setting the mind firmly. They prefer what they call the open mind on all questions. The result of such openness is, of course, emptiness; the wide-open mind is a windswept expanse. Commenting on this devotion to the open mind with no set to it, Mr. Chesterton points out that the purpose of an open mind is the same as that of open jaws, "to close it on something."

To set the mind is emphatically needed in the realm of religion. It is a rigorous necessity all too often passed over in favor of invertebrate mooning and sentimental feeling. One minister has said, "Many of the members of my congregation seem to have joined the church on 'confusion of faith,' " not loving God with the mind. Just as shoes are very often left outside the entrance to a Mohammedan mosque, so minds are often checked at the entrance of a Christian church, to be recovered after the service is over.

Some minds are never "set" in religion in any vigorous way. Richard Potter, the father of Mrs. Sidney Webb, was a rich and able man, but in his religious thinking, or rather in the lack of it, he used the ideas he learned as a little child. His daughter remarked of him, in his middle and old age, that he repeated the prayer taught to him at his mother's lap: "Gentle Jesus, meek and mild, look upon a little child."

Some set the mind on the flesh, as Paul says here. That becomes a decisive mind set, shaped by repetition and use, all energies directed to the great goal of life, the things of the flesh, a bewildering and alluring variety. That is the terrible side of the integrated mind. Many people have repeated the ill-digested psychological terms they have learned in a way that indicates that they think integration is in itself a good thing. The integrated and unified mind can be a terrible thing. A person can be integrated around a whiskey bottle, a roulette wheel, or a racing sheet. But, to set the mind on the Spirit is life and peace (v. 6). God's gift in Christ is freedom from the law of sin and death. But it is only when we set our mind on the gift that it becomes a saving power.

26. THE UNAVAILING FLESH

Those who are in the flesh cannot please God. ROM. 8:8

This word "flesh" so prevalent in Paul's letters, has been fenced in too rigidly in much contemporary thinking. It is commonly applied to the gross sins of appetite, and thus, its connotation is too limited. Move the word away from Corinth and Rome and set it down in present-day Seattle or Chicago, or any American community. "Flesh" has become a bad word. Even the man who rejoices in 280 pounds of flesh feels that such phrases as "to live according to the "flesh" (Rom. 8:5) and "with my flesh I serve the law of sin (Rom. 7:25) picture the sad condition of the profligate in the gutter. Of course they do, and they picture a lot else besides.

People generally feel that the man who "lives to the flesh" lives on Skid Row, and we can almost hear the bang of the saloon door as he is thrown out on the street. Or in common thought, higher up on the economic ladder, the "mind of the flesh" is marked by gluttony or lechery.

We need to be reminded again and again that the word "flesh" as used by Paul has a much larger meaning than "carnality." The man who lives "according to the flesh" lives on Evergreen Drive as well as on Skid Row. He can be, and frequently is, a slim, graceful figure, the glass of fashion and mold of form, and yet, he may be "in the flesh."

It would be hard to find a better description of "living by the law of the flesh" than that given by A. E. Taylor. He says that people who live by the flesh are "those who make the words 'I want to' the legitimization of every desire." There are people who do exactly that. The words "I want to" are the supreme court of their lives. There is nothing higher. Words such as "ought," or "constrained," those mountain peaks of the dictionary, are still Greek to them. They have never been translated into their daily language. They have been well called "earth bound." The man who "lives by the flesh," then, is the man who is "left to himself." He has cried out to so many appeals, "Let me alone," that it is a fitting punishment that such is what has happened to him, he has been "let alone," alone with just the thoughts and emotions of the "natural" man. The translation of Rom. 8:5 made by J. B. Phillips puts the picture sharply: "The carnal attitude sees no further than natural things." It is the near-sighted life. The contrast to this is the man who lives by the spirit, who reaches out for the things beyond the fences of the flesh, to the enhanced powers of the soul.

27. THE GREAT FORGOTTEN TEXT

Any one who does not have the Spirit of Christ does not belong to him.
ROM. 8:9

Of course, there are many texts which could be called, without any cynicism, the "great forgotten text," words of Jesus, for instance, such as "Love your enemies." They have been well forgotten in a tragic case of Bible amnesia.

But some texts seem peculiarly forgotten, especially in ecclesiastical practice. It seems ironic that they appear in the Bible, in plain print, so that all may read. It often seems as though they had not been translated into native tongue, but have been left in some unknown original tongue, such as the word "selah," which keeps appearing in the Psalms, with no one paying any attention to it.

High on such a list would be this sentence in Romans: "Any one who does not have the Spirit of Christ does not belong to him."

As we look about us, it is often hard to realize that this sentence is printed in plain, readable English, and has so appeared for centuries. So often no attention has been paid to it. Men read it, presumably, and then "it flies forgotten as a dream dies at the opening day." Life in the spirit denotes the spirit of God dwelling within a person. The term is equated with the spirit of Christ. But it also means possessing Christlike qualities. The result of having the spirit of God dwelling in a person is the spirit of Christ shaping and informing one's action. If our emotions and actions do not reflect the spirit of Christ, we are none of his.

What if that were made a test of orthodoxy! What upsets would follow! But it *is* a test of belonging in the Christian fellowship. For the test of the presence of the spirit is not aesthetic. It is not ecclesiastical. It is *ethical*. The power of the spirit is the power of *goodness*. The test of our belonging to Christ is whether what we are doing is what Christ would have us do. The test is whether there grows in us the fruit of the spirit, listed in Gal. 5:22, "Love, joy, peace, patience, kindness, goodness, faithfulness, gentleness, self-control."

This is a truly terrible text. For it means that nothing counts with God except possessing and showing a Christlike spirit. Nothing else counts—the boast of heraldry, the pomp of power, miter, and robe, all the salutations in the market place—all add up to zero. We have that in Jesus' exact words:

Not every one who says to me, "Lord, Lord," shall enter the kingdom of heaven, but he who does the will of my Father who is in heaven. On that day many will say to me, "Lord, Lord, did we not prophesy in your name, and cast out demons in your name, and do mighty works in your name?" And then will I declare to them, "I never knew you; depart from me, you evildoers." [Matt. 7:21–23]

The things mentioned as claims on the bounty of the Lord really stand for the curriculum of a theological seminary. And those were not enough. There is the "Lord, Lord"; that is worship, is it not? And a beautiful and fruitful art it is. The words "prophesy in your name" represent preaching. And it has been of measureless power through the years and centuries. "Cast out demons." Surely that is what the skilled counselor does, casting out the demons that blight personality. "Mighty works in your name." That surely is administration. But add it all up together. Precious as those skills are, they are not enough. They may win the sad verdict, "I never knew you." If we do not have the spirit of Christ, if there is self-seeking competition and brag, if we apply the social-standing test to God's word, or the color test to God's church, we are none of His.

28. THE MIGHTY MONOSYLLABLE

Rom. 8

The word "if" has been called, with some show of reason, the "biggest word in the language." It is one of the biggest, if not in the language of erudition, at least in the living language which we use for daily life. For the really "big words" in the dictionary are not the long words, such as "transubstantiationalist." They are the short, stubby words, which breathe, as, "do, be, no, man, wife, home, love, life."

The word "if" is a mighty monosyllable. It is a door which stands in front of life's finest possibilities, like a stern, armed sentinel on guard. In a negative way, it is a door which opens on every kind of disaster. When we do not meet the "if" which guards life's prizes, the door slams shut. There is a bang of finality about it, the grim finality we hear in the words of the parable of the Wise and Foolish Virgins, "and the door was shut." We can put our ear close to the page and still hear its slam. In fact, there is no sound which suggests "the end" quite so powerfully as the closing of a door.

Every fair possibility depends on the opening of the door "if." Recall the many excursions of prophecy, with the imposing title, "The Next Hundred Years." The body of the revelation is a dazzling array of wonders to come. At the end there appears the *"if"—if* we do not have a war that blows up the world.

In the eighth chapter of Romans we see and hear the swinging door of "if." Man's highest potential and his highest joy, are reached through an "if." The word punctuates the whole chapter. In this wonderful description of the new creation in Christ, notice the "ifs" on which it depends. Listen: "You are in the Spirit, *if* the Spirit of God really dwells in you" (v. 9); "*If* Christ is in you, . . . your spirits are alive" (v. 10); "*If* the Spirit of him who raised Jesus from the dead dwells in you" (v. 11); *"if* by the Spirit you put to death the deeds of the body you will live (v. 13); "*if* children, then heirs" (v. 17); and that towering Mt. Everest of faith, "*If* God is for us, who is against us?" (v. 31).

Also, we go over the cliffs of spiritual and moral disaster through an *"if."* "*If* I do what I do not want, . . . sin . . . dwells within me" (Rom. 7:20); "*if* you live according to the flesh you will die" (v. 13). If instincts walk the quarter-deck, in command of the voyage, we are on a trip to destruction.

World peace and man's survival hangs on a demanding "if." Woodrow Wilson put it in his last speech before his stroke. At Omaha in September, 1919, he said, "I can predict with absolute certainty that within another generation there will be another world war, *if* we do not concert the method by which to prevent it."

Some people never clearly see the "if" in front of achievement. The world is so full of a number of things that we want them all. In our early years we are like children romping through a toy store. We choose this and this and that. Then, if we have sensitive minds and ears, we hear an authoritative voice, "Just a moment. There is a price tag attached to that article. Look at it carefully. It isn't free."

We hear it back in the Old Testament, "*If* ye are willing and obedient, ye shall eat of the good of the land" (Isa. 1:19). In any event, the people who are in a hurry, and are eager to "skip the preliminaries," never enter into any kingdom of power. You can be a competent surgeon *if.* You can be an effective teacher *if.* The sentry, "if," guards the garden of marriage with a flaming sword. You can have a happy marriage and blessed home *if* you can throttle the insistent "I," *if* you can subordinate yourself and love, "up to the level of each day's quiet need. . . ."

All through this chapter, the door to life's richness and power swings open, "*if* Christ is in you . . . your spirits are alive" and "*if* any man be in Christ, he is a new creation." And that door to life which is life indeed, "If God is for us, who is against us?"

That brings delivery from every jail into which man can be cast.

29. SONS OR MACHINES

You have received the spirit of sonship. ROM. 8:15
We are children of God. ROM. 8:16

The basic truth of the Christian gospel meets a sharp and increasingly painful need of men at this moment with a new significance. It is a widespread loss of a sense of status which is cutting into men's spirits in a new way. We are in a growingly mechanical world. Into that world comes the personal gospel for an impersonal world. This assurance brought by Paul, "We are children of God," comes into our situation with the relevance and freshness of a five-star final extra. Part of the ordeal of this generation is that we are in an increasingly depersonalized world. It is as though great impersonal forces are running over men like a fleet of steam rollers. The shadow of automation deepens about us. The fearful ogre of our day is not a dragon spitting fire, but a mechanical man, a giant Univac, who looks as though made out of stove pipes.

In the background of this impersonal quality is the tragic fact that the times have made it hard to believe in human live. Our sensibilities have been blunted by the scale upon which human misery has been presented to us since World War I. It has been difficult for a great multitude to believe in the value of human life.

There is a notable spiritual insight, one among man, in the story of Jesus' temptation in Matthew. Satan is represented in the first temptation, as attempting to insinuate doubt in Jesus' mind about his status—to break down his consciousness of sonship. He said, "if thou be the son of God." If that sense of sonship could be impaired, the rest might follow. In our world today, the sense of a unique worth is taking a hard pounding. If that is impaired, the way to disaster is open.

A picture of the impersonal onslaught on individual personality is given in a novel of totalitarian regime, *One,* when the leader says to a man, "I will *pulverize* your identity." There is a growing process of pulverizing identity.

We find this impersonal process pictured in a confession from a man in a large office force:

> *The fellows up in personnel*
> *They have a set of cards on me.*
> *The sprinkled perforations tell*
> *My individuality.*
>
> *And what am I? I am a chart*
> *Upon the cards of I B M*
> *The secret places of the heart*
> *Have little secrecy to them.*
>
> *It matters not how I may prate*
> *How charged with punishments the scroll.*
> *The Files are masters of my fate*
> *They are the captains of my soul.*
>
> *Monday my brain began to buzz:*
> *I was in agony all night.*
> *I found out what the trouble was:*
> *They had my paper clip too tight.*

It is not only the preacher who feels this impersonal quality of life. Here are the words of Harry Stack Sullivan, the psychiatrist, in his *Interpersonal Theory of Psychiatry:*

The deepest problem of people today is loneliness, isolation and the difficulty of self-esteem in our society. Whereas the problem in Freud's early decades was sexual repression, and the chief problem in the early thirties, when Karen Horney wrote, was disguised hostility, today it is loneliness.

Loss of status plays a large part in that condition. And here is the supreme timeliness of the gospel, a personal gospel for a depersonalized world. The gospel declaration is that man is not a machine, not a chemical accident, not an educated ape, but a child of God. Christ as the champion of personality meets a growing and aching need. A tremendous word for today is an old one, "He calleth his sheep by name." That means much in a world where numbers seem to many people to be supplanting names. That is something to sing about. So we sing about it, "O Love that will not let me go."

30. HEIRS AND HEIRLOOMS

If children, then heirs, heirs of God and fellow heirs with Christ. ROM. 8:17

This is another picture in Paul's great description—his gallery of pictures, of the powers of the Christ-filled life. The new life in the spirit is the theme running through the towering eighth chapter of Romans.

The subject of an heir is the theme of some of the world's great literature. All the world loves an heir in disguise in story form. *Ivanhoe* and *Great Expectations* are only two examples of a great many, where the narrative is accompanied by the question, "Will the heir get the inheritance?"

Often the story is that of the missing heir, played out occasionally in real life. Perhaps the most notable life drama of the missing heir theme is the incredible story of Mrs. Henrietta Garrett of Philadelphia. Hardly a dozen people attended the funeral on a wet, gloomy day in November, 1930, when an old lady of eighty-one years was buried, unknown to fame and to the world. Only two of those at the funeral could be classed as relatives! But life sprang one of its topsy-turvy surprises when the probate court broke out the news that this widow who left no children did leave a fortune of seventeen million dollars, and no will could be found. Thousands of people hurriedly rose up to call her blessed. She became one of the most beloved women in the world. In twenty-five years the estate had grown to thirty million dollars, and twenty-six thousand people claimed to be heirs!

Not many people are missing heirs in the sense of claiming a fortune or part of it. But there is an unnumbered host of others who never press any claims in a probate court. They do not press their claim anywhere. But they are missing heirs of a great inheritance from God. There is no sense of sonship or inheritance. This is the theme of a great detective story in Christian history. It is not the story of a sleuth laying a hand on a person's shoulder, saying, "You are the criminal." It is the long story of the heralds of Christ saying to a person, "You are an heir of God. Claim your inheritance."

That is always a word in season, yesterday, today, and forever. It is the legacy of the spirit of God which brings the power of God into life, enhances a person's capacities, so that he is literally "beyond himself," and he is led out of the dark prison of frustration and futility. That is a staggering legacy to claim!

But it is true of this word of Paul's (as of others, see comment on Rom. 8:15 and 12:2) that it comes with peculiar timeliness and urgency to this present generation. For there is an increasing number of people who have no sense of being heirs, or of having been left a legacy by a Father.

The spiritual condition of a great host is paralleled by one of the tragic spectacle of a physical host of wandering people who are in search of identity. These are refugees, escapees, DP's, defrauded people who are stateless, who have lost nationality, herded into concentration camps, or wandering the earth like Cain, with a mark on their foreheads for no crime, except for the "crime" of being born. These people lack proof of identity, in many cases their native lands have been erased from the map by the Communist eraser.

Like these stateless folk, there are multitudes of people who, too, have lost their spiritual identity. In their own thought of themselves, they come from nowhere and are on their way to nowhere. They are heirs of nothing except the ills that flesh is heir to. So they have lost the greatest motive for living and the greatest motive for power, described in the Gospel of John, "Jesus, knowing . . . that he had come from God and was going to God, . . . girded himself," the sense of origin and destiny in God. But multitudes have no sense of origin and destiny with which to claim an inheritance. On this condition of so many, Erich Heller has written memorably in his *The Disinherited Mind*. He quotes feelingly from Kafka in diagnosis of the ill: "Yet I feel no certainty about anything, demanding from every single moment a new confirmation of my existence . . . in truth, a disinherited son." Professor Heller's thesis is that "man has gradually lost his identity, his private harmony, so to speak, with the universe. . . . God has abandoned him; or rather, he has abandoned God." He says that this is the theme of much modern literature, man disinherited, no sonship, no heir!

The great inheritance is portrayed in the magic words of human speech, "our Father." When we can use that great language, when we can say "thou" and not "it", we are no longer displaced persons, or disinherited persons, but by the power of the spirit, sons of our father.

It is natural for Paul to continue, "fellow heirs with Christ." That gives a closer definition of "heir" and enlarges its range. We are fellow heirs in three respects. We inherit the relationship, our Father. We inherit a family, our brothers in Christ. We inherit the task of Jesus, to play a redemptive part in life.

31. THE ENDLESS DIALOGUE

I consider that the sufferings of this present time are not worth comparing with the glory that is to be revealed to us. ROM. 8:18

The greatest arguments of history are those which man holds with himself. There have been endless affirmations and equally positive rebuttals. Man is not only the animal that laughs. He is the debating animal. Shakespeare gives a lively and, withal, a realistic recording of one of these millions of debates. Launcelot Gobbo speaks in *The Merchant of Venice*, "Well, my conscience says, 'Launcelot, budge not.' 'Budge,' says the fiend. 'Budge not,' says my conscience. 'Conscience,' say I, 'you counsel well.' 'Fiend,' say I, 'you counsel well.'" So it goes, about it and about. Such impassioned debates have gone on since the dawn of time, when man began to have a sense of the future. Of all the dialogues which man has had with himself, the endless one is that between today and tomorrow. Shall I settle for cash on the barrelhead, right now, so that I can jingle the coin in my pocket, or hold my resources for greater gain tomorrow? Some people make it a short and conculsive debate, soon over. Their theme song in life is "I've got coins that jingle, jangle, jingle." We all debate the question, in many realms, material, ethical, and spiritual, "Shall I be a capitalist, saving for the greatest return, or a spendthrift?"

We hear in one ear the insinuating voice:

> *Ah, take the Cash and let the Credit go,*
> *Nor heed the rumble of a distant drum.*

In the other ear, we *do* hear the rumble of a distant drum, "not worth comparing with the glory that is to be revealed to us."

In every realm we are lured by the chance of a quick sale and profit-taking. Too often the devotees of "take the quick profit today and forget the calamity tomorrow," the land skinner, and the slaughterer of forests, have won the debate over the best use of our natural resources.

Yet, it is the mark of a mature mentality to realize that the weights, as Paul balances them, are with the choice to postpone the expenditure of capital resources, and to vote for the high tomorrow over the quick and easy today. The suffering of today seems so real, painfully real; the weight of glory tomorrow so far away, and intangible. Comfort, no matter at what a spiritual price, so often has allurements over the vague reward of glory.

Yet the martyr's faith weighs the days, with the vote for the greater weight tomorrow. "Above this darksome circus shine the stars." There is always a tragedy about the words "paid in full." When all the profit of life is paid immediately, there is a dreary finality about it. No mysterious remainders of life, no glory of tomorrow to look forward to; the whole thing is receipted. There it is, "paid in full." The high adventure of life is over.

The supreme instance of this is seen in the temptation of Jesus. In a real way every temptation was a dialogue between a quick, comfortable today, with its deceitful good, and a long weight of glory. Thus the temptation to cash in—"make these stones bread," *now,* "throw yourself down from this pinnacle," *now,* "take over the kingdoms of this world," *now.* Jesus said to them all, "You shall worship the Lord your God, and him only shall you serve," the God of the glory of tomorrow and the glory of serving Him.

32.   A WAITING WORLD

For the creation waits with eager longing for the revealing of the sons of God.   ROM. 8:19

We are in a waiting world. We are learning to count in a new and tragic way. Every day records its fearsome counting, such as is sounded off before a bomb explodes on a testing ground. "Five, four, three, two, one, zero. Bang!" We are breathlessly listening, not for the last trump, but for the last bang. T. S. Eliot assured us a generation ago that the world does not end with a bang but with a whimper. Since that time, we have decided, on the basis of scientific "advance," that the probabilities are in favor of a bang as the end of the world.

But the waiting, here set forth as a prelude to world salvation, is a vastly different kind of waiting. It is waiting for a revelation of a different kind of *people,* the sons of God. Salvation is to come, not from machines, but from men of love and brotherhood, men set on life rather than death. The creation waits for a revelation from God. Salvation from the final bonfire is an affair of the mind and heart, of the soul, if the wise ones will permit the use of such an anachronism.

It is not only the man of religion, not only the preacher, who waits with eager longing for the coming of the means of world survival, but scientists and philosophers and indeed all who can see with unbandaged eye. Here is Bertrand Russell wondering out loud if scientific man can survive. He quotes one gloomy statistic on the side of scientific man's not surviving:

Consider one single matter: The expenditure of public money on scientific and technological research in the past eighteen years. What has been the purpose of this expenditure? About ninety-nine percent of it has had as its aim the perfecting of methods of mass extermination.

Again he asks:

Who are the heroes whom we in England most admire? The answer is easy. Compare the height of the Nelson monument with the height of the statues to Shakespeare, Newton and Darwin. This will give you the exact proportion in which we consider the extermination of enemies more important than services to mankind.

I think it is possible that the governments of East and West alike may decide that their enmity is suicidal, and many come together in a determination to make science the servant of man rather than of homicidal lunatics.

This demands a morality which will be new only in the sense of being acted upon. . . . If this lesson can be learned in time, science can lay the foundation of a new golden age.

Waiting! But not for any revelation from God or minds propelled by the spirit of God. Bertrand Russell rejects all that. Yet he sees the needs with painful clearness and has again and again demanded "Christian love." In many ways, he seems to throw the Bible away, and quote from memory.

There are various kinds of waiting in the world. Many among us are waiting with eager longing for bigger and better missiles. Some are waiting with a naïve faith for a new political order or merely till "our party" gets in power. If the world should ever come to destruction, the last thought of many politicians will be "How will this affect the next election?" Others are just waiting, in a sort of mental and spiritual vacuum.

There is an active waiting contemplated in the words "waiting for the revealing of the sons of God." It is like a wise farmer waiting for spring. He is waiting on the action of heaven, of the sun and sky. But at the time he is preparing for the coming of spring, so that he may co-operate with the powers of heaven. Here is an instance of creative waiting.

Indomitable persistence matched with infinite patience changed the mild nature of Louis Pasteur into a driving force. Before he had attained maturity he had decided that the three words which held the deepest meaning were will, work, wait. So, our world is waiting for the "sons of God," who can bring the creative power of God's love into action for world salvation.

33.   CREATIVE GROANING

The whole creation has been groaning in travail . . . and not only the creation, but we ourselves . . . groan inwardly.   ROM. 8:22

Groaning is a matter we know something about. We do it enough to know all about it. We do know plenty. For we do a plentiful job of groaning.

We groan over the morning paper. There is usually more than enough to call for loud groans. Charles Lamb suggested that there ought to be a "grace before reading a book," as well as before a meal, for a book calls for a return of thanks to God. In a different manner we need a "grace before reading a newspaper," for we need to be fortified for the ordeal. We call our time a postwar era. Shall we also adopt Toynbee's term and call it a "post-Christian era" or a post-sanity era?

We groan over the income tax and over the shrinking dollar of inflation. And many groan deeply over a worry-induced ulcer.

Of course, Paul's use of the word "groaning" did not mean this kind of groan. It meant a kind of sense of corruption and futility in the creation, which has been described in verse 19, earlier, as "waiting with eager hope for the revealing of the sons of God." Paul seems to be thinking of the sorrow of nature, something akin to what Hardy calls the "long drip of human tears." The groan is a cry for release of pain.

But there is a related meaning from the strong metaphor which Paul uses, that of childbirth. There is also the groaning, the travail, of those who are struggling to bring a new creation to birth. All those who work to bring about a new order of life do "creative" groaning. It is so when any better order of life is brought about. It was so in the Constitutional Convention of the American Colonies which brought to birth the United States. The journals of that gathering emit a loud series of groans. But between groans they kept at it for the glory that was to be. There was creative groaning in the birth and growth of the Christian church and of the building of peace.

We have, individually, groans of many sorts. Some people groan as naturally and almost unconsciously as breathing. Many people groan when they do not get their daily shot of flattery in the arm. A common occasion of loud groans is when someone else is getting a larger share of this world's loot than we are.

Paul describes a different kind of groan, the striving to be adopted as sons of God, the desire for inward rather than outward possession. Such a deep yearning is seen in Brother Lawrence, continually struggling to be a more Christlike man. He never gave up the struggle.

Our world needs more groans, not cries of complaint, but of aspiration. We need to hear the groans of workers under a heavy load, struggling to make a better world.

34.   PATIENCE AND HOPE

But if we hope for what we do not see, we wait for it with patience.
ROM. 8:25

In the preceding verse we read of the hope of adoption as sons. We read, "In this hope we were saved." The passage presents two things of permanent importance, both meeting a contemporary need, the right of the Christian to hope, and the coupling of hope and patience. They are old words which need to be firmly said today.

As has been already pointed out a few pages back, among some theologians of the present, hope barely rates as a Christian virtue. It is more regarded as the mark of a naïve, unrealistic, not to say juvenile, mind. A man of hope is one who has not learned the facts of life. Yet here we read, "In this hope we were saved."

Of course, it cannot be said too strongly that hope is not immoral optimism. It is not the happy eagerness of great expectations. Hope must have a moral foundation and texture.

Political hope, for instance, is sprinkled with easy baseless hopes. Here, for instance, is Lloyd George, addressing the House of Commons on Armistice Day, November 11, 1918. "I hope we may say," he said with emotion, "that thus, this fateful morning, came an end to all wars."

Yet a few weeks later, he was sitting in on the big poker game of the Paris Peace Conference, seeing that his country got a big slice of the spoils.

Here is President Herbert Hoover joyfully looking into the crystal ball, August 11, 1928:

We in America today are nearer to the final triumph over poverty than ever before in the history of any land. The poorhouse is vanishing from among us. We have not yet reached the goal, but given a chance to go forward with the policies of the last eight years, we shall soon, with the help of God, be in sight of the day when poverty will be banished from this nation.

Such was blind "hope."

Many Christian writers and speakers have made an overcompensation in revolt from empty optimism, which had no relation to the gospel. The result has been that sometimes Christian hope has been thrown out with unchristian optimism.

One psychological snare should be clearly remembered and avoided. There is often a real titillation of the feelings in giving way to despair. This is not seen vividly in men of Christian faith. But there have been on the part of some a tendency to wallow in despair.

Also, it is to be remembered that an active, positive hope is harder to hold than a pessimism or despair. It requires a much deeper and far-seeing look at the situation. Christian hope is like the solidly based hope that believes in the coming of spring, though. That is definitely what Paul says, hope in what is not seen.

> There is a day in spring,
> When under all the earth the secret germs
> Begin to stir and glow before they bud.
> The wealth and festal pomps of midsummer
> Lie in the heart of that inglorious hour
> Which no man names with blessing, though its work
> Is blessed by all the world.

It takes hope to see any wealth of midsummer in a rainy day in March. But hope has anointed eyes. When patience is not woven into the strand of hope, then hope is rarely more than wishful thinking. Patience is not to be confused with indifference, or with apathy, although it often is so confused. Patience is a very active quality of mind and heart. It is an equipment of the spirit so great that it is a military virtue. It is not a rest camp relaxation. It is an athletic virtue, without which hope cannot endure. Think of the patience required in a man who runs a two-mile race. In fact, that metaphor

of a race is the classic picture of hope plus patience in the New
Testament: "Let us run with patience the race that is set before us,
looking unto Jesus" (Heb. 12:1–2, AV).

35.   GOD WORKS FOR GOOD

In everything God works for good with those who love him.   ROM. 8:28

These words mark one of the high spots of the Revised Standard
Version of the Bible. It means much more to have the translation
"God works for good" than that of the King James translation that
"All things work together for good." The King James translation has
seemed to a large number too automatic, like a clock that has been
wound up and ticks on regardless of everything. Of course, the root
meaning of the two translations asserts God's help. But the phrase
"God works in everything" is so much more personal—and believable
—than the implied *things* work. Moffatt translates in the same manner, "those who love God . . . have his interest and aid in everything." Goodspeed renders the same thought, "God works with those
who love him."

A clear presentation of this difference is found in C. H. Dodd's
translation, "God co-operates in all things for good." Undoubtedly
more Christians have had a feeling of doubt as the Authorized
Version renders this than have ever voiced the doubt. There is a
block to our acceptance. We cannot say, "Everything is for the best."
Against it there is too much that seems insurmountable evidence,
even to Christian faith. But we can say, God works in every situation,
no matter how difficult. We deal with a personal God, not with an
order of things.

This concept is a tremendous affirmation and reassurance. So often
we are in the mood of the parable of the Wise and Foolish Virgins,
"as the bridegroom was delayed." How slow the consummation is
that we desire. Life seems to be one long wait. Patience, in Matthew
Arnold's line, becomes "too near a neighbor to despair." Those outside the household of faith ask bluntly, as Thomas Hardy did, "Why
does not Christianity throw in the sponge and say 'I'm beaten,' and
let another religion take its place?"

The fact that God works in any situation, the assurance that we
have his interest and aid in everything, heartens us onward on
every journey, dark or light. A traveler in West Africa records that
"West Africa is a land where the improbable is normal and the im-

possible occurs often enough to make life interesting." With God working in everything, the "improbable" is normal. We know that in the darkest spot of earth some love is found.

It is the love of God, in everything working for good.

36. WHO SHALL SEPARATE US?

Who shall separate us from the love of Christ? Shall tribulation, or distress, or persecution, or famine, or nakedness, or peril, or sword? ROM. 8:35

Swelling words! Yet the words themselves are not more amazing than the demonstration which has been given of them in life experience. An innumerable host of people have *not* been separated from the love and faith in God by these things, even when they have appeared in their worst kind of slings and arrows of outrageous fortune.

Consider Paul's own demonstration in detail of the truth of these words. He wrote that not peril, sword, nor anything else could separate. Here is his record of experiences in his own life that did not and could not separate him from God . . . "Three times I have been beaten with rods; once I was stoned. Three times I have been shipwrecked; a night and a day I have been adrift at sea; on frequent journeys, in danger from rivers, danger from robbers . . . in toil and hardship, through many a sleepless night" (2 Cor. 11:25–27). Not much of a picnic! And yet, these had no power to separate him from God. He looks back and says, inwardly (that is incredible, except to those who have experienced faith), "I am content . . . for when I am weak, then I am strong" (2 Cor. 12:10).

These are powerful "separators" which Paul lists, but not powerful enough. The words mean, of course, that none of the tribulations named will cause God's love to be separated from us. He will go with us through it all. But there is a danger that such sufferings may cause us to separate ourselves from God, from faith in His love.

But, looking in the opposite direction, think what *has* separated people from the love of God, by their own separating choice, and from faith in God. This might do for a rule-of-thumb appraisal—prosperity is much more likely to separate us than adversity. Very often, adversity unites; prosperity separates. The filled barn separates rich fools from faith and love. It leads to the disaster of self-satisfaction, "Soul, take thine ease." The lust of the eye is a separator, the dazzling array of life's possible accumulations. The upholstered chair has been a sharp separator.

Faith in the love of God has been a powerful upholder of the mind and heart. Here is William James, describing a time in his early life when he was in the grip of a deep despair:

Fear was so incisive and powerful that if I had not clung to scripture texts like "The eternal God is my refuge," and, "Come unto me all ye that labor and are heavy laden," and, "I am the resurrection and the life," I think I should really have gone insane.

A vivid suggestion of what keeps us from being separated from faith in God's grace was given, quite unintentionally, by a motion picture actress, Deborah Kerr, in a newspaper interview on her experience in making the film *Quo Vadis*. At one point lions rushed at her when she was tied to a stake in the Roman Colosseum. A reporter asked her, "Weren't you afraid when the lions made a rush at you?" She replied, "No, I am one of those actresses who read all the script of a movie. I had read to the end of the script, and I knew that Robert Taylor would come and rescue me."

A good sentence to keep in mind and heart: "I had read the script to the end." Not trivial. That is a true picture of a shining host of Christians in the first century, and of every century. They have read the script to the end and they know how it ends: "I have overcome the world. If God be for us, who can be against us?"

God has the last word. The cross is not the last word. The resurrection is the last word. So, nothing can separate us.

37. MORE THAN CONQUERORS

In all these things we are more than conquerors through him who loved us. ROM. 8:37

Christianity is a religion of surpluses. It cannot operate on a spiritual deficit economy.

The disciple of Christ must show a plus over the righteousness of the scribes and Pharisees. There must be more. It is not enough for us to salute those only who salute us, thus sentencing ourselves to the narrow jail of a mutual admiration society. It is not enough for us to avoid transgressing a law. We must do more, go into the motive of action. Indeed, the steady beat of the word more, more, more, goes all through the gospels.

So, we are more than conquerors over adversity, not in our own power, but through him who loved us. Or sometimes we must say, we *ought* to be more than conquerors, or *may be* more than conquerors. Just to be conquerors over adversity is a tremendous human achievement. Through all history there are spots of gleaming light, marking the almost unbelievable endurance of man's mind, body, and spirit. But we should be more than conquerors over evil. There must be more than endurance. There must be more—joy enduring through disaster. There must be more than just "standing it." It is within the power of the children of God to turn evil into a positive blessing. More than conquerors.

One picture of the need of the more than conquest, in a quite literal sense, is the history following World War I and World War II. America and her allies were conquerors. But more than physical conquerors were needed to match the days of destiny. Man cannot shoot his way to peace, not even with 5,000-mile missiles. There is a spiritual task of weaving a strong fabric of peace.

But these words are more than an exhortation. They say more than that we ought to be more than conquerors. They are the reassurance that we *are* conquerors through him that loved us.

38. "I AM SURE"

For I am sure that neither death, nor life, . . . will be able to separate us from the love of God. ROM. 8:38

Great words, "I am sure!" And terrible words! They have been terrible words about things concerning which a person has no right to be sure. Many of the great tragedies of history have happened because men have said "I am sure" prematurely and at the wrong place. The unrivaled block to progress toward truth in many realms, scientific and political and social and religious, has been a sureness of a belief not open to test. Someone has spoken of the "sound sleep of a decided opinion." Often there has been grievous justification of that description. Sometimes a sleep so sound that no alarm clock can disturb it.

Multitudes of men, women, and children have been hurried to untimely funerals because physicians have said "I am sure" about medical old wives' tales which had no proof. They have said, I am sure that bloodletting is the sure cure for disease, thereby very often taking away a person's last chance of recovery. In the yellow fever epidemic in New Orleans in the early nineteenth century some "authorities" were sure that a brass band would bring a cure by disturbing the atmosphere with percussion. The band paraded and pounded, the atmosphere was thoroughly disturbed, but the yellow fever was not.

In political life there has been a disastrous devotion to unfounded legends. The cave man, as he shaped his stone clubs, was "sure" that the way to peace was to make clubs so terrible that his enemies would be "scared to death." We look back with pity on the ignorance of the cave man, but we solemnly go on the same theory. One of the most terrifying things in our trembling world today is that never in history have new powerful weapons been made that they have not been used.

In religion, what desolation has been wrought over the earth by bigoted certitude which has said, "I am sure." Men professing the Christian faith in a God of love have said "I am sure" that the way to promote the gospel of love and to serve the church of Him who gave His life a ransom for many is by torture, burning, and the headsman's block.

In science, of course, there has been a steady and beneficent march away from premature and unjustified omniscience into a dedicated search for truth. Such a progress was made imperative in a way described by Alfred North Whitehead. He said, "When I was a young man, I was taught science and mathematics by brilliant men. . . . Since the turn of the century I have lived to see every one of the basic assumptions of both set aside. . . . And yet, in the face of that the discoverers of the new hypotheses in science are declaring 'Now at last we have certitude.'"

There are still giant strides to be taken. Paul's declaration, "I am sure that nothing can separate us from the love of God," is a vastly different kind of conviction. It is a faith in love, in a God of love as the ultimate power in the universe. And with Paul it was a faith founded on experiment. We can reach the same conviction by making the same experiment. We can respond to the invitation "Come and see." We can live as though God is love and find that life has a new lift and power as a result of that experiment. Thus, "the experiment becomes an experience." Then in the face of anything we can say with Paul, "I am sure."

It is not an easy faith to hold. If it is to give life a firm support it demands the investment of the whole of life, all its energy in acting as if it were true. But when that is done, we can look out on any scene and be unafraid with any amazement.

39. ANYTHING ELSE IN CREATION

Nor anything else in all creation, will be able to separate us from the love of God. ROM. 8:39

This is a translation that fits the atomic age. It is a rendering which also Moffatt and Phillips join, Phillips phrasing it, "nor anything else in God's whole world." This translation is a great gift to our day. There is no new idea added but the ancient assurance is given new range and depth. This culminating phrase of the eighth chapter of Romans reads as though Paul were thinking, "If I have forgotten anything that cannot separate us from the love of God, here it is—any other creature." But to our day, the word "creature" suggests something in a zoo, or lions and tigers bounding along the landscape.

But the phrase "anything else in all creation" reaches out through all space. It covers atom bombs, missiles, satellites, "anything else" that is to come.

Such enlargement of the range of God's love and power is greatly needed in our day. For there has come into being a strange, indefinable feeling that outer space is outside of God's jurisdiction. In that respect many people are like the ancient Hebrews in their idea, which finds expression again and again in the Pentateuch, that God is localized, tied to a place. The idea found expression that in getting into Palestine, the Israelites were likely to get out of bounds, and that God had no control over events off His localized spot.

Of course, the image of our world in the mind of men today has been infinitely enlarged. And the old idea that many held of a cozy God presiding in a cozy world does not fit the expanding universe. We must put new dimensions into an old faith. "Our God is a great God." The Ancient of Days is still in control of the Latest Thing. The most important things in the world are not the new things but the old things.

True, we are living in a new world. It has even invaded the nursery. Here, in a bit of fugitive verse, is "The Space Child's Mother Goose":

> *Mary had a little lamb*
> *Its fleece electrostatic*
> *And everywhere that Mary went*
> *The light became erratic.*

> It followed her to school one day,
> Electrons all a jingle
> It made the children's hair rise up
> And finger tips a tingle.
>
> The teacher tried to turn it out
> Her body was not grounded
> The sparks were seen for miles around
> And she's not yet rebounded.

But the old is more basic than the new. God is the Lord of space. Here is the most important thing about space, that all space is under the dominion of God, that there is no God-forsaken place. Here is the ultimate truth about space.

> Whither shall I go from thy Spirit?
> Or whither shall I flee from thy presence?
> If I ascend to heaven, thou art there!
> If I made my bed in Sheol, thou art there!
> If I take the wings of the morning
> and dwell in the uttermost parts of the sea,
> even there thy hand shall lead me,
> and thy right hand shall hold me.
>
> [Ps. 139:7–10]

In these days we have had much legal discussion on the question, "Who owns the moon?" But there is a prior question, "Who owns the earth?" The answer, still good in an age of hydrogen, cobalt, and "anything else," is "the earth is the Lord's and the fullness thereof."

With this regirded faith, we can go at the task of thinking God's thoughts after Him, and creating the conditions that make possible peace and survival. For we know that our labor is not vain in the Lord.

40. "PAIN THAT NEVER LEAVES ME"

I have great sorrow and unceasing anguish in my heart. ROM. 9:2

These words express Paul's agony over his kinsmen, the Jews who reject God's culminating revelation of Himself in Christ. J. B. Phillips translates vividly, "Feel very depressed, like a pain that never leaves me." The words still convey a twinge of pain. Paul never wrote of his own sufferings, his tour of the parts of Asia Minor and Greece, the rioting and beatings, with anything like the pain with which he writes of his sorrow for his kinsmen who reject God's gift in Christ. He writes, "I wish that I myself were accursed," so keen is his feeling.

That should be the permanent feeling of the Christian as he looks out on the world's sorrow, need, and sin, "a pain that never leaves," "unending anguish." This is not a trick that you can do with a lugubrious face. Jesus gave explicit directions on the use of faces. He said, "Anoint your head and wash your face." It is the hypocrites who "disfigure their faces" that they may get a reputation for piety. The inward hurt must go with a radiant face.

This is the deep dimension of the mind and heart of the Christian, "unceasing anguish." Where that is lacking, the personality is on the surface. The church is a caricature of its Master when it is made up largely of superficial people, charming, intelligent, friendly, alert to many of the winds that blow but not gripped by any "pain that never leaves me." They are like brightly colored butterflies that light on the surface of a meadow.

Lack of any pain goes with a well-insulated heart. It also accompanies a remoteness from the world's bruises. W. Somerset Maugham diagnoses the condition in his comment on Henry James:

He did not live, he observed life from a window. . . . Something escapes you unless you have been an actor in the tragi-comedy. In the end the point of Henry James is neither his artistry or his seriousness, but his personality, and this was curious and charming, and a little absurd.

Unless we are actors in the real life drama of humanity, we will have no real depth. Without that, a person can have very attractive qualities as a house guest or picnic companion, but Jesus did not call his disciples to a picnic. He mentioned a cross.

We reach back a number of years to a portrait of one of these charming persons, skimming the surface of life, to one author's description of Portia. Whether this is an adequate analysis of Portia or not, it does portray a large company who have no aching pain.

There is a commanding grace, a high-bred airy elegance, a spirit of magnificence, in all that Portia does and says. . . . She is full of penetrative wisdom and genuine tenderness and lively wit, but as she has never known want, or grief, or fear, or disappointment, her wisdom is without a touch of the somber or sad; her affections are all mixed up with faith and hope and joy.

These words recall Jesus' judgment when he met a very attractive character: "One thing thou lackest."

To such people, the plea in Christopher Fry's *The Lady's Not for Burning*, applies:

> *Be disturbed, madam, be disturbed,*
> *To the extent of a tut,*
> *And I will thank God for all civilization.*

Turn to the positive side of this statement. In 1841 a shy, sickly New England spinster went to Sunday School one day in March, and as a result the treatment of the mentally ill was changed all over the United States. For what Dorothea Dix saw that day in the House of Correction at East Cambridge, Massachusetts, the barbaric cruelty, gave her an unceasing anguish. She had "a pain of compassion that never left her." She became one of the most effective reformers the United States has ever known. The pain of sympathy, of empathy, is the supreme equipment for service. And it is more—it is an equipment for *seeing*. There is a physiological function of tears. A completely dry eye is a blind eye. A moist eye has the power of seeing. This is true in social as well as physical life. In that high and blessed sense we are called to be "chronic sufferers."

> *May my tone*
> *Be fresh with dewy pain alway.*

41. NEVER PUT TO SHAME

No one who believes in him will be put to shame. ROM. 10:11

We sing, usually in Lent, when we sing the hymn at all any more,

> *Jesus, and shall it ever be,*
> *A mortal man ashamed of thee?*

Yet even among those who hail Jesus as Master and Savior, it is not too uncommon to find various kinds of shame, frequently hidden from consciousness. A softer word, probably more fitting, is used by Moffatt, Goodspeed, and Phillips: "disappointed." It is not rejection of Jesus; just a saddened note of disappointment. But also, there is often an element of being ashamed of Jesus. Frequently not above the threshold of consciousness, but it is there. It comes from many reasons, some trivial, some deep. For one thing, there is no secure place in many minds for a spiritual world. No sense of a world which lies beyond this world of sense. And hence, no world in which that vague thing, spirit, can find a secure habitation. It is intangible, living only a sort of verbal life, compared to the material facts of life, so hard, so solid, so deceptively "real." Strange, isn't it, how religious people in such large numbers have allowed that word "real" to be kidnaped by the materialists and applied exclusively to the physical material of life. We get a curious trace of this in Addison's hymn, "The Spacious Firmament on High." Writing of the movements of the sun and earth, he says:

> *What though no real voice nor sound,*
> *Amidst their radiant orbs be found?*

Quite a gift to the unbelievers, that only the physical is real!

People grow ashamed of Jesus because his ideas and allegiance demand such a clash with their "set." Increasingly the first commandment is, "Thou shalt worship the gods of thy 'set,' and them only shalt thou serve." And when Jesus comes into sharp conflict with the gods of Wall Street, of the codes of the suburbs, to line up on the side of Jesus seems quixotic.

Sometimes the faint note—or louder one—of shame has its roots in an intellectual disparagement of Jesus. Christian belief does not have quite the intellectual prestige needed in modern elite circles. Also, with some, Jesus acquires a faint musty odor, as being something left over from a more simple time. It is a kind of period piece. It is kept as a beloved antique, like an old cobbler's bench now used as a magazine table.

Yet the words of Paul, "No one who believes in him will be put to shame," have proved profoundly true in the experience of an unnumbered host. The basic reason why there is a gnawing sense of shame about a dedicated faith in Jesus is that faith has not gone deep enough. It has not produced an enduring experience. Religion is given a once-over-lightly treatment. Jesus himself indicates the weakness of unstable sound as a foundation for religious thinking and living. "The rains descended, and the floods came." The situation is like the reproach which a great music teacher gave to a pupil, "You play the piano with a feather duster. You do not strike down deep enough to get out the music there is in the instrument." Exactly! There is glorious music in the "instrument" of Christian faith, when the deep places are reached. A genuine experience provides a joyful and triumphant alternative to meek surrender to other gods. It speaks in this language, "For me to live is Christ." It asks:

> *Ashamed of Jesus? Sooner far*
> *Let evening blush to own a star.*

42. AWE CONQUERS PRIDE

So do not become proud, but stand in awe.   ROM. 11:20

There is a keen insight here, in that awe is opposed to pride. More than that, awe, in the high original sense, preserves from pride.

This whole section in Romans is a warning to the Gentile Christians against the pitfalls of presumption and conceit, over their being admitted into the family of God, redeemed by Christ. They had, in the picturesque language of Paul, been grafted in the tree of Christ to take the place of the unbelieving Jews, who had been separated from the root. But they are warned lest they too are rejected because of unbelief. They need to be saved from conceit, by a deep awe.

In our time, awe is an emotion which is rapidly passing out of the experience of great multitudes. The only way in which many people use the words is as a false synonym. People ask, "Isn't it awful?" for something which has no awe in it at all. Indeed, the very word "awe" is passing out of use. One of our dictionaries gives the meaning, "power to inspire reverence," as *archaic!* The words "fear" and "dread" as meanings for awe are given as *obsolete!* About that we can admit that it is true, and God pity us!

When we say of so many trivial things that they are "awful," it illustrates our degenerate use of words. We use up all our really great adjectives on inconsequential things, so that when some really major event occurs, we have nothing to say!

But when the feeling of awe passes from a life, the life is stripped of one of its highest endowments. The sense of mystery fades into the light of common day, and a very murky light it is. Albert Einstein asserts that when we can no longer wonder we are as good as dead. He writes:

The most profound emotion we can experience is the sense of the mystical. It is the power of all true science. He to whom this emotion is a stranger, who can no longer wonder, and stand rapt, is as good as dead.

There is so little sense of the infinite and majestic which would lead people to say, as is recorded of Jacob, "How *awesome* is this place! This is none other than the house of God" (Gen. 28:17). That is the root meaning of "awful." But with us, it is corrupted to mean "What a nuisance." In that sense many words really do "end with a whimper."

One reason for this is that many young people have never really been exposed to awe. Even in religious feeling, that high quality of wonder and awe gives way to something more "practical." This is recorded of Mrs. Sidney Webb:

Mrs. Beatrice Webb had a mystical belief in prayer, which she found both stimulating and soothing, though too often, perhaps, she spoke to the Almighty as if he were a higher grade Civil Servant whose interest in the Minority Report on the Poor Law she hoped to elicit.

Many with a far more orthodox belief in Christianity than Mrs. Webb had, nevertheless have a trace of regarding the Almighty as a useful, very much higher grade Civil Servant. In this connection every minister and everyone with a concern for the Church should keep in mind the words of Francis Bacon: "What is real atheism but to handle holy things without feeling?"

So pride is substituted for awe. It is so much easier to manage, so much less embarrassing, so much more satisfying to the ego. But it is a pitiful exchange; to go from awe to pride really *is* going from the sublime to the ridiculous. It is exchanging the sun for a penny candle which we burn to our own importance. In the translation of J. B. Phillips, conceit should give way to a "certain wholesome fear."

The basic trouble of some very popular versions of the Christian religion in our time is that there is too much God as a benevolent Santa Claus in it and too little awe of a sovereign deity. There is need for recovering the uplifting emotion which finds outburst in such words as, "With God is a terrible majesty" (Job 37:22); "Let all the earth fear the Lord; let all the inhabitants of the earth stand in awe of him" (Ps. 33:8); "My heart standeth in awe of thy word" (Ps. 119:161). Against such, there can be no strutting pride.

43. THE GREATEST JOURNEY IN THE WORLD

O the depth of the riches and wisdom and knowledge of God! ROM.
11:33

Note the exclamation point at the end of the sentence above. It registers the emotional mood of the New Testament.

The greatest journey in the world is the journey from a question mark to an exclamation point. Here in these exclamation points in the climax of the more strictly theological portion of Romans is the glorious record of the journey for one man. Paul's great journey in life's experience began with a question mark on the Damascus road, "Who art thou, Lord?" It ends with this exclamation point of answer to the question. It ends with the exclamation point following one of the most exuberant affirmations of the New Testament. Fittingly that exclamation point answers a question mark. We read, "Who will deliver me from this body of death?" (Question mark.) "Thanks be to God through Jesus Christ our Lord!" (Exclamation point.)

Consider two other journeys from a question mark to an exclamation point. There is the question put to Jesus sent by John the Baptist, in a mood of wondering depression, "Art thou he that is to come or shall we look for another?" It is a baffling question in our own day. So much of the trend of current history impels us to ask wonderingly, "Have we made a mistake? Things haven't worked out as we expected. Perhaps Jesus is not the answer. Perhaps we had better look a little farther."

Jesus gave the only sufficient answer from the facts of experience, what they had seen and heard in his acts. Then later came an answer in the shout of the Palm Sunday throng, "Blessed is he that comes in the name of the Lord!" (Exclamation point.)

Of course, there were no punctuation marks in any of the manuscripts of the New Testament. But when the task of translation was begun, it was inconceivable that its high meaning could be conveyed without a whole galaxy of dancing exclamation points.

Life is poor with no exclamation point. It is like a typewriter. There is a question mark, a dollar sign, a period, for the final end. But no exclamation point, thus! Such a life never breaks out into singing.

But Christian faith does put an emphatic exclamation point into life.

> *Take all away from me*
> *But leave me ecstasy*
> *And I am richer then*
> *Than all my fellow men.*

The Christian ecstasy is marked by exclamation points. They are in the gospels. They have been repeated in experience every century and in every part of the world. There was the recognition of Jesus' character by a Roman centurion at the crucifixion, "This was a son of God!" (Matt. 27:54). There is the greeting of the risen Christ, "Hail!" (Matt. 28:9). There is the jubilant report of the two who had walked to Emmaus, "The Lord has risen indeed, and has appeared to Simon!" (Luke 24:34).

Our world today is a bewildering, even a terrifying, mass of question marks. H. G. Wells observed way back in 1906 that the smoke over the mills of some American cities formed a dark question mark in the sky. To him the question mark hung over our whole industrial civilization. In this day, an even more threatening symbol is the mushroom cloud arising from an atomic explosion. It says clearly to us, Question mark?

Those who are the trustees of the gospel must bring the gospel's exclamation points, one of faith, "The Lord God omnipotent reigneth!" and the exclamation point of obedience, "Follow me!"

44. WITH EYES WIDE OPEN

With eyes wide open to the mercies of God. ROM. 12:1 (Phillips)

These four words, "with eyes wide open," add much to the meaning of the phrase, "by the mercies of God." They "stab our spirits broad awake." They picture with vividness how we should look at the mercies of God. But so often we fail to do it. In regard to God's gifts, we do a form of sleepwalking. Instead of looking with wide-open eyes again and again, we play a game of Blind Man's Buff. God's mercies become like pictures on the walls of some rooms of our homes. We can live with them for years without even seeing them.

This is particularly true of those mercies of God, new every morning, which are right in front of us and at our feet. We take them for granted, and that pernicious habit always develops cataracts in both eyes. G. K. Chesterton has commented in his characteristic, surprising way on our passing over the great mercies we grow blind to. He says we thank God for the presents in our stockings at Christmas, but we ought to thank God we have legs in our stockings!

Elizabeth Peabody was once asked how she happened to run into a tree on the Boston Common. Her explanation was simple. She said, "I saw it but I did not realize it." That's our trouble, isn't it? We do not realize what we see. To do that demands eyes wide open to God's mercies. Do not go through this amazing world like a one-day-old kitten. Cultivate the art of "staring."

45. IN AN AGE OF CONFORMITY

Do not be conformed to this world but be transformed by the renewal of your mind. ROM. 12: 2

What a command for an age of conformity! The person who hears it and obeys it will be hearing a different drummer from the blaring brass band marching down our main streets today. And he will be listening to a distant drum. And the person who, in many ways, will not be conformed, will be badly out of step.

These words leap the centuries and the oceans, and land right in the midst of life in the mid-twentieth century in America. For it is not without good reason that ours is called an "age of conformity." There has always been the worship of false gods in every society. But our time has invented new rituals for the worship of and obedience to our most popular idol, the goddess of success. She has been renamed by one who always refused to bow the knee, the "bitch goddess" of success. She inspires today a slavish devotion.

Now, of course, there is no value on nonconformity just for the sake of being different. That is a mark of an immature mind, often of an exhibitionist one. Conformity in many aspects of life is a necessity to effective society. One gauge of railroad tracks is better than a dozen. Much merely being different springs from the motive that animated Samuel Rogers, the poet. Asked why he said so many disagreeable things, he explained that he had a weak voice and that unless he said something nasty nobody would listen to him.

Yet there is much conformity to this world for personal advantage. For the forces making for conformity today are stronger than ever before in history. They were strong in the first Christian centuries when persecution was rife. Today, there is no fire and sword, as a rule, in the United States. There have been painful exceptions to that in racial conflict. But agencies of mass production, newspapers, TV and radio and the policies of business corporations exert pressures impossible in other days. Powerful forces seek to make people into one mold. The end result is pictured by one writer: "Men dressed in interchangeable gray flannels, drive interchangeable station wagons, from interchangeable ranch houses, to take interchangeable commuter trains to interchangeable jobs in interchangeable offices." That is by no means the worst. The pressure tends to make the *minds* interchangeable. J. B. Phillips in his translation pictures the situation: "Don't let the world around you squeeze you into its own mould." People are told what to like in books, plays, ideas, and what to do in social practices, and multitudes accept the commands with docility. The alternative to rebellion is unthinkable. It is "being different." Many people would rather be behind the hearse than behind the age. Emerson described it with tragic words:

When you say, "As others do, I renounce, I am sorry for it, my early visions, I must eat the good of the land, and let learning and romantic expectations go till a more convenient season"—then died the man in you.

Paul was deeply concerned over the breakdown of spiritual and moral character, over the imminent loss of allegiance to God which this world's pressure brings. Peter Maurin succinctly describes one

> *Who tries to be somebody*
> *By trying to be like everybody*
> *Which makes him a nobody.*

Such spiritual conformity to majority standards leads to degradation, for the word means literally "de-gradation," a grading down of values, values which have been the highest possessions of men.

But Paul does not rely only on earnest exhortation. In these verses he gives two resources of unfailing power. One is renewal. As Henry van Dyke wrote vividly and truly, "You may have to live *in* a crowd, but you do not have to live *like* it, or subsist on its food. You may have your own orchard. You may drink at a hidden spring." There is a hidden spring, the renewal of the mind in the life of God in the soul.

The other resource is found in the preceding verse. It is *dedication*. "Present your bodies as a living sacrifice" (Rom. 12:1). "Present" means "dedicate." Moffat so translates it. Phillips renders it "give . . . your bodies." The way to victory over the squeezing forces of the world is to dedicate the mind and heart to the will of God. A dedicated life is a nonconformed life.

46. THE RENEWED MIND

Be transformed by the renewal of your mind. ROM. 12:2

Paul brings no easy, outward remedy to the problem of resisting the pressures to conform to the codes and ways of the world. One of the greatest and most repeated blunders of history has been that of bringing outward remedies to inward ills. Paul knew the massive pressures to which the Christian was exposed in the effort to remold his mind. He knew "imprisonments, with countless beatings, often near death" (2 Cor. 11:23) that called for a great power to resist, not a change in outward shape of conditions, but a transformation of the mind, a change that ran through the whole being, an inward renewal.

The word "renewal" is a familiar one to our time. A large part of the enormous mass of advertising is devoted to remedies for renewal, to devices to repair the ravages of time. We strive to renew almost everything, our hair (that is a major industry), our skin, our teeth, our ears, and also renewed houses. But alas, not so much effort to have the mind renewed. By desperate earnestness, we strive to renew the outside of the head, but leave the inside of the head alone, as of far less importance.

We are slow to learn that we cannot keep our religion at full strength, indeed, at any strength, automatically. We can do it with the oil heater in our house. We can set the thermostat at 70° in October and never give our heat a thought till May. It goes automatically. Religion does not, although people act as though it did. When our faith is treated in that way, soon all that is left of it is "the ghost of an old amazement." If we are to be saved from the big squeeze to mold us in the world's image, the mind and heart must be renewed by fresh coming of the life of God in the soul. Specifically, this demands nothing more mysterious than prayer, which is, of course, the most mysterious thing in the world. The mind is reinvigorated with old memories. Memories demonstrate the amazing proposition that time can be used again. That is a very present help in time of resistance to evil. What actors in a play which has had a long run often seek to recover is "the illusion of the first time." That is what the renewal of the mind by communion with God brings. Only it is not the "illusion," but the recapture of the first fine, careless rapture of first experience. It is the parallel in the life of the mind to the miracle of spring. It is not the "first time" when it comes to our past childhood. But it does bring a deep and amazing renewed power and joy.

A loved name among some of the Puritans was the name "Renewed," such as appears on some lists, names such as "Renewed" Wiseberry and "Renewed" Robinson. It is a name to strive for and live up to.

47. YOU CAN PROVE IT

So that you may prove in practice that the plan of God for you is good.
ROM. 12:2 (Phillips)

This translation brings Paul's thought into clear visibility, much
more clear than the other translations, "that you may prove what is
the will of God." The essential meaning is the same, but the rendering, "you may prove in practice that the plan of God for you is good,"
etches the meaning more sharply on the mind.

"Proof" is a strange word to use in connection with Christian
faith. We cannot prove it as we can prove that the sum of the
angles of a triangle equals two right angles. It is true, as has been
said, that a "God proved is a God dead." Religion must get into the
realm of faith.

Yet Paul uses the word "prove" and rightly. There is a firm foundation of conviction of Christian faith. Christianity when truly conceived brings no bandage to men's eyes. It asks them to make an
experiment in broad daylight. It invites, "prove in practice that the
Plan of God for you is good." It can be done. It has been done. One
of the great days in the history of science was that day on which
Galileo, in the early 1590's, tested the dictum of Aristotle, which
had been unchallenged for nineteen hundred years, that a heavier
body fell to earth faster than a lighter body, by dropping two balls
of different weights. Galileo proved that bodies of different weights
fall with equal velocities and with a uniform acceleration. Galileo
did not, as the legend has it, drop these balls from the Leaning
Tower of Pisa. But he dropped them from somewhere and they
landed with a thud which reverberated through the centuries. Experiment is the method of science. And in the sense used in these
words of Paul, it is the method of the Christian religion.

This word of Paul echoes one of the first invitations ever given
to accept the teaching of Jesus, Philip's invitation to Nathanael,
"Come and see" (John 1:46). Our gospel is not in word only but in
demonstration. It is life's greatest adventure in curiosity, in demonstration, "Come and see," "Prove in practice."

We can see the proof in practice of the affirmation, "My grace is
sufficient for thee." We see it proved not only back in the book of
Acts, but just around the corner, today. We can prove in practice,
"Lo, I am with you always." Millions have proved that "the Great
Companion" is more than a figure of speech. When they have truly

prayed, "O Master let me walk with Thee," they have walked with him. Multitudes have proved in practice, "I can do all things in him who strengthens me."

Prove it in practice.

48. A CLOSE LOOK IN THE MIRROR

I bid every one among you not to think of himself more highly than he ought to think. ROM. 12:3

This advice is always a word in season. Paul knew his human nature. Note how wide a sweep he gives to this plea, "to *every one* among you." That includes us all.

There have always been people troubled with spiritual elephantiasis. The dictionary says that means "enormous enlargement," and that is their chronic trouble. There are always men who are ready to slip into Napoleon's coat or Socrates' toga, just to try it on for size. Their magnitudes are confused. They resemble Edward Gibbon in one respect, that he was said to have confused himself with the Roman Empire.

There are many timely things to be said about this plea of Paul's for a right estimate of self. A hard trick! Consider two.

The greatest danger at the present time, with youth particularly, is at the other end. It is not the danger of overestimating one's ability and value, but the danger of *underestimating* them. The present generation is not notably a bragging generation. There is hardly a whisper about youth building a new world, and doing a better job than their vicious and stupid elders did. Those were stock themes of the 1920's, but long since passé. But the "conceited ass" is not a very common figure. That model has gone out of style. The present danger is underestimating one's importance in the world's work. This comes not so much from humility, as from indifference. Youth is particularly afraid of being an "eager beaver." Hosts of young people are far more interested in security and pension systems and fringe benefits than in spiritual adventure. After the "lost generation" and the "beat generation" and the "silent generation," there have appeared many who might fairly be called "the indifferent generation." There is great need to bring again to many young people and older ones of this age a sane estimate of their importance to the common welfare and common destiny.

There is also our time's own special need to think with sober judgment of themselves. There are many exaggerated estimates which people make of themselves. Some people always operate in a bull market in regard to their own stock. What is needed is a downward readjustment of delusions to fit the facts. In the reading of a sane estimate, a goodly measure of humility, and as Paul pleads here, a measure of faith are the greatest help. This process has some of the saving process currently known as self-acceptance. It forswears the freak mirror so dear to us with its fantastic heights and sizes. It substitutes a candid mirror which throws back the image of what we really are. This reduction of exaggerations is a painful experience but a saving one. It gives us a sane estimate of our capabilities, neither unduly swelled nor shrunk. Thus we can see ourselves as God sees us and as we are.

Christian faith is an instrument, a means of right thinking. It peers through all pretensions like an X-ray. When we do that honestly we take one more step. We see ourselves as, by the grace of God, we may be.

49. "WE BELIEVE, THEREFORE"

Having gifts, . . . let us use them: if prophecy, in proportion to our faith. ROM. 12:6

"Prophecy" here means "inspired preaching." Genuine Christian preaching, this word of Paul makes clear, is determined by faith. It is shaped and empowered by the preacher's personal faith; not by oratory, or a musical voice, or even by erudition, but by the prophet's faith.

That is an old truth that needs stress and recovery with each new generation of prophets, and with each new set of controversial questions that arise. For sometimes men prophesy, not in proportion to their faith, but according to their idea of what will be accepted and popular. Quite a different measurement of the message from this one of Paul.

Ronald Knox has put this measurement of the message brutally but vividly. He said that some preachers ask, in writing their sermons, not, "What is the will of God on this matter?" but "How much will Jones swallow?" And if Mr. Jones is having throat trouble, as he sometimes does, and does not swallow easily, the parts of God's message which Jones will not swallow are considerable. "Really, you know, there is no use irritating our hearer." So it works out, that the author of the preacher's message is not the Lord God Almighty, but the great god Jones.

This works out very dolefully in our day in the matter of racial tension. It is a difficult thing, at certain times and places, even a dangerous thing, to prophesy God's word according to the measure of one's faith. So the preaching is done in proportion to one's timidity. This sometimes happens to church leaders, from whom the churches have a right to expect inspired courageous prophecy. But they do not prophesy in proportion to their faith. One minister said in defense of his silence, "I do not find the word 'integration' in the New Testament." That let him out!

Whenever there is any subject on which a church may not speak its full faith, the result is a divided church, a kind of schizophrenia. It was so preceding the Civil War. Up until the 1830's, slavery was a tabooed subject for the most part. Free discussion of the hottest issue of American life was under edict. The witness, the very life of the church, was sapped of strength. It was frustrated, hearing the command of a Bluebeard, saying there is one room you may not enter, one subject which you must not discuss.

The word of God must run free. "Prophecy, in proportion to our faith."

50. MERCY WITH CHEERFULNESS

He who does acts of mercy, with cheerfulness. ROM. 12:8

It is surprising how closely in the New Testament giving and mercy are linked with cheer. "The Lord loveth a cheerful giver." But with so many of us, giving fills us with a glee like a trip to the dentist. And extracting a coin becomes an operation like extracting a tooth, without Novocain. Perhaps Paul realized the need for stress on cheerfulness. Indeed there is sometimes as much stress on cheerfulness as on generosity itself. Rightly, for there is no real generosity without cheerfulness.

All too often there is stoic mercy instead of Christian mercy. It is performed with a heroic spirit; every muscle in the face announces clearly, "I am going through with this if it kills me." Like their painful saving for a Christmas Club, people seem to feel that they are laying up merit somewhere. It's really not a cheerful affair. The recipient of the mercy often detects—and resents—this. As one "client" of almsgiving cried out with sure insight, "You can't save your soul on me!"

There is a bay in the wide Kennebec River just above Bath, Maine, with a name which we might well ponder. It is Merry Meeting Bay. A church ought to be a merry meeting, not frivolous, but a coming together of people who have had a merry experience of the joy of the Lord.

Even when money is not involved there is often a dour lack of cheer—like a bleak January landscape—in the face of the giver. Such acts of mercy as forgiveness or the overlooking of an injury or slight are dutifully carried out, but there is no merrymaking about them. The result often is as though no mercy has been shown. It is as though the words had been said, through clenched teeth, "I'll forgive you this time, because I am a Christian, and you are mighty lucky that I am. But don't imagine that I'll forget or that you can come around as though nothing had happened!"

That is not mercy. Just an imitation by one who does not know what mercy is.

Mercy flows from a deep spring. "Freely you have received, freely give." The cheerfulness that should go with mercy is not forced. It is unconscious. One has received in such great measure, love so amazing, so divine, that a brimming spring of joy is opened up. Wordsworth traced it in his noble sonnet on Milton:

> Thy soul was like a star and dwelt apart,
> So didst thou travel in life's common way
> In cheerful godliness.

Mercy and cheerfulness go hand in hand.

51. "THROW AWAY" LIVING

Hold fast to what is good.   ROM. 12:9

This is a word in season for all seasons. It pleads for the wisdom for a lifetime against the improvisations of the moment, for the centuries against the hours. But it is peculiarly a word in season to a nation and generation such as ours, which has been deliberately fashioned by sellers and advertisers to adopt a cult of obsolescence. The watchword of so much of our mechandising and industry is not "hold fast to what is good," but "get rid of it as soon as possible. Get a new model. Change every year." Otherwise you will be out of fashion, an "old-timer." "Hold fast to the good"—that is a plea for a solid, enduring life against the showy, passing novelty.

Also, and emphatically, this is a word in season, and how good it is, to a generation trained to throw so many of the usable implements of life away. Then, partly from habit and partly from the spirit of the times, many people go on to throw away the precious possessions of life and of our intellectual and spiritual culture. We seem to be in an era of "disposables." So many things are to be thrown away—plates, cups, knives and forks, tablecloths and napkins, many articles of clothing become part of "throw away living." It has even been suggested in jest, but even that is evidence of the trend, that the way to beat the parking problem in cities will be to have people drive to the city in disposable automobiles.

The words represent something much deeper than dishes and clothing to be disposable. There has been among many people a tendency to "throw away" things of the spirit and mind. During the past few years there has been a tragic tendency, owing partly to mass hysteria, to throw away some of the great inheritances of American freedom. Many people, some of them in high office, have by their actions said, "What use do we have for the guarantee of American liberty in the Bill of Rights? Throw them away!"

So, also, many have thrown away the great heritages of the Christian faith. They engage in throw-away living when it comes to their personal life. Their attitude toward the restraints of Christian living is an impatient "Throw it away." Many people think thus of the great heritage of the Sabbath day, and of the moral and spiritual heritage of sexual control.

A towering word for a time given to the allurements of "throw away living": "Hold fast to what is good."

52. THE ART OF HATING

Hate what is evil. ROM. 12:9

Many of us do not hate evil any more. We explain it and account for it. That is less wearing on the emotions. We are told by some of those learned in psychological lore that to hate evil is too simplified a reaction. It is an emotional response instead of an intellectual comprehension. (Apparently, to have both is forbidden.) Naturally, many of us cringe before the charge of being too simplified in our ideas and remedies. We must be complex and subtle or die. The nastiest word hurled about these days is "naïve." So, instead of the simple response met so often in the Bible, "to hate evil," there is often substituted a wise tolerance. One bad result has been the disappearance of horror from our look at evil. That is rather widely regarded as a growth in good taste. Of course, it is a mark of good taste to outgrow a morbid hankering for horror tales in theater and movies. But in real life, ethical and religious, horror serves a real purpose. A sense of shocked horror has played a large part in reforming the worst evils. It was true of John Howard stepping into eighteenth-century jails in England.

We need a recovery of the emotion of horror. We need it to sustain the blessed emotion of hatred of evil we had when the end of World War II displayed the murder camps of Buchenwald and Dachau. But that horror did not range far enough or last long enough. It did not proceed to a shock of horror at the policies and goals which helped to produce World War II, and which, unless checked, will be on their way to produce World War III. The whole nuclear threat to the survival of humanity has not stirred the horror that it should have. We need to learn to hate evil.

If we lose the capacity to hate, we lose the definiteness of our moral sense. Logan Pearsall Smith describes his baffling experience in telling a group of young people that something was "wrong." That was a strange word to them.

The incident which had caused the laughter of those youngsters was not a thing to joke about. I expressed my conviction briefly; but the time-honoured word I made use of seemed unfamiliar to them;—they looked at each other and began whispering together. Then one of them asked in a hushed voice, "It's *what,* did you say?"

I repeated my monosyllable loudly.

Again they whispered together, and again their spokesman came forward.

"Do you mind telling us how you spell it?"

"I spell it, I spell it with a W!", I shouted. "W-R-O-N-G—WRONG!"

A great host of synonyms for the word "wrong" have come into common use, words less dogmatic, more sophisticated. But none mean the same thing. It is a good word to use. God pity us, if it becomes obsolete.

It is easy to hate conventional evils. It is easy to hate kidnapers, sneak thieves, and the man-eating shark. That is why this has been a popular platform with many politicians, who want a popular issue—"Down with the man-eating shark!" There is need to see and feel and consequently hate deeper evils. These are not necessarily more subtle but less visible to the casual glance. In international relations, an evil not so visible as armed aggression, but one which has stood in the way of a livable compromise, is the idea, which our own country has labored under, of a complete victory over our enemy, and having him get down on his knees and sign on the dotted line—on our terms.

What Carlton S. Coon records as the attitude of early man—as it still marks nations of today—is a matter of horror. He writes:

Moving out of the Neolithic age may be the world's most difficult problem. It is the retention by atom age men of the neolithic point of view that says, "You stay in your village and I will stay in mine. If your sheep eat our grass, we will kill you. Or we may kill you anyhow to get all the grass for our sheep. Anyone who tries to make us change our ways, is a witch and we will kill him."

It is easy to denounce juvenile delinquency. It is not so easy to see and hate the indifference of citizens and cities which refuse to pay for facilities for recreation of young people or to oppose the dominance of financial gain, which carries over from our culture to young people. The Bible and history cry, "Hate evil."

53. FLAGGING ZEAL

Never flag in zeal. ROM. 12:11

The word "flag" is a picturesque one. It gives the same general idea as does the translation in the King James Version, "Not slothful in business." But it gives an increase in drive and intensity. The figure of a limp flag hanging down like a wet rag is memorable.

Don't flag. One may be tired. Life is an affair of physical and emotional hills and valleys, not a taut line, always on a level. Just as a mediocre writer is always at his best, only a dull, insensitive spirit is always the same. Of course, as long as we are alive, we get tired, that is, if we are really doing anything. But, as one has said of the ministry, he gets tired *in* it, but never tired of it. We "flag" when we get tired *of* effort.

Some people, Christian people, always carry their flag *at half mast*. When we see them, and gaze into their lugubrious eyes, seeming on the verge of flooding with tears, we are impelled to ask, "Who died?"

Others are not as sad a sight as that, but carry their flag limp. It hangs inert with no more spread than a decorous flap. Indeed, nothing in their manner or speech gives proof through the night (or day) that their flag is still there.

Such people rarely ever let the flag of their spirits float, seaward and skyward, high and wide. Such limp hanging of the flag, like a wet towel on a clothesline, is a libel on Christian faith and experience. For earth has not anything to show more fair than a person who strides on through toil and tribulation with unflagging spirit. That stride is beautifully portrayed on a plaque relief of Canon Barnett, of East London, on one of the supports in St. Paul's Cathedral. It is the figure of a sower striding vigorously along, scattering seed. Underneath are the words, "Fear not to sow on account of the birds."

Paul was urging zeal in the service of God in the spread of the gospel. The indolence he deplored is a lack of concern over what ought to be the disciple's chief concern. As it was in the beginning, it is now. The pleading comes to all disciples to show unflagging zeal for bringing the gospel. One of the most effective sermons on behalf of evangelism was preached by a postman when the Christmas rush was over. A friend was extending condolences over the sad plight of the postman, staggering under mountains of mail. The postman said, surprisingly, "That is not the hardest part. The hardest part is to see in the post offices large piles of undelivered gifts. They did not have the right address." Gifts and messages of love, undelivered. Never flag in zeal, lest the gift of God in Christ be an undelivered gift.

54.   BE AGLOW!

Be aglow with the Spirit.   ROM. 12:11

Aglow—a good word to add to the bright lexicon of youth, or of deep middle age, or to the last act of life's drama. To be aglow in the sense used here does not mean to have a professional smile which can be turned on and off like an electric switch. Such a synthetic glow is much better off than on. As one man said, in justifiable irritation, "If it comes to be a choice between Pollyanna and Scrooge, I vote for Scrooge." To be "aglow with the Spirit" is a far different thing, of a deeper and permanent radiance.

Paul in writing these words was probably not thinking of the face. The glow which comes from the Spirit and which issues in serving the Lord, as this verse declares, is a far greater thing than that. It is an affair of the heart and not of outward appearance.

However, to be aglow with the Spirit often does include a radiant face. Indeed, it ought to, unless the face is frozen. Someone said

to a friend, "You have such a February face." Too many Christians
with February faces, or, at least, inclement March faces. A congregation with February faces is Satan's company of shock troops. A
dull, glum face on a Christian is a libel on the gospel. It gives the
impression that religion is nothing to write home about. But sometimes we can read the persuasive message of the spirit of God in
a person's face.

We must admit that the gift of a radiant manner is not one which
we have all received. Some gifted souls are endowed with it. They
deserve the tribute often paid, "When he came into a room, it was
as though another candle had been lighted." Most of us have seen
such a manner. We know people of whom such a tribute as this is
not exaggerated: "He can order a can of sardines and give you the
impression that it is a distinguished and impressive thing to do."
Or we can believe, from those whom by the grace of God we have
known, that this tribute to a Christian saint can be true: "Although
dying, he could brighten up a room."

But what Paul is writing about—the "aglow with the Spirit"—may
be the possession of every disciple. The whole being is incandescent,
lighted from inexhaustible and deep sources. The mind is aglow.

O glory of the lighted mind, lighted by the Spirit of Him who
called us out of our darkness into His marvelous light! What a book
could be written—pray God it may be—of the lives of men and
women who have contributed a glow to the world. They wrote no
Epistle to the Romans, no *City of God,* no *Pilgrim's Progress.* They
made no missionary journeys, and did not put to flight any armies
of aliens. Nothing but a glow. Yet they let their light shine so that
men, seeing it, glorified their father in heaven.

The Christian faith which is not aglow has never been pictured
more sharply than in the damning words of Edward Gibbon in his
description of Greek scholars in tenth-century Constantinople:

> They held in their lifeless hands the riches of their fathers without
> inheriting the spirit which created and improved that sacred patrimony.
> They read; they praised; they compiled. But their languid souls seemed
> incapable of thought or action. A succession of patient disciples became
> in their turn the dogmatic teachers of the next servile generation.

We do not have to go back, alas, to Constantinople or the tenth
century. We can find some of the same lackluster languor in our
own day and place. The power of a church with men and women
aglow is pictured in other words. It follows this model:

> *Three, with a new song's measure,*
> *Can trample an empire down.*

55. HOSPITALITY

Practice hospitality.   ROM. 12:13

One of the regrettable marks of our century and country is the decline of hospitality. The architects and builders, and the cost of living which shoots up like a missile into the sky, have pretty well erased hospitality from our culture. Phillips has given the meaning of the term as Paul used it in detail, "never grudging a meal or a bed to those who need them." The small house of today, the apartment, the ranch house, has no room for guests. Progress is made in this manner, first no room for guests, then no room for books, then the final advance, no room for children.

Physical hospitality, the bed-and-board kind, being impossible, the desire to show hospitality dies down and the joys of life, to say nothing of its emotional and intellectual enlargement, shrink.

This is a matter of major importance. It would be hard to overrate the part that hospitality, both to friends and to strangers, has played in the history of the Christian church. We get many short glimpses, like a peek through the door left ajar, at the homes in which the itinerant preachers were entertained, Paul and Peter, Silas and Barnabas and Timothy. There was the home of Aquila and Priscilla, of Jason, of Cornelius, and many others. The secret weapon of the early church was the home. The practice of hospitality is difficult but it is a necessary art and sacrifice.

Beyond the physical use of the home in hospitality is the necessity of mental hospitality. To equip our minds with a door that swings wide in welcome to new truth is a necessity to growth, intellectual and spiritual. Of course, there can be too much hospitality of mind, so that the mind becomes like the waiting room of a union station. So much rushes in pell-mell at the door to find a large, indiscriminate welcome, that there is a melee of incoherence. Such a man with a union station mind was the minister who was said to have included Freud and Marx and Jesus in one all-comprehending muddle. That is a perverted extreme to be avoided if the mind is to be preserved as a thinking instrument. But there must be a selective hospitality. That is envisioned in the injunction, "Prove all things." If there is a closed door, there will be no more chance for a new idea to get into the mind than there is for a breeze to blow through a billiard ball.

A common tragedy—tragedy is the right word—occurs when there is no hospitality, no open door to the great ideas of life, when there is a stout bar to any entrance of the truth of Jesus to the house of the heart and mind. "Behold, I stand at the door and knock," but if the bolts are never shot back, there will be no feast within. There will be a life, denuded of high possibilities, condemned to a low level. One kind of spiritual destitution is arrestingly described, not by a preacher in a pulpit, but by an observer, novelist and dramatist, J. B. Priestley. He writes about some people in a new suburb:

> No lasting vision of a nobler life haunts them. The reason for this is that such is their present style of life that no vision of any kind haunts them. Most of them are living too near the surface of things. They are leading too trivial and flat an existence. They are living what I call a car and radio life. . . . A life that hardly moves away from a school boy fussing with such things obviously lacks fullness and depth. Three quarters of the rich channels of communication of the mind are closed up. The whole universe has shrivelled. A large portion of these young people marry and settle into a little bungalow, join the local tennis club, acquire a radio set and a car, and then might be simply a pair of cave dwellers, for all the relation they have to the world of spirit.

The trouble was not that they lived in bungalows, but that they lived bungalow lives.

"If any man hears my voice and opens the door, I will come in."

56. HARMONY—BUT NOT UNIFORMITY

Live in harmony with one another.   ROM. 12:16

There is a tremendous difference in the translation above in the Revised Standard Version and the rendering of the same Greek words in the Authorized Version, "Be of the same mind one toward another." The essential meaning is the same, of course. That is secured by the words "one toward another." Those words make it clear that "the same mind" does not mean the prison lock step, but rather the unity of the spirit in the bond of peace.

But the greatest tragedies of Christian history have followed when men have read the sentence as though it were, "Be of the same mind," period. That has brought about the pressure of flame and sword, the "persuasion" of the headman's block, and Christian torturing Christian in the Inquisition with the torture of the thumbscrew and the rack. The command taken literally, "Be of the same mind," has lit the fires of Smithfield. It has led to the State Church of England hounding and persecuting dissenters and Catholics in the seventeenth century. It banished Roger Williams and Anne Hutchinson from Massachusetts.

In our time there is a very different, but spiritually and socially vicious, use of the injunction, "Be of the same mind." It has given unprecedented power to our business culture to secure mental and spiritual conformity—even conformity of dress and hair-do, as well as ideas. The top powers of our culture have so emphasized, and perverted, the values of "togetherness" that it has resulted in the smothering of individuality. That is in special degree the curse of suburbia. "This is the first and greatest commandment, 'Don't get out of step.' And the second is like unto it, 'Don't think for yourself.'" Sometimes the compulsion of college standards where, theoretically, the mind should be awakened (thank God it so often is) keeps the mind asleep. For some unfortunates it has been well described as "four years under the ether cone." That makes a supreme concern for the Protestant churches, for their strength is coming increasingly to be in the suburbs. This calls for a struggle with "sameness of mind." For in some suburbs, the sound of opinion is like fifty phonographs turning out the same tune.

Provincialism, when it expresses the innocence of childhood, is a charming thing. We all love and cherish the child's description of Charleston, "where the Ashley and Cooper Rivers come together to form the Atlantic Ocean." But there is nothing charming about the provincial adult who equates the codes of South Carolina with the laws of the universe, or accepts any other belated provincialism.

The harmony urged by Paul is a harmony of spirit, which respects the mind of one another and reaches out to others in brotherhood.

57. "IT DOESN'T MATTER"

Don't say, "It doesn't matter what people think."   ROM. 12:17 (Phillips)

This translation is an exciting addition to the familiar rendering of the Authorized Version, "Provide things honest in the sight of all men." Of course, it is not a literal translation. A good many grace notes are added. It is really a sort of musical cadenza. The dictionary says that a cadenza is "that portion of a concerta where the soloist is permitted to build some improvisations upon the straight musical facts which confront him." That is what this sentence is, a vivacious improvisation on the straight words. But what an enlightener! The plea of Paul is not to cause an injury to the faith and fellowship by our indifferent behavior. Don't say, "It doesn't matter."

These words are said daily in many connections. In reference to some things the words "It doesn't matter what people think" are gloriously right. In reference to other things, they are shamefully and viciously wrong.

In many connections, these are the words of a free soul. He looks the whole world in the face and to its jibes and to any of its assaults he calmly says, "It doesn't matter." As Paul put it when charges of disloyalty to Jewish law and tradition were made to him, "By the way that men call heresy, so serve I the God of my fathers."

When followers of "the way" are called old-fashioned they need not cringe. That adjective, so terrifying to some in our day, like a bully swinging a club, has no power over them. The town gossips may gabble, "Really, my dears, you have no idea how quaint, really priceless, they are. They actually have family prayers!" Followers of the way feel, "It doesn't matter what people think," and it doesn't. They may be out of the running in the town's rating, but they are in God's race, running the "straight race."

Dedicated Christians are sure to be called narrow. How could it be otherwise if they have entered the narrow gate? Some neighbors will complain that the lives of these dedicated ones are hardly wide enough for a cocktail tray. It doesn't matter. A man and woman, who have shared their goods, not grudgingly or of necessity, but liberally, with human need, and for the cause of Christ, can wear an old coat like an aristocrat, or a five-year-old hat like royalty (which they are) and say "it doesn't matter what people think."

Others bear privations and stern limitations cheerfully, without envy or bitterness. They have an inner possession so great, so joyful, they can say, with Paul, "I have learned in whatever state I am, therein to be content." People may think them poor. "It doesn't matter what people think."

With reference to some other things, it *does matter* tremendously what people think. The quality of the life, the goals it chooses, the outgo in service—these things matter immeasurably. For they are not only life's real treasure. They are also the things which bring credit to the Christian faith. If men feel and say that such things do not matter, they betray the faith.

We hear much of making mountains out of molehills. There is the reverse of that commonly practiced by a large number. They make *molehills out of mountains!* The great spiritual mountains of the realities of spiritual and moral truth, they shrink into little inconsequential molehills. There are no mountains in their landscape of living, no hills to which they look up—just a flat desert, with here and there a little molehill.

With such things, it *does* matter!

58.   TAKE THE INITIATIVE

Overcome evil with good.   ROM. 12:21

This whole passage, "if your enemy is hungry, feed him; if he is thirsty, give him drink; . . . overcome evil with good," is a vigorous plea to take the initiative in dealing with people and in dealing with evil. It affirms the power of a moral and spiritual initiative. It is a plea to get out of the passive voice into the active voice. In many ways, this is the most thrilling shift in position we can take. Jesus put it for all time, "The Son of man came not to be ministered unto, but to minister" (Matt. 20:28, A.V.). Out of the passive into the active!

But so many never really make the momentous journey. It is so much easier to live in the passive voice, to be *acted upon* rather than to act, to be *served* rather than to serve. To be ministered unto is like folding yourself into an inert state, like wrapping a soft woolen blanket around you.

When we overcome evil with good, we take the first step. We seize the initiative from evil. That is the strategy of Christian action; we don't wait, we "get the jump" on evil. Taking the initiative gives an immense advantage. Feed your enemy, give him drink, overcome evil by the strategy of first action.

A shrewd businessman was giving a suggestion to a newly elected editor. He said, "Watch your incoming mail. If you don't, you will be all the time answering questions put to you by others, dealing with their issues, and have no time to create a positive program of your own." In other words—take the initiative. General U. S. Grant was an adherent of the initiative. He said, "The art of war is to find out where your enemy is, get at him as soon as possible, strike him as hard as you can, and keep moving on." No anxious waiting to repel something!

In recent years, theology has opened new understanding of "the divine initiative." "While we were yet sinners, Christ died for us." In dealing with people, taking the initiative as described here is a risk. Jesus took that risk. He was told by the "respectable" classes,

"You will get in wrong if you become the friend of sinners." He "got in wrong." There was the risk, "Some will disappoint you." Judas disappointed him. He had no guarantee that people like Mary Magdalene would stick to him. He took the initiative.

To overcome evil is never a sure thing. But God's strategy of victory is to take the initiative. "Do not be overcome . . . but overcome."

59. THE ULTIMATE DEBT

Owe no one anything, except to love one another. ROM. 13:8

Not many years ago, this would have seemed to many people the *ultimate nonsense.* Today, it is rapidly acquiring the standing of *ultimate truth.* Certainly a generation ago, to advocate a sentimental thing like love would have sounded, to many who took pride in hardheaded realism, like a program of idiocy. But torrents of water, water mixed with blood, have gone under the bridge since then.

Today, not only to the religious, but to those looking at the facts of our world, which has a precarious existence between hydrogen bomb and intercontinental ballistic missile, with satellites looking down from above, love is the necessity of survival. We have had that proclaimed by many voices which have no ecclesiastical accent. They are not pulpit utterances. They come from laboratories. We read the words of Bertrand Russell. In these words he is not subcribing to the Apostles' Creed. But he is saying something about love as a possibility of salvation. He made an address at Columbia University. Many of his listeners were surprised to hear him make an emphatic plea for Christian love in the world today. As he made it he had an embarrassed air, somewhat like a boy caught stealing jam. He said:

If we want a stable world, the root of the matter is a very simple and old fashioned thing, a thing so simple that I am almost ashamed to mention it, for fear of the derisive smile with which wise cynics will greet my words. The thing I mean is love, Christian love, or compassion. If you feel this, you have a motive for existence, a guide to action, a reason for courage.

Incidentally, in that last sentence there is a notable sermon with a three-point landing. This is echoed in a score of books, among them Erich Fromm's *The Art of Loving.*

Here is a statistic on the necessity of love in a threatened world. In the first edition of the *Encyclopaedia Britannica* in 1768, there were four lines on the atom and five pages on love. In the latest edition there are eight pages on the atom, and no separate entry on love. There had better be full treatment of love!

60. GOD'S ALARM CLOCK

The night is far gone, the day is at hand. ROM. 13:12

Always in the background of Paul's thought is the day of the Lord, the parousia, the coming of Christ. In the earlier letters to the Thessalonians this seems more imminent than in the later ones, but the expectation is never absent. However, the result of that expectation is the same as the necessity to Christian committment is with those who do not look forward to the same kind of a literal second coming of Christ. The urgency is the same. "Cast off the works of darkness and put on the armor of light." Paul was always deeply concerned with the issue of belief in action.

Salvation, which includes the present life in Christ and the future full deliverance from sin, is both present and future. Both for today and for the unknown future, "Put on the Lord Jesus Christ." Beyond that general meaning for every day, there is, surely, in these words, a specific meaning for our day of arousing intensity.

In 1820 Missouri was admitted into the Union as a slave state, thus raising the slavery issue. Thomas Jefferson wrote, "Like a fire bell in the night, it awakened and filled me with terror." The tragic years of the Civil War forty years later proved how far-seeing his awakened eyes were.

Like a fire bell, God's alarm clock rang suddenly and loudly when the atomic bomb was exploded over Hiroshima on August 6, 1945. That alarm bell announced that the day of opportunity was very far spent, and that it was time for the world to awaken from sleep. For the day, not of salvation, but of destruction, was nearer than we thought. As no event in history has ever announced in such screaming tones—it is time to cast off the works of darkness, and conduct ourselves becomingly, as becomes those who hope for the world's survival.

But, the evidence is too strong that in this day of atomic threat, a great many are still sleepily trying to turn off the alarm and turn over for more sleep. As has been said, "Ideas ought not to be bedridden in the dormitory of the understanding." The idea of world destruction is bedridden in too many minds. These ought to be days when

> *God's trumpet wakes the slumbering world,*
> *Now each man to his post!*

God's alarm clock has sounded. Yet it is still so largely a slumbering world. True, we are frantic about missiles and conquering outer space. But so many never truly awakened to the creation of peace. The nations are still all intent on the works of darkness—the obliteration of the human race. The churches today are called to keep the alarm sounding. One man said of his bulldog, "He spends nine tenths of his waking hours asleep." That is not confined to bulldogs.

God's alarm has sounded. It has not announced, as one has gloomily said, man's inability to make a biological success of himself. But it has announced a danger unlike any that has ever existed. For there are enough nuclear explosives in possession of the United States and Russia to put an end to the life of man on earth.

Napoleon III of France, at the time of the *coup d'état* which made him emperor, had nearly every drum in Paris punctured. So there was no alarm! God grant that this supreme task of the ages may not find churches with punctured drums! It is high time to awake from sleep!

61. LIFE FROM THE INSIDE

Put on the Lord Jesus Christ. ROM. 13:14

There is no need to add the words, Put on the Lord Jesus Christ *from the inside*. That is stressed in the whole of the New Testament. "Cleanse the inside of the cup." Christ must be put on, not as a cloak thrown around one, but as an inward change, a transformation of the heart, spreading from the inside out into all the actions of a life.

It is like the glow of health, put on from an inward well being, not applied from a bottle. This distinction is well to keep in mind in a day when one of the major industries of the United States seems to be putting on something on the *outside* of the head. A large part of the incessant advertising on television is devoted to persuade viewers to put on something, on the face, on the scalp, on the hair. A casual onlooker gets the impression that there must be a different product to put on the hair for every hair of the head.

There has been in history, and it still goes on today, in many connections, a bad sense of "put on Christ." That is with the meaning that it is all "put on." It is an outward covering, a camouflage, for an inward reality that has no spirit of Christ about it. Often the drive to power has been disguised as Christian. Even human slavery has been disguised as a provision of God. "That execrable villainy," to use the description by John Wesley, had the name of Christ "put on" it, to cover it up. "Going, going, gone, nine hundred dollars, a man made in the image of God, on the auction block, a fine piece of property." In the frenzy of Christmas commercialism, greed has "put on" Christ as a means to bigger and better sales.

But this injunction of Paul's means, put on Christ from the inside. It is a *chemical* change, not a physical one.

> No ear may hear His coming,
> But in this world of sin,
> Where meek souls will receive Him still,
> The dear Christ enters in.

As Paul puts it in another figure, "Christ liveth in me." Or another, "The life I now live in the flesh I live by faith in the Son of God" (Gal. 2:20). We need to be reminded that we live *outward*, that what is nearest to the center is most real to us. When Christ is at the center of our life, the new creature becomes possible.

Inward change is the deepest need of our world. Not new weapons, not new organization, but new minds. Spiritual diseases will not be cured by outward remedies. When a person has typhoid fever, it is not a true remedy to put on rouge and lipstick. If a well is poisoned, it does no good to paint the pump. Our world is poisoned. It needs inward change. As Lewis Mumford has said, "Organization alone will not save us. Salvation depends on a change in the individual human heart. Only as the individual man curbs his rapacity will the greed and rapacity of the state be curbed." Wordsworth said it memorably:

> We look
> But at the surface of things; we hear
> Of towns in flames, fields ravaged, young and old
> Driven out in troops to want and nakedness;
> Then grasp our sword and rush upon a cure
> That flatters us, because it asks not thought:
> The deeper malady is better hid.
> The world is poisoned at the heart.

Put on the Lord Jesus Christ—from the heart.

62. TIED TOGETHER

None of us lives to himself, and none of us dies to himself.   ROM. 14:7

It ought not to take much persuasion to enforce this truth in this day of the world. It is a day of "fearful propinquity." We live and die together. In the fullest sense, if we do not learn to live together, we will die together. This truth has been completely demonstrated in the twentieh century from 1914 on. As one modern poet has written, "We must love each other or die." There is no place to hide —from death.

Two or three years before World War II broke out, a thoughtful man in Australia, a keen student of world affairs, concluded that a world war of unimaginable devastation would soon break out. So he set himself to find the safest hide-out to which he could go. He studied a long time, and finally settled on a remote and sparsely populated island in the South Pacific. The name of the island was Guadalcanal. That "hide-out" became the center of one of the world's most terrific bombardments.

Yet it is proving a gigantic task—at times it seems an impossible task—to shape the human mind to fit the outward conditions. It was said, a few years ago, no doubt unfairly, of a prominent political figure in the United States, that he had "one of the finest minds of the eighteenth century." There are too many people looking out on the twentieth century with eighteenth-century minds. Some of the tribes of ancient Gaul used to go into battle all tied together. But today the whole population of the globe goes into a world war or world peace—men, women and children—all tied together.

Sometimes what keeps men from an intense, shattering realization of this common fate of all peoples is just plain provincialism. People think they are a special brand. Often this is so incongruous as to be laughable. The headline of a story recently in *The Manchester Guardian,* telling of a disaster in the Far East in which hundreds of people were killed, and millions of dollars worth of property damaged, was "Manchester man injured abroad." This is matched by the story of an eclipse of the sun in 1925 which appeared in a Buffalo paper under the heading "Local News."

Sometimes the cause is something far worse—callous indifference. Perhaps in many cases, it should be called sleepy indifference. The adjective is softer but the frightful result is the same. A grim instance

of this appears in the description by Orville Prescott of the uncon-
cern of George Santayana, in his latest years:

In his old age Santayana has withdrawn farther and farther from the
world until the long, historical perspective with which he regards human
affairs seems callous and inhuman. The infamies of facism did not per-
ceptibly distress him; the cruelty of communism does not arouse his righteous wrath. Such aberrations are no more than his professionally low
opinion of mankind expects. Such an aloofness from the good fight
which men must always wage against tyranny and injustice is under-
standably infuriating to men of goodwill. If it were widely imitated world
slavery would be the inevitable end.

We can hear a pin drop at the end of the earth. We can see the
North and South Poles as readily as the front yard. Indeed, they have
become the front yard. But the communication of common feeling,
of brotherhood, is still to be achieved. Isolation has been broken
down by incredible invention, but no sufficient saving realization of
living and dying together has yet been brought about. Yet the truth
of spiritual relationship is as Booker T. Washington put it years
ago. He said to an audience of white people:

No member of your race in any part of the country can harm the
meanest member of mine, without the proudest and bluest blood in
Massachusetts being degraded. When Mississippi commits crime, New
England commits crime, and by so much, lowers the standards of your
civilization.

Our world needs a unifier—a spiritual unifier. Two world wars
have provided one unifier—death. We need the teaching of Him in
whom all things hang together. Above every other sovereignty—that
of tribe, group, or nation—must be the sovereign of man.

63.   HELL IS PAVED WITH STUMBLING BLOCKS

Never . . . put a stumbling-block or hindrance in the way of a brother.
ROM. 14:13

It is fascinating to watch Paul at work here. He takes a controversial question—hot in the hour of conflict—and lifts it out of the
furnace up to an entirely new level. He lifts it from the level of "me
and my stomach" up to Christ's level, where concern for my stomach, whether to eat meat that had been offered to idols, gives way to

concern for the souls of men. On that new level we see the enormity of leaving stumbling blocks as we pass along on which men and women may grievously fall. To put a stumbling block in the way of a brother is to be guilty of murder, the murder of a soul.

We are all familiar with the statement that there are more accidents in the home than on the highway. When we come to look closely at the causes of accidents in the home, we discover that a chief cause is stumbling blocks. In any list of "How to avoid accidents in the home," one of the first pleas is "Don't leave toys or anything else on the stairs or in hallways." Stumbling blocks have been deathtraps.

So are moral and spiritual stumbling blocks deathtraps. We have heard that hell is paved with good intentions. *Hell is also paved with stumbling blocks.* Hell must be the best-paved place of any.

This word is Paul's vivid picture of the responsibility of personal conduct. In families, we see clearly the crime of putting stumbling blocks in the way of youth. Often children stumble over a *bottle*. A bottle of strong drink has caused a stumble; the turning point on which the life of a parent has centered has been, "me and my gullet."

Sometimes the stumbling block is *example* in general. Parents, not on malicious purpose—but just as disastrously as though malicious—cannot control their desires with any consideration of what harm the children might take from example. Paul gives a crowning blow on example when he explains, "Surely we shouldn't wish to undo God's work for the sake of a plate of meat!" (Phillips). But that is exactly what a parent often does! Sometimes the stumbling block in the way of children is more intangible. It is the empty place where a father ought to be. He ought to be by the young person's side at times of choice. He is too busy. So the young man or woman stumbles for lack of guiding friendship. There was an old Civil War song, sure to bring tears: "There Shall Be an Empty Chair." Sometimes the empty chair is father's. Sometimes it is mother's. The empty space causes a stumble.

So many stumbling blocks and hindrances have prevented spiritual progress that might be made. A church largely wrapped up in itself has been a tragic stumbling block to serving the community filled with people with many kinds of acute need. The indifference of good people to a town's welfare has often been a hindrance to advancing that welfare.

64. FOUR MIGHTY WORDS

For whom Christ died.   ROM. 14:15

One of the best commentaries ever made on these four mighty words was the sentence of T. R. Glover, "Four words destroyed slavery, "For whom Christ died.'" Our hope is that the same four words will someday destroy war, someday destroy racial discrimination and segregation, someday destroy exploitation.

St. Paul brings here the crowning argument against allowing our selfish indulgences to injure people by the example we set. The people who might be injured are a special brand of people, the elite of the earth. *All* people are a special brand; *all* people are the elite of the earth. They are the men and women "for whom Christ died." That is the most powerful argument for unselfish conduct that was ever forged. With the eyes of the heart enlightened by that love so amazing, so divine, men can see their neighbor, whether across the street or across the world, in a new dimension, as "the brother for whom Christ died." Lewis Mumford has written of the power of an idea when it is incarnated. He says, "The beginning and the end of making ideas socially operative is in the incarnation of the idea in a human person." Lift that truth up to its highest demonstration. The incarnation of God's love in a person, Jesus Christ, has made the idea "socially operative." The word became flesh and dwelt among us, and has had power beyond any other idea that ever entered the mind of man.

Four words finally destroyed slavery. A book on America of a century ago reproduced a handbill advertising a raffle in the southern part of the United States. Two chief items were raffled: a dark bay horse, Star, described as "aged five years, a square trotter," and a mulatto girl, "Sarah." This piece of merchandise was described as "about twenty years, general housework, valued at nine hundred dollars and guaranteed." A horse, and Sarah!

But others saw the brother for whom Christ died. A Vermont judge in 1812 made a resounding echo of this verse. He heard the plea of a slaveowner for the return of a slave who had escaped to Vermont. The claimant showed a bill of sale to prove his ownership. The judge replied that he would order the arrest and return of the slave only if he "were shown a bill of sale by Almighty God."

The truest description of the Christian doctrine of man was made in the early days of the Christian church by a deadly enemy, Celsus.

His was the oldest literary attack on Christianity of which any details have survived, about A.D 178. We know of it from Origen's reply, *Contra Celsum*. Celsus wrote, "The root of Christianity is its excessive valuation of the human soul, and the absurd idea that God takes an interest in man." Exactly! Paul never made a much better description himself! Celsus penetrated to its very heart.

It should never be forgotten that these four words are a profoundly theological affirmation. There is no power in the foggy idea that Jesus was a sympathetic person who sent his good wishes to everybody. Nor is there power to destroy evil in a general fog of sentimentality. The Christian faith roots in specific fact and specific revelation.

A few years ago an outdoor theater was opened in Cold Water Canyon in Beverly Hills, California. Over the entrance to the auditorium was to be inscribed, "Amongst our eternal hills we build a shrine, sans creed, sans dogma, inspiring all mankind."

There is a good answer to that in one word, really the only fitting word, "Fiddlesticks!" All mankind will never be inspired by an intellectual vacuum. Here is what has inspired man, "For whom Christ died."

65. WELCOME!

Welcome one another. ROM. 15:7

Damon Runyan, in one of his short stories, writes that one of his characters greeted another with a "medium hello." That phrase deserves a long life, for it describes perfectly the kind of a welcome some people give. It describes perfectly what Paul did *not* mean when he wrote, "Welcome one another." He was urging both Jews and Gentiles to bear with the limitations of each other, to let the dividing differences be overcome by a Christlike love.

The words a "medium hello" describe also the church which gives a languid welcome to strangers, that is, to those who are *really* strangers, people on the other side of the high picket fences of economic class, nationality, or color.

There is a warmth about this plea, "Welcome one another." Instead we often tolerate one another.

Note the words, the motive and motive power, "as Christ has welcomed you." That is a welcome which demands no card of admission in the form of a carefully articulated passport, no signature on a dotted line of opinion. The ideal is pictured in Edwin Markham's phrase, "the friendly welcome of the wayside well." It is perfectly expressed in Jesus' words, "Come unto me, *all* ye that labour and are heavy laden" (Matt. 11:28, AV).

The welcome to any person, any brother in the family of God, ought to be like the welcome of the father to the returning prodigal. The father could not have seen him from afar if he had not been watching for a long, long time, eager to run with open arms if he appeared. Just imagine what would have happened if the returning prodigal had met his elder brother before he met the father. There would have been no robe, no ring, no feast. He would have gone away. Now take that out of the realm of imagination. For that is what *has happened* again and again to some who would have come unto the Father. They met the elder brother—perhaps they met us— on the church steps. At best they got a frigid welcome, a medium hello.

It is easy for a church to print in its advertisements, "Everyone welcome." It is hard to translate that into the language of human friendship.

A church might well seek the tribute paid to a man by a friend, as told by Archer Wallace. The man said, after walking around town with him, "You seem to know even all the dogs and cats in this town." The man replied modestly, "I may know all the dogs, but I am not so sure about the cats." Notice the welcome he had to all the dogs. Admission to his friendship was not limited to a specific brand of greyhounds, nor to aristocratic Great Danes.

So the church should welcome all. The church should not be the Republican party at prayer nor the Democratic party at prayer, but a fellowship of Christ where there is neither bond nor free, but all are one in Christ Jesus.

So, as individuals, we should welcome one another, not keeping them out in the vestibule but welcoming them into the living room of our lives. W. H. Auden has written a sentence which can stir the imagination to a lively activity. He writes, "Ascribe it to prevenient grace, intuition or sheer luck as you will, one of the greatest things in any life has been the meeting of the right helper at the right time." Thousands and thousands of life stories illuminate that truth with shining letters.

Welcome one another. For you may be the right helper at the right time!

66. I AM PROUD

I have reason to be proud of my work for God.   ROM. 15:17

Pride has taken a terrible beating in recent years. It has been charged with a sum total of evil which is appalling. The religious insight of theologians, Biblical scholars, psychologists, has shown human pride to be not a minor blemish on character but a major evil in individual life and history. Self-righteousness, self-assertion, and self-satisfaction have been forms of pride which have gone before the fall of man into grievous sin.

Pride builds a strong wall gainst a person's entrance into Christian experience. The gates into that experience are repentance and humility. Pride cannot stoop low enough to get in.

A loss which has with many people attended this spiritual gain has been the slighting or forgetting of great virtues which have been in what has been called "honest pride." Perhaps there should be another word for the deep and genuine joy one takes in participation in something great. Paul exults in this kind of joy. In the Epistles to the church at Corinth he apologizes several times for what he calls "boasting." But it is not boasting. It is high pride. It is legitimate pride in a great and noble heritage—"of the people of Israel, of the tribe of Benjamin, a Hebrew born of Hebrews" (Philip. 3:5). He was proud of the gospel, and his connection with it. "I am not ashamed of the gospel of Christ" (Rom. 1:16, AV). ("Proud," Moffatt.) "As the truth of Christ is in me, this boast of mine shall not be silenced" (2 Cor. 11:10).

A person may be too proud to stoop to corruption or bribes; too proud to lie; too proud to betray a trust.

Paul is proud of his ministry. That pride is tempered with the phrase, "in Jesus Christ." The only things of which one has a right to be proud of are those which express the spirit of Jesus. Yet all too often, there has been sinful and empty pride over the wrong things, place, reputation, and power. John Masefield gives a searing picture of pompous ecclesiastical pride:

> *the portly presence of potentates goodly in girth.*

The Lord's spiritual have had a tendency to be goodly in girth and ungodly in pride. The very phrase "princes of the church" does not suggest a carpenter of Nazareth nor one who humbled himself to the death on a cross.

Paul rejoiced in the right kind of pride. Pride is a noble noun, the kind of pride in ministry, the kind that can be described "in Christ Jesus." That is the ministry to people. It is beautifully described by Henry Sloane Coffin, "To take the hands of men and women and put them into the Hands of God." The words of an actor, Granville-Barker, make an unintended description of the high service of Christian ministry. He describes the skill of a producer as "his ability to make actors and actresses rise above their normal talent, and form, with other actors and actresses what it would be over-simple to call, although this was its achievement, a living pattern." The joy and pride of ministry is in bringing the enabling spirit of God into a person's life, enabling him to "rise above his normal talent."

This is not only the true pride of an ordained minister, but of those called so beautifully in Paul's letter, "Christ's men and women," and as Phillips adds, "from head to toe."

Emily Post has a suggestion of value in this connection. She writes, "Go through your house sometimes as though you had never been there before. Look it over as though you were a stranger."

Look over your ministry, as though you were a stranger. Can you say with Paul, "I have reason to be proud of my work for God"?

67. "FULLY" PREACHED

I have fully preached the gospel of Christ. ROM. 15:19

Who would dare make such a claim today? Only a person who failed to plumb the depths of the gospel or measure its range. Or one who failed to see and to feel the ordeals of the world today or its aching need. Paul, in this passage, is thinking and writing principally in geographical terms. He covered the territory of Asia Minor and Greece. He claimed that he was the first in many places and the work goes on. In this verse, his own achievement is completely ascribed to "the power of the Holy Spirit."

This adverb, "fully," bows us to our knees. Such an adverb is too high for us. We cannot attain to it. That word "fully" leads out in so many directions. As we look at them we see that we have come short of the glory of being Christ's minister.

First *the depth of the gospel.* Karl Barth has suggested the soundings to the deep gospel in his words tilting at superficial presentations of Christ. He describes scornfully the type of minister who preaches Christ as a sort of "village sage" or "city sage," and is "content to counsel people shrewdly instead of confronting them with the redeeming God." It is, alas, not too uncommon, a preacher adept at telling folks "six ways to be happy," but not confronting them with the redeeming God. When the gospel is preached in half portions, or quarter portions, we may ask with the Pope, who asks, in Browning's *The Ring and the Book,*

> *Is this little, all there is,*
> *Is this salvation?*

When psychology and self-help are substituted for the good news of redemption, we may well ask, are these little preachments all there is?

Secondly, *the God of all comfort.* To bring the resources of God's grace to the individual in need is a difficult task, if we do not preach the gospel fully. It is so much easier to speak in general terms, eloquently, than to bring the comfort and fortification of God to people who sit in darkness. The task of God's messenger is to bring His truth and His power "out of the everywhere into the Here," the "Here" of the individual life.

Thirdly, *into the battlefield.* The Son of God goes forth to war against the evils and the dark powers of this world. We do not preach the gospel fully, nor even try to, unless we follow in his train in that warfare. It is so much easier to preach "partly" the gospel, leaving out the parts that go into the dangerous, controversial areas of our world. So we can spend our time massaging the prejudices of a group, or accepting the moral and spiritual limitations of a group, and living happily behind those stout barricades. Robert Louis Stevenson made an exclamation that might profitably be included in the ritual of ordination to the Christian gospel, "For God's sake, give me a young man who has brains enough to be a fool." In battle against the massive powers of evil of this world, the willingness to be a "fool for Christ's sake" is a necessary equipment. A person whose chief concern is his own neck, rather than his Master, will stay in the safe "rest areas" of God's holy war. To preach the gospel fully is to challenge the dominant philosophy of "success." As one American historian of our time has pictured it, "The new faith (in the 1920's) in the sanctity of success permeated the churches, the courts, the colleges, the press. . . . The factory was the temple, work was worship, and business verged on a new religion." Extreme, no doubt, but recognizable. One tendency in a church which blocks the outgoing reach of service is that of drawing to itself people and resources. The centripetal power of a church is a force to resist in many ways. True Christianity is centrifugal—"Go ye into all the world."

We can imagine Jesus going through the streets of our cities and towns—the streets of the kind not included in the official chamber of commerce tour, and seeing the need and neglect, and asking, "Has my gospel been fully preached here?"

To preach the gospel fully is to seek to arouse the mind and heart of the country, to choose the policies that make for the possibilities of peace in a manner commensurate with the frightening need.

Can America take the initiative in leadership in something more than a frightened preoccupation with missiles and bombs and other preparations for mass destruction? If the gospel is fully preached, there must be *intensity of conviction that stirs the mind and heart*. It was that way in the beginning. At the first Christian sermon, Peter's at Pentecost, the hearers did not yawn and sleepily go their way. They were "cut to the heart." A fully preached gospel must be one that cuts. It is to such intensity of conviction that men respond. Men want a call to action, rather than a soothing lullaby. As Chesterton has said, "Men want drums."

In a fully preached gospel there can always be heard a roll on the drum.

68. CASTLES IN SPAIN

I hope to see you in passing as I go to Spain. ROM. 15:24

Castles in Spain are not Real Estate. But they are part of the goodly estate of one who lives life up to the brim of its possibilities. Castles in Spain represent the reach of man beyond his grasp.

Paul had great dreams of a journey to Spain to carry the gospel to the very end of the world. Those dreams were his Castles in Spain. Gorgeous Castles they were, too, with cloud-capped pinnacles and domes. Spain, with the Pillars of Hercules, was the very jumping-off place of the earth, the farthest reach of man's imagination. It was the ultimate of the world. Paul had been determined to stamp on the great cities of the world, its great nerve centers, Ephesus, Athens, Corinth, Rome, the marks of the Lord Jesus.

He was determined to stamp the same marks on Spain. He had heard in his inmost soul words that shook him to the depths, "Go ye into all the world."

A castle in Spain is the unachieved. The beckoning dream, still to be overtaken, is a life preserver in an individual life. It saves us from sinking down into the mire of contentment. When there are no castles in Spain on the far horizon, life collapses, as far as any effort goes.

The church needs to plan and dream of journeys, "on my way to Spain." It must sing,

"*westward leading, still proceeding.*"

So in its endeavors it must proceed to the end of the earth, to the last outpost, the Spain at the end of the long trail. One of the glories of Christian history is that it is *almost* true, if not quite, that no people have ever received the gospel except at the hands of an alien and foreigner.

It was a Jew who brought the gospel to Rome, a Roman who took it to France, a Frenchman who took it to Scandinavia, a Scandinavian who took it to Scotland, a Scotsman who evangelized Ireland, and an Irishman in turn who made the missionary conquest of Scotland.

A little accidental happening in a church in London in the 1920's gives a vivid picture of the world church. At the Guild House, where Maude Royden preached, two notable visitors signed the guest book on successive days. The first was Dr. Wilfred Grenfell, of Labrador. The second was Dr. Albert Schweitzer. Under his name, Dr. Schweitzer wrote, "The hippopotamus greets the Polar bear." In Christ's church it does. That outreach must never be paralyzed.

69. KEEPING FAITH IN AN ALIEN CULTURE

That I may be delivered from the unbelievers in Judea. ROM. 15:31
That I may not fall into the hands of the unbelievers. (Phillips)

Paul lived under pressure. We get a brief and arresting summary of some of the varied pressures in his list of dangers, "dangers from robbers, . . . danger in the city," and thirteen others (2 Cor. 11:26 ff). It reads like the memoirs of a man who had been squeezed by a vise. We, in a day when the Christian has many pressures applied to him, may well make this prayer of Paul, "Stand behind me in earnest prayer . . . that I may not fall into the hands of the unbelievers."

The particular danger Paul hopes to escape is not one which we meet today. Paul was praying deliverance from the non-Christian Jews in Judea. They regarded him as a traitor and archfool. We know from the book of Acts how great the danger of violence was.

The pressure or danger from unbelievers is entirely different, but something to pray intensely about. The pressure of unbelief around us is a sort of atmospheric or barometric pressure, the pressure of what is in so many ways a non-Christian culture. We need to pray for strength that we "may not fall into the hands of the unbelievers." Our danger is not that we may renounce our faith in some dramatic manner. It is the far more subtle, and usual, way, that we do not realize to what an extent we become influenced and shaped by the secular, nonspiritual mind of hosts of people around us. It drifts into the mind like a fog, resulting in low visibility of spiritual realities.

One temptation, of course, is to try to withdraw from the world, so that we may not be exposed to its infections. We can say this is an evil generation, and try to fly away to some separated life. But that is impossible, and far from the mind of Christ.

Thomas Carlyle, writing to Emerson, made a strong denunciation of shamefully trying to run away from one's time. "A man has no right to say to his own generation, turning quite away from it, 'Be damned.' It is the whole past, and the whole future, this cotton-spinning, dollar hunting, canting and shrieking, very wretched generation of ours. Come back into it, I tell you."

We are in a situation like that of the Jewish exiles. They said, "How can I sing the Lord's song in a strange land?" Their problem was that of keeping faith in an alien culture. That is never an easy task. It was a hard problem. Many of the Hebrews couldn't do it. They became "the lost tribes" of Israel. They were lost in Babylon when they lost their religious faith. We, too, become lost tribes of God, if we fail to keep faith in an alien culture today.

70.   ROLL OF HONOR

Greet . . . my fellow workers. ROM. 16:3

In one of the short stories of James M. Barrie, a man rushes out of a hotel in London, jumps into a hansom cab and orders the driver, "Drive back ten years!"

If we only could!

Also we have the strong feeling of how wonderful it would be if we could drive back, or fly back on a magic carpet, to some historical scene at which we would like to be among those present. That is true of the churches of the first Christian century. If we could only drive back about 1,850 years and pull up at a gathering of Christians in a Greek or Roman city. If we could see them, stealing down dark streets, looking back to make sure there were no secret police, and turn into a little house!

We have no magic carpet, except that of the imagination. That can take us on marvelous journeys. The finest, most glorious first aid to the imagination for a journey back to the earliest Christian churches is this 16th chapter of Romans. Here is the company gathered before us. We just step in. This chapter enables us to say, commandingly, "Backward, turn backward, O Time in your flight," if we read this chapter, carefully and prayerfully.

The 16th chapter of Romans is a roll of honor, a tremendous chapter. It has sometimes been regarded as a sort of anticlimax, just a list of names, a comedown from the great heights of the 8th and the 12th chapters of Romans. All wrong. People are always a *climax* to any truth. They are the operating clause which validates truth. Here are the people who demonstrate the gospel.

And what a demonstration! Notice two things about this list of people on the roll of honor, people who are awarded God's Distinguished Service Medal. Two things are mentioned over and over—*necks* and *hands,* the risking of life and hard work. How firm a foundation for a church. "Prisca and Aquilla, . . . *workers* . . . who risked their *necks.*" We take such good care of our necks. We don't like to "stick our necks out." These people did not regard saving their necks as the chief end of man. They risked laying them down on the block.

Notice the tributes to work—"Phoebe, a *helper* of many; Mary, who *worked* hard; Urbanus, our fellow worker; Persis, who has worked hard in the Lord"; "those workers, Tryphaena and Tryphosa; Timothy, my fellow worker." Not a "flowery bed of ease" in the whole chapter.

It is a thrilling atmosphere, God help us all, it should be the native air of the church of Christ. We can feel the warmth of fellowship, even on the printed page. Too often in our churches we are like a bag of marbles. We touch but do not adhere. There is no formal word here like "fellowship" but there is the real thing, "fellow prisoners," "beloved in the Lord," "host to the whole church," "our brother Quartus."

God's physiology—God's tools—necks and hands!

71. THE CHURCH IN THE HOUSE

The church in their house. ROM. 16:5
Give my love to the little church that meets in their house. (Phillips)

This verse has called forth many times a comment that should be repeated over and over. Hence this repetition. This comment

consists of two observations, a pair of twin observations. One is that
because the Christian church began in a home, it should always
retain the marks of its birthplace, the love and warmth of a home.
The second is because the home was the birthplace of that gift of
God, the church, the home ought always to retain some of the qualities of a church, the worship of God and the presence of his spirit
in its whole life.

These observations ought always be held in remembrance, for
each needs the other, the home and the church. By the grace of God,
they move together.

Note the affection which appears in Phillips' translation, "the
little church that meets in their house." The word "little" does not
refer primarily to size; it is the "affectionate diminutive." Rightly!

I love thy church, O God.

72. NOTABLES

Men of note. ROM. 16:7
Outstanding men. (Phillips)

Whenever a man says in these days, "Our church has men of
note," we know exactly what he means. They are "men of note,"
noted in Dun and Bradstreet or the Social Register, rather than in
the Lamb's Book of Life. They might very well be men of note in
both books, and, praise God, they often are.

But to us the words "men of note" have a very different meaning
than to Paul. Phillips uses the word "outstanding." To us, an outstanding man is one who stands out from the crowd in distinguished
achievement. When a church has "men of note" in its membership,
this phrase denotes, usually, such men as the president and vice-
presidents of the First National Bank, several professors, quite outstanding, Mr. Robinson of Robinson, Robinson, Robinson and Robinson, the leading law firm of the state, and other notables. Thank God
for them all. But in this roll of honor of the church in the house in
the 16th chapter of Romans, a different measurement is at work.
Look at it—"first convert in Asia"; "approved in Christ"; "eminent in
the Lord." This is God's hall of fame, not man's. God's measuring
rod has been used, not man's.

The First Epistle of Paul
to the Corinthians

73. "AND"

Paul, . . . and our brother Sosthenes. 1 COR. 1:1

The word "and" is one of the greatest and most beautiful words in the language. Before we say "nonsense" to that extravagant statement, reflect on it. Here, as in many other places in Paul's letters, and in millions of places in life, it represents the fortifying power of friendship and companionship. In the opening sentence of five of Paul's letters, we read "Paul and"—somebody else. That represents a sustaining fellowship. It was not just Paul, but Paul plus—Paul plus the reserve force of love in a yokefellow. The words "and someone" do not indicate a joint authorship, but a joint moral and spiritual strength.

Trace that golden word "and" through Paul's letters. "And our brother Sosthenes" (1 Cor. 1:1); "and Timothy" (2 Cor. 1:1); "and all the brethren who are with me" (Gal. 1:1); "and Timothy our brother" (Col. 1:1); "Silvanus and Timothy" (1 Thess. 1:1 and 2 Thess. 1:1).

We do not know about Sosthenes. Probably a convert, he perhaps wrote the letter from Paul's dictation. The inclusion of these names in the salutations is an evidence of Paul's fine courtesy. But more, it is an evidence of friendship. His strength was as the strength of two or three, those who were beside him, with lifting power to his heart and mind.

What a field of service these salutations offer to the imagination and dedication. People, included after the word, very rarely get into an encyclopedia or even a Who's Who. But they are enrolled in God's Book of Life. Those who stand by a friend have an inseparable part of his achievement and service. This word "and " is part of the very genius of the Christian life and fellowship. We do not walk alone. It is Christ *and* his disciples; Paul *and* Sosthenes.

Often on the brightest pages of history it is written, "John Smith, *and wife*." Burma saw the heroic drama of Adoniram Judson, *and wife* Ann. It was beautifully and truly said of Canon Barnett and his wife that their two lives burned as "a single flaming candle" in the darkness of East London. Often it has been written in extra-illuminated letters, a man or woman, and mother. Think of St. Augustine, *and mother*, or John Wesley, *and mother!*

The word pictures memorably the high office of friend. Such sustaining friends, even though inarticulate so far as the world is concerned, do not die with all their music in them. It comes out melodiously in other lives. Such sustaining friends are God's "reinforcements." Many a battle has been won by reinforcements.

74. ENRICHED

The grace of God which was given you in Christ Jesus, that in every way you were enriched in him. I COR. 1:4–5

These words sound like a letter of congratulation to people who have come into a great fortune. That is exactly what it is! Paul gives his hearty gratitude that these people in Corinth have received a great legacy, in being heirs of the grace of God.

We frequently hear the expression, "He struck it rich." One man gave a turn to that expression, which sounded like an echo of Paul. On his announcing that he had "struck it rich," a friend asked eagerly, "Gold?" "No, God," he answered. Anyone who has received the grace of God in Christ has "struck it rich."

The words enriched "in every way" spread out like a magic tent till they cover the whole of life. Look now at the intangible enrichment to life, a wealth not to be touched, weighed, or counted by hands or tools, but nevertheless, the most *real* thing in the world.

Begin with the largest enrichment. It is that of relationship in an age of loneliness. Here is the legacy, "Beloved, now are we the sons of God." That is capital which increases immeasurably one's spiritual and intellectual bank account. It makes wonderful savings for a rainy day! There is a sharp timeliness about this fortune, this legacy. Any time is a lonely time without the companionship of God. But in many ways our time is peculiarly liable to be a time of loneliness. Ours is increasingly a mechanical world. Even the sky has been taken over by fearsome machines. One of our modern poets, Phyllis McGinley, has pictured with painful sharpness the awful emptiness when love between humans is all there is to cling to. The poem is entitled, "Mid-century Love Letter."

> *Stay near me. Speak my name. Oh, do not wander*
> *By a thought's span, heart's impulse, from the light*
> *We kindle here. You are my sole defender*
> *(As I am yours) in this precipitous night,*

Which over earth, till common landmarks alter,
Is falling, without stars, and bitter cold.
We two have but our burning selves for shelter.
Huddle against me. Give me your hand to hold.

So might two climbers lost in mountain weather
On a high slope and taken by the storm,
Desperate in the darkness, cling together
Under one cloak and breathe each other warm.
Stay near me. Spirit, perishable as bone,
In no such winter can survive alone

That word "mid-century" rings a little bell in the memory. For it recalls another "mid-century love letter"—this time the middle of the nineteenth century. Matthew Arnold in his unforgettable "Dover Beach" has dealt with the same theme, the empty world with no divine reliance, when the only love was the only refuge.

Ah, love, let us be true
To one another! For the world, which seems
To lie before us like a land of dreams,
So various, so beautiful, so new,
Hath neither joy, nor love, nor light,
Nor certitude nor peace, nor help for pain;
And we are here as on a darkling plain
Swept with confused alarms of struggle and flight,
Where ignorant armies clash by night.

But into the life, enriched by God's grace in Christ, there comes another love letter. Here is the mid-century love letter which fills an empty world, whether in the mid-twentieth century or the mid-first century, "God so loved the world, that he gave his only begotten Son."

Among the "every ways" in which life is enriched by God's grace is family life. The relationship of a family is not that of the casual acquaintance of a journey on a railroad train. It is an eternal love which binds immortal souls. Baron von Bunsen put this in classic form when he said to his wife on his deathbed, "In thy face I have seen the eternal."

So many people dream of the time "when my ship comes in." There they wait, vainly scanning the horizon for a mythical treasure ship. St. Paul here announces, and his successors as the heralds of the good news must announce, the ship has docked. The treasure ship, with incredible riches, is here. Beloved now are we the sons of God.

75. WITH ONE VOICE

Be united in the same mind and the same judgment.   1 COR. 1:10
*I do beg you, . . . by all that Christ means to you, to speak with one
voice.*   (Phillips)

These words are a part of Paul's tremendous plea to the church in
Corinth to let harmony prevail over their conflicts. That church was
having an acrimonious and violent civil war. Its party cries were
like the partisan banners at a political convention.

Nineteen hundred years later there is measureless need for harmony, for "the same mind and the same judgment" in the world
and in the church. There is a crucial need for the churches to speak
with one voice.

One of the common words of our current speech is the word
"split." We have split personalities, split families, split nations, split
churches, and a split world. We need the power which can bind
men, churches, and nations together. In the church we cannot sing,
"one in faith and doctrine," in a way to bring conviction to ourselves
or outsiders. We had better try the next line of the hymn, "one in
charity." That is more immediately possible. Bring into operation the
motive power Paul applies here, "By all that Christ means to you."
That is the only unifying force strong enough to bind diverse minds
together. Keep that in the foreground. In Christ's name, put in the
center the things which we hold together, rather than the things we
hold separately. Let Christ increase, and the Founders of our particular group decrease.

To achieve the same mind and the same judgment is easier at the
top level of denominationalism than at the bottom; at the level of
top leadership it does not seem too hard. Conferences and assemblies
will pass glowing resolutions that would persuade the innocent that
a united church was just around the corner. But on the level of the
local churches it turns into a task for miracle workers. One mystery
appears in bringing divided churches to one mind. It is strange how
many words of Jesus men believe in relation to individuals, but
reject them in relation to denominations. There is the word, for instance, "He that loseth his life shall find it." Men and women are
ready to grant that in personal life. But they stubbornly refuse to see
their own local church or denomination make any experiment in
losing anything, for the common good. We must deal with the task

where Paul dealt with it, with the people, not with resolutions. He brought the motivation of God's love.

One truth increases the urgency of the one voice. When the plea to "get together" comes to the nations of the world from a divided church, it carries little persuasion.

76. DIVIDED LOYALTIES

Was Paul crucified for you?   I COR. 1:13

At first glance this seems like a foolish question. It was not a foolish question to Paul, nor a rhetorical question. It was an impassioned question. He was seeing a church dedicated to love as revealed in Christ, going down on its maiden voyage in loveless contention.

This question does not seem foolish, if it is translated in terms of more recent and partial loyalties. This question has pertinence to us in these terms: Was it Martin Luther who was crucified for you? Was it John Wesley who died on the cross for you? Or John Calvin? Or Alexander Campbell? Or were you baptized in the name of the historic episcopate or the apostolic succession, or of any of these founding fathers? Some apparently were. And who are these? In Paul's words, ministers through whom you believed. Let them not become, as they might become, idols of a sort. This question calls for one resounding answer, "I am of Christ."

77. WORD AND SACRAMENT

For Christ did not send me to baptize but to preach the gospel.
I COR. 1:17

Here is an audible echo of

> Old, unhappy, far-off things
> And battles long ago.

It has been a well-fought battlefield for centuries. Is the Word more important than the sacraments? In general, Protestants and Catholics have been lined up in battle array on opposite sides of the field.

While this text does throw some light on Paul's position, it does not end the debate. Paul was not giving the Word of God on that question. He was guarding here against another thing, the dangerous calamity that the Christian converts might get more attached to him than to his Master. Would that all pastors had had the same great concern and dedication!

Paul believed completely in the power of the Word in preaching. Strangely enough, one of the clearest statements of the relative importance of the Word in Christian experience comes from a friar, the author of *Dives and Lazarus,* who made a plea for preaching in the Middle Ages. He wrote:

It is more profitable to hear God's word in preaching, than to hear any mass. For by preaching, folk can be stirred to contrition and to forsake sin and the fiend, and to love God and goodness, and to be illumined to know their God, and virtues from vices, truth from falsehood, and to forsake errors and heresies. But if any come to mass in sin, they go away in sin, and shrews they come and shrews they went.

That last sentence, of course, represents a very inadequate appreciation of the mass and communion service. Yet, it does have an insight into the relative values of ceremony and the proclamation of the Word. In the proclaimed Word there is prophetic power. What ceremony could serve the spiritual and moral effectiveness of Amos, Hosea, Micah, and Isaiah? George Adam Smith paid a perfect tribute to Micah by saying that in his words one can always see the "pinched faces of starved peasants peering through the fences." Where else but in the Word can we find the holy anger of Jesus over those who devoured widows' houses, or against those in our own day, who, for their own gain, block low cost housing?

Preaching God's Word in Christ enables men to see the human parade as it goes by with all its grievous need, flayed and harassed, like sheep without a shepherd, and the sacrament of the Lord's Supper, deeply received, supplies tremendous motive power. But the Word may bring inwardness of insight. When the Word is muted, there is danger that creeping mechanism may invade, as it has invaded often, the sacrament. In the days of Charles II in England, there were ministers known as "silenced ministers." They were ministers of nonconformist beliefs, who were silenced by state command. Today there are "silenced ministers," not by any government command, but by their own hesitations and fears. An emphasis on sacraments, and a minimizing of the prophetic Word, has been a refuge for those who have hauled down the belligerent flag. "The entrance of thy word giveth light." In the fight against evil, God uses His Word. "With the breath of his lips shall he slay the wicked."

Incidentally, J. B. Phillips' translation has a cutting edge for the minister who is out to "make a killing" in statistics. It reads, "Christ did not send me to see how many I could baptize." There was no quota in the first-century church!

78. DEFLATED WISDOM

Has not God made foolish the wisdom of the world?   I COR. 1:20

The history of the world, from the first century to the twentieth, and particularly the first half of the twentieth century, might be attached as a footnote to this verse. This verse is a question. If you want an answer, look about you.

We must tread carefully here. The debt of mankind to science and to all kinds of exact knowledge, and to man's wisdom in the use of knowledge, can never be measured. The sum total of benefit to human welfare and comfort outruns the imagination to conceive. For it all, we ought continually to get down on our knees and thank heaven, fasting. What Paul here calls the "wisdom of the world" is the arrogant assurance of the "know it all." He was a citizen of Paul's day as well as of ours. What God has made foolish is the complacency and dogmatic self-satisfaction of the "wise" people (Paul lets his irony go full force on that adjective!) who dismiss all knowledge except their own limited kind. He is the self-esteemed man who *knows*. Paul describes him, and the description fits some, at least, of the present-day counterparts of the man of Paul's "wise man," "scribe" and debater of this age. As Paul observes, he dogmatically brands any spiritual reality as "nonsense."

Frank Lloyd Wright has defined an expert as "man who has stopped thinking. He knows." Not all experts, thank God. Many of the most renowned experts of earth press on in the deathless search for new knowledge. But the definition does fit many in Paul's day, and ever since. Where is the wisdom of those who opposed new truth? Where are the debaters (and how they could debate!) of Galileo's age who scornfully hurled the verdict "nonsense" at Galileo's fantastic story of the revolving earth? Where is the wisdom of those who had a hilarious time over every great invention ever achieved? Where are the people who threw shoes on the first telegraph line ever erected, calling on Mr. Morse to deliver their shoes? Where are the wise ones who had such fun ridiculing the Wright brothers, including the man on the New York newspaper who discharged a reporter for turning in such a ridiculous story?

So we may ask where is the scribe to whom the Christian gospel was "nonsense"? That gospel transmitted by believers has been the greatest and most permanent contribution of the whole Greek culture.

Yet a large part of the world is still thrown into a trance of befuddled admiration of the wizard of the laboratory, the bomb and the missile. He has become the popular idol, to whom lifted hands of prayer are raised. On January 30, 1958, one advertiser took a whole page of *The New York Times,* with a devotional tribute to the "man who knows." His gigantic figure is shown, much deeper in thought than Rodin's "Thinker," before a blackboard filled with equations, beside which the equation, $E = MC^2$, must seem like first-grade arithmetic. The scientific wisdom of our times is in his hands. Yet a deeper look at the threatened world will indicate that the future is not secured even by a ten-thousand-mile missile nor a space ship to the moon. The hope of our world is not the material wisdom of the wise, not the man who knows all factual knowledge, but the man who believes. The hope of the world lies in the ways of brotherhood and the actions that weave the fabric of peace. In other words, in following what Paul calls in this passage "the wisdom of God."

The intricate wisdom of today, as a saving wisdom of the world, has been made foolish. When Blériot, the French aviator, flew the English Channel for the first time (July 25, 1909) there was great celebration and an orgy of prophecy. One newspaper became lyrical, saying this means the end of frontiers and a decline of nationalism. For, it asked, what could they mean in a world where aviation had erased frontiers? Five years later that wisdom of the wise was "stultified."

In many different ways this material wisdom, then and now, could be summed up in "salvation from a machine." Lewis Mumford has pointed out:

Most of the advances which Bacon and Leonardo, and Della Porta and Glanville anticipated and a grand succession of later inventors realized, were devices for saving time, for shrinking space, for enhancing energy, for speeding motions, for accelerating natural processes, devices which equipped man with Seven League Boots, and Magic Carpets, releasing people from physical restraints of here and now. But note the curious twist that actual experience has given to all these early plans and aspirations, the faster we travel, the less we actually see and experience on the way; the larger the area of communication, other things remaining the same, the more limited the area of understanding; the greater our physical power, the more formidable become our social and moral limitations.

Seven League Boots and Magic Carpets are vain things for safety. For the greater the wisdom of mechanical sort alone, the less hope of man's salvation.

It is not the wisdom shown to be foolishness, to which we must turn, as a Savior, but the folly of Christ.

79. LOOKING FOR A PANACEA

For the Jews ask for miraculous proofs and the Greeks an intellectual panacea. I COR. 1:22 (Phillips)

Deep in the heart of quite a large section of the human race is the love of a panacea. There has been an eager search for it, like the search in the Middle Ages for a philosopher's stone which would change any metal into gold. So there is a yearning and a deluded hope for a formula that would change all of life's baffling complexities into simplicities. The words of the Authorized and Revised Standard Versions, "the Greeks seek wisdom," are translated by Phillips into "seek a panacea." A panacea is a cure for all diseases, which will do the whole job of solving life problems at once. We get an echo of this search for a mythical panacea in the phrase we so love to use, "once and for all."

Military victory has called forth a mighty faith as a panacea for war. World War I was a war to end war. The Allies were going to do that job, "once and for all." We raised an altar to the great god Panacea. But World War II came and we sang, "When the lights go on again all over the world," never to go out again. They went out. Panaceas have a way of going out.

We have escaped from that particular delusion. But we still, as the ancient Greeks, "seek wisdom." We seek a panacea and for our day, many have found it in science. We want a million brilliant new scientists, all equipped to annex the moon. And we want them the day before yesterday!

Education has been a regulation panacea—just have more and more information pumped into the minds of young people and all will be well. Pre-1914 Germany pushed that trust to the limit. Reinhold Niebuhr said that there was more education per square head in Germany than anywhere else in the world.

In religion, also, there has been the easy and vicious oversimplification that seeks to find a panacea, a remedy for all diseases of life. Men have regarded the first step of the religious life, making a decision, signing a card, walking down an aisle in a public place, as the whole thing. That particular panacea has distorted the whole Christian gospel and has worked untold damage. A particular form of words as a reliance against all evil has terribly oversimplified the long, arduous, complex task of being a disciple of Jesus Christ in a bewildering, confusing world. It is a world which requires moral decisions with no easy "once and for all" about them.

The Greeks seek wisdom, but we preach Christ crucified, not as an easy word to say, nor as a magic panacea to cure all diseases, but as the power of God working within us and as the wisdom of God to guide us.

80.   ARE WE FOOLISH ENOUGH?

For the foolishness of God is wiser than men.   I COR. 1:25

This is a dangerous text. For it can bring false comfort to a person when its meaning is distorted. We step into a trap when we identify our own foolishness as "the foolishness of God." When we load up all our foolish actions on to God we are giving Him too much credit. We deserve quite a bit ourselves!

It is a present help in time of trouble, when, instead of looking at ourselves as we really are, we call our mistakes and blunders "the foolishness of God." It is a dangerous practice for it prevents our seeing ourselves clearly. It ministers to complacency and makes us impervious to criticism. It prevents growth in the grace of our Lord Jesus Christ.

The foolishness of God which is greater than man's wisdom is God's act of redemption in Jesus Christ. That is the victory that overcomes the proud wisdom of man.

Are we sufficiently "foolish"? Do we really trust enough in God's revelation of love as the most powerful force in the world? We pay honor to the wisdom of God. But we so often guide our steps by something else. In other words, so often we feel that the wisdom of practical men is better than the foolishness of trusting in love. For so many today, to be told that they are not practical, makes them weak in the knees. They buckle under at such a terrible charge! For the highest admiration of such a great number in our practicel culture and society is the "practical man." He looms high as an object of worship, a chief idol like the statue of Zeus which was one of the wonders of the ancient world. Sometimes even in the field of religion genuflection is made to the practical man. A minister's highest recommendation, at times, is that he is a practical man, he can raise the money, can attract substantial people, and is a wizard at public relations. No vague mysticism about him.

But when we look closely at the practical man, in the light of history, we see that the practical man often is one who repeats the mistakes of his ancestors. Practical men ridiculed the proposed voyage of Columbus, and Jenner's vaccination for smallpox. G. K. Chesterton has given an enlivening, and true, picture of the "practical man," whose greatest gift is for pooh-poohing any new venture of faith. He has painted a harrowing picture of what happens when a man has no philosophy at all.

The best reason for a revival of philosophy is that unless a man has a philosophy, certain horrible things will happen to him. He will be practical; he will be progressive; he will trust in evolution; he will do the work that is nearest; he will devote himself to deeds, not words. Thus, struck down by blow after blow, by blind stupidity, and random fate, he will stagger to a miserable death, with no comfort but a series of catchwords such as those which I have catalogued above.

In the eyes of many of his contemporaries, and multitudes since, Jesus was not a practical man. He brought into his thinking other and greater factors than those which paid financially and in a short time.

In deeper ways, he was the most practical man who ever lived, for he brought to light the truths which work out in practice. Bernard Shaw's comment stands, "Jesus remains unshaken as the practical man; and we stand exposed as the fools, the blunderers, the unpractical visionaries."

Paul was thinking and writing of the power of the cross of Christ in human life. A beautiful picture of what Paul is discussing here, the power of love over all the material devices of force, is found in Rudyard Kipling's poem, "Cold Iron." It is one of the most deeply religious things which Kipling ever wrote, and has a sure insight into the Christian gospel. A baron has rebelled against his king and brought an army. Before the battle, the baron boasts of his powerful weapons and asserts that "iron, cold iron is the master of men all." The rebellious baron is defeated and taken prisoner. He is brought before his king and expects the usual penalty. Here the story becomes highly symbolic. Instead of revenge, the king sets before his enemy a table, and serves him bread and wine. The baron finally says with conviction:

Iron, cold iron is the master of men all.
The iron nails of Calvary are master of men all.

There is history as well as poetry in the poem. The love revealed
at Calvary has proved the master of men. The foolishness of the cross
has proved more powerful than the shrewdest wisdom of men. The
endless battle between the cocksure wisdom of the world and the
love incarnate on the cross is pictured in the words of John Gals-
worthy:

The idealist said in his heart, "The God of force is dead or dying."
He has been proven the fool the man of affairs always said he was. But
the fools of this world—generally after they have gone—have a way of
moving men which the wise and practical believers in force have not
. . . the battle between the God of love and the God of force endures
forever. Fools who follow the God of Love, drowned out and beaten to
their knees, in due time will get up again and plant their flag a little
farther on. The German fool, Schiller, said, "All men are brothers."
And so shall the fools say again when the time comes, and again and
again, after every beating.

This is true in the long run, and we have a God of the long run.
We have a gospel of the long run. If we cease to believe in it, if we
become so infected with the skepticism of the world, and regard the
foolishness of God's love as "sheer nonsense," we have lost the saving
power of God.

81.   FEAR AND TREMBLING

I was with you in weakness and in much fear and trembling.   1 COR. 2:3
Nervous and rather shaky.   (Phillips)

Paul is giving to the Corinthians a list of his handicaps as a
speaker and public figure. He lists three, "weakness and fear and
trembling." But with his handicaps, it was a case of "the last becomes
first." For these have turned out to be, in human experience, great
assets, indeed, among the greatest that any speaker can have, indispensable elements of power.

Trembling is an equipment for distinguished service. It is a strong
verb here, for Moffatt translates it "great trembling" and Goodspeed
renders it "a great deal of fear and trembling." Some fear and trembling before an audience never leaves a speaker of the front rank. A
minister complained to an older veteran that he was humiliated that

he never got over a feeling of fear and trembling in preaching. The wise veteran replied, "Pray that you never do get over it. For when you do, there is nothing left, but to embalm the corpse and nail down the coffin. You will be a finished speaker—completely finished!"

This is not a perverse idea, for trembling is an indication of sensitiveness of spirit and of mind, a disturbing awareness of opportunity and responsibility. More than that, trembling indicates the possession of that pearl of great price, humility. Blessed are the humble, for their's is the kingdom of the platform and pulpit. When a person is amazed at the wonder that anyone should listen to him five minutes, the Lord is with him. But when, instead of that humility, a person has a brassy, calloused self-confidence which feels the great privilege which this audience has of listening to him, his strength is gone, as definitely as that of Samson after Delilah got through with him.

How many of the great heralds of the gospel have had weakness and fear and trembling. There was Frederick W. Robertson, one of God's great preachers of all time, and a great trembler. Perhaps, today, his fear and trembling might be diagnosed as a deficiency in nervous temperament, but he did demonstrate gloriously that it is a fearful thing to fall into the hands of the living God as His ambassador and undertake to speak in Christ's stead.

There is a deeper cause for trembling for a preacher, and indeed anyone who teaches the Word of God. There is the danger that in handling the Word of God he may become accustomed to it. Then the wonder is gone. The shepherds of Bethlehem, at hearing the message of God from the skies, were "sore afraid." That is the feeling which every messenger should have. The sin against the Holy Ghost is handling the things of God lightly. Pray that we may retain the power of trembling, the saving gift of fear.

82. BEYOND EYE AND EAR

What no eye has seen, nor ear heard, nor the heart of man conceived, what God has prepared for those who love him. I COR. 2:9

These words are Paul's description, really a rhapsody, rather than an exact description, of the secret wisdom of God. This wisdom is not attained by study, by laborious days and nights, nor by any initiation, such as was common in the mystery religions, but by the gift of the Spirit.

This gift is beyond the senses, beyond eye and ear, beyond touch

and taste and feeling. This gift is beyond the boundaries of the pl
cal attainment. It is a journey into wonder. The whole thri
history of the modern world, for five centuries, has been truly a j
ney into wonder, all the way from Columbus to the unveiling of
the latest life-saving drug. Each new generation has had inspired
curiosity, the vision which has guided all scientific searchers into the
wonders of an unknown world. But in what "God has prepared for
those who love him," there is a more momentous journey into wonder. It is a journey past "the last frontier." That so-called last frontier of man has been moved many times in recent years, exploration
has moved so rapidly. Some years ago, the last frontier was in Central Africa. Then it was moved to the Antarctic, where the thrust
into the unknown with men, dogs, and machines has continued in a
heroic story. Today, that last frontier has been placed in outer space,
and it doth not yet appear what we shall be in the crossing of that
last frontier.

But, in the highest and deepest sense, the last frontier of man is in
the spirit. It is beyond what eye can see and ear hear, in the spirit,
that horizon on the rim of our knowledge where the known shades
into the unknown, the seen into the unseen, the human into the
divine, man into God. That is the last frontier in this great passage
of Paul—man's relation to God.

God has prepared many gifts "for those who love him." The centuries have demonstrated an infinite increment of rich rewards in
experience of those who have accepted the gift of God in Christ.
But the greatest gift is that beyond the last frontier, relationship to
God. It has filled life with wonder and has proved a strong reliance
in time of need. These words of Anne Douglas Sedgwick, the novelist, show forth the reality and power of God's gift beyond eye and
ear. It is a true journey into the wonder of God's love, made by a
countless host. Mrs. Sedgwick wrote in a letter in the midst of a
painful illness:

Now, added to everything else, I can't breathe unless lying down, my
ribs collapse. Yet I can't drink my food sitting up. Life is a queer struggle. Yet it is mine and beautiful to me. There is joy in knowing I lie
in the hands of God. When you wrote, "Your spirit can surmount anything," I felt a strange tremor of response, from an indomitable thread
of life within me. It is mine, but I feel it communicated from God.

That was news from beyond the frontier, authentic tidings—"I felt
it communicated from God."

That relationship to God can create an "inner environment" of
the spirit that is inviolate against all outward changes. In that, it is

like the temperature of the body. It is constant whether it is June or January, whether the wind blows east or west. God can create the weather in our souls that will transform the inner scenery. One lively illustration of the inner scenery with outward surroundings is that describing how Leigh Hunt, who was confined in Horsemongers Lane Gaol for slandering George IV, turned a vacant ward in the infirmary into "a noble room."

I papered the wall with a trellis of roses, I had the ceiling covered with clouds and sky; the barred windows I screened with venetian blinds; and when my bookcases were set up with their busts and flowers and pianoforte, there was perhaps not a handsomer room on that side of the water.

Here in the prison of flesh, there can be created "a noble room" for the spirit, beyond the power of eye and ear, which God has prepared for those who love Him.

83. IT DOESN'T MAKE SENSE

But the unspiritual man simply cannot accept the matters which the Spirit deals with—they just don't make sense to him, for, after all, you must be spiritual to see spiritual things.   1 COR. 2:14 (Phillips)

Phillips' phrase "don't make sense" is a massive verdict on the Christian gospel made by many people in Paul's day, and is a verdict often pronounced today. This phrase by which Phillips translates the Greek (rendered by the Revised Standard Version "they are folly to him") makes Paul's point very sharp, in colloquial language.

The first thing to be said about this now, is just what Paul said about it then. The people completely ignorant of spiritual matters are not competent judges. In no other realm do we accept total ignorance as a qualification for judging. The gospel is not on trial before the natural, unspiritual man. Dean Inge, discussing once his capacities as a musician, said that he could not tell the tune "God save the weasel" from "pop goes the king." That is just a fact about Dean Inge, but not a fact about music! Beethoven is not on trial before the first grade music class. Michelangelo is not on trial before the clay modeling class of the kindergarten. It is a strange fear which some Christians have of the adverse judgment of those who have no qualifications to judge. Here is a man, for instance, who has spent forty years a prisoner in a chemistry laboratory, giving an offhand

opinion that religion does not make sense because it cannot be found
in a test tube. The well is deep and he has nothing with which to
draw. That judgment is like measuring a mountain with a three-foot
rule. Chesterton made an answer which covers the ground pretty well.
He recalls the time when he made the surmise that "perhaps those
might not be the best judges of the relation of religion to happiness,
who, by their own confession, had never experienced either."

The second thing, though, to say to the man who asserts that
religion does not make sense, is to say "that is the glory of religion."
It is a charge Christians accept gratefully and proudly. A parallel is
found in Job, "Oh, that I had the indictment written by my adver-
sary! Surely I would carry it on my shoulder; I would bind it on me
as a crown" (Job 31:35). Christians do wear as a glittering crown
the indictment that spiritual things do not make sense. Christianity
does not make sense to a parcel-weighing world. Nothing about it
makes sense—not a baby in a barn, nor a Savior on a cross, nor
loving your enemies, nor the forgiveness of sin. That is the glory of
it. It lifts life to a new dimension—wonder. It is made up of the
things that cannot be and are. Religion is not geometry. If you could
prove it, it might be mathematics, but it could not be religion. "A
God proved is a God dead." The artist, Russel Cheney, writes of the
power of wonder in art, "I could stay along in classes happily, having
work laid out to do, a fairly good craftsman-dilettante, and all that
has nothing to do with this outside force—you called it the unknown—which takes you right off your feet." In the spiritual realm,
God is the "outside force . . . which takes you right off your feet."

The power of the spirit in life, power for living, "doesn't make
sense" either. Through the power of God which possessed them, men
have extended themselves unbelievably, that is, unbelievable to the
devotees of the great god, Common Sense.

Some years ago, T. R. Glover wrote an amusing but true little
story of an agnostic who, out of the goodness of his heart, undertook
to transform a drunkard, without bringing in any religion, nor anything that did not make sense. He tried to cure him by dragging him
past the doors of saloons, sitting up at night teaching him sound doc-
trines, and in general giving him the care which a fond mother would
lavish on a two-year-old. The only flaw in the treatment was that
whenever the man was called out of the city on business, he would
return to find his charge roaring drunk! "And then," said the
agnostic, "some rough looking people in red jerseys with an atrocious
band appeared, and I don't know exactly what happened, but anyhow he can walk right by a saloon by himself now." Of course, Dr.
Glover comments, he was not "by himself." That was the world-

changing fact! He had found a new force in life, a hand was on his shoulder. Christianity is much more than a "common sense" railway time table. As Dr. Glover says, "it is a knock on the door, the promise of a friend, the gift of a Presence."

If Jesus had had no mystery, no amazing wonder in his life and teaching, he would have been forgotten long ago. He would have been like the nineteenth-century didactic moralizer, Samuel Smiles. Smiles was once very widely read and his books on *Self-Help, Thrift,* and *Duty* were a veritable gospel to many of his generation. Now he is as dead as the late Jacob Marley. But in his day he was read far more than Keats, Wordsworth, and Coleridge put together. He was always clear and reasonable and—platitudinous. If Jesus had just made sense, he would have been just a first-century Samuel Smiles, a forgotten curiosity.

"God chose what is foolish in the world to shame the wise."

84.   THE APPRAISER

The spiritual man judges all things.   1 COR. 2:15
The spiritual man . . . has an insight into the meaning of everything.
(Phillips)
The spiritual man is alive to all true values.   (Goodspeed)

This verse gives a sharp etching of the spiritual man as "appraiser." An appraiser is an expert judge, a man with keen, instructed eye who estimates the quality, size, weight, and values of things. He has played a great role in American history, a figure familiar to many. "John Jones, appraiser," has been a man to reckon with. He puts a value on a whole estate. Often it has been a calamity to the eager heirs to have him come and turn his piercing eye on everything. The family diamond brooch is turned over to him, a piece of legendary value. "Sorry, madam, pure paste," The priceless piece of furniture, alleged to have come over to Salem, Massachusetts, in 1662. Early American furniture. "Very sorry, madam. This is not Early American, 1662. It is Late Grand Rapids, 1932."

Or the man who judges all things may reverse the common estimate. He lays down the magnifying glass. "This," he says, "is the real thing."

The spiritual man judges all things. He is "alive to all true values" in the world's dazzling bazaar. Jesus gave a memorable picture of two appraisers at work, men who knew comparative values:

The kingdom of heaven is like treasure hidden in a field, which a man found and covered up; then in his joy he goes and sells all that he has and buys that field.

Again, the kingdom of heaven is like a merchant in search of fine pearls, who, on finding one pearl of great value, went and sold all that he had and bought it. [Matt. 13:44–46]

There is in London a church with a striking name, quickening to the imagination, "The King's Weigh House." That is what a church of Christ ought to be, a sanctuary where the things of life are brought and weighed on the King's scales, and given their proper weight.

Jesus weighed the world twice. He did it once at his temptation. He looked at the prize, the kingdoms of the earth. He appraised them carefully. They were worth—nothing! Nothing in comparison to a higher value, doing the will of God. He weighed the world again—on Calvary. The world of men needing to be saved was worth —worth everything. He appraised it so highly that he gave his life, a ransom for many.

We all go through our years on a lifelong shopping trip. The world is a globe-shaped department store. We choose. There are glittering baubles and pearls of great price. The high art of life is to tell the difference. We all face the danger of shopping for cheap values. With the great prizes of life ours for the asking, we are liable to end up with a toy balloon for which we have paid everything. Dr. Frederick Grant tells an amusing story of his college days:

In 1910 when the students' dormitory at Nashotah burned, we had the biggest and stoutest man in the senior class. At the last minute he had gone back to the closet off his bed room, in order to salvage a bag of hickory nuts, that had broken and spilled over the floor. We got him out just before the roof fell in.

So many people salvage a bag of hickory nuts, comparatively, from their journey through life.

It is a difficult art, that of putting a price tag on things. But we must all practice it. Some blundering estimates have been made. Jesus mentioned the most appalling one—"What shall it profit a man to gain the whole world and forfeit his life." A shining ball, of course, but what an infinite price, his soul!

We can pay far too great a price for anything, and have a terribly poor bargain.

"The boast of heraldry, the pomp of power, And all that beauty, all that wealth e'er gave," can be so poorly appraised and paid for at a calamitous price. Think of the buyer of cheap goods, men with no "insight into the meaning of everything," Demas, who loved this present world, and the rich young ruler who chose great possessions over the discipleship to Jesus. Think of missing that chance for a few acres and livestock! There are a million examples of the stark truth that "the trouble with money is that it costs too much."

There is so much distorted vision. A Harlem gangster explained to the police that "when you are 'high' with drugs, you can look across the street, which is littered with garbage cans, and say everything looks fine." So shoppers have picked up trash and, lacking any insight into life's meaning, have said "it looks fine." People have made place as well as wealth the big bargain. Some have bought a ticket of admission to the "country club set" and have paid for it with their deepest convictions. Men have bartered almost their souls for "success," an office dressed with a little brief authority.

Others have judged all things rightly, as David Livingstone did, "I set no value on anything, except in relation to the cause of Christ."

As Paul writes in the next verse, we have an instrument which will give us an insight into the meaning of life. It is the mind of Christ, or, as Phillips translates it, "the very thoughts of Christ!" When we test the world's offering by his mind, the things that were small to him become small to us, and the things that were great to him become great to us.

85. ORDINARY MEN

Are you not . . . behaving like ordinary men?   1 COR. 3:3

This is a very serious charge which Paul brings against the Christians at Corinth. There is jealousy and strife among them, and they are showing qualities which would be displayed in a quarrelsome fish market. They have sunk from the high level of being Christ's people to that of ordinary men.

Paul's reiterated and vehement emphasis all through his letters is that Christians are called to be *extraordinary* people. He points out that we have an extraordinary God, an extraordinary gospel, and an extraordinary power.

The greatest danger which the individual Christian and a Christian church face is that of sinking to the ordinary level, at which there will be little difference from the pattern of life around them. Arnold Bennett, on rereading some of his writing, confided to his journal that he was surprised to find how often the word "extraordinary" occurred. He felt it was far too often, and told himself that he would have to watch it. Yet, that word is emphatically in the language of Christian faith. A Christian and a church must be extraordinary to be Christian.

That is as it was in the beginning. Put a stethoscope down to the opening pages of the book of Acts and you hear a heartbeat and movement. This record reveals an extraordinary people. They are alive. They came on the scene at an extraordinary time, and they were people to match the time. They were recognized as extraordinary, as "those that came to turn the world upside down." Pliny, in his famous letter to the Emperor Trajan, was so impressed by their steadfast loyalty, that he paid them the high tribute of calling them "pig-headed." Some of them stood up and told the astounded high priests that they must obey God rather than man. Nothing ordinary about that!

Our great danger is that of losing the distinctive qualities in our life that make us a peculiar, a different people. The most vicious and damaging attack on the Christian faith is not that made by any multitude of violent atheists or agnostics. The church can resist that, for "the chruch is not a candle, blow on." The devastating blow is given when Christians become so ordinary that they give onlookers the impression that being a Christian does not make any difference.

Today we live in extraordinary times. For such days, ordinary people are not enough. A drama critic said of a lavish production of Hamlet that it was "wild and whirling occasion, and routine competence is not enough." We are surely in a wild and whirling occasion today; routine competence and ordinary people are not enough.

Our danger is, in some ways, just that of melting into the general mass, of blending with the background. This present mass has been described by Ortega y Gasset, the Spanish philosopher. In the early 1920's, he

warned that Western civilization was threatened . . . not by the barbarians from without, but by the barbarians from within. Ortega defines the barbarian as the mass man, the self-satisfied man. . . . He holds up no high standards of behaviour for himself. . . . He is the average man, who takes pride in this mediocrity. If he admires anything outside himself, it is success. He admires the smart operator, the getter-by, the fixer, the man who can beat the game.

In holding to Christian convictions and patterns of conduct, the Christian often suffers from what is called in mountain climbing "high altitude lethargy." Part of the training for climbing is preparing the body to keep driving after that sets in, as it does set in. The Christian must be trained to keep driving in the "high altitudes" of Christian conduct, which mark one off from the ordinary. Otherwise, he embraces an easy, undemanding, very ordinary religion. James A. Michener describes a Buddhist in Japan telling him how well satisfied with Buddhism he was and why. He writes:

Buddhism suits us exactly. It does not concern itself with this life, only with the life after death. Therefore it does not set up a system of daily behavior, an ethical pattern, or a weekly demand for weekly church going. Buddhist services are conducted in Chinese and cannot be understood by worshippers, and Buddhist priests have very little effect on daily life.

That seems exactly the kind of religion that an "ordinary" Christian has—"little effect on daily life." Lord Melbourne, Queen Victoria's beloved prime minister, certainly as "ordinary" a man, as far as the Christian faith was concerned, as ever bore the name Christian, said, "If we are to have a prevailing religion, let us have one that is cool and indifferent."

The alternatives to acting like ordinary men, and the power to achieve the extraordinary, are constant themes of Paul. "It is no longer I who live, but Christ who lives in me" (Gal. 2:20). "To all who received him, who believed in his name, he gave power to become children of God" (John 1:12).

86.   GOD'S BOOMERANG

He catches the wise in their craftiness.   1 COR. 3:19

These words form the plot of one of the world's great stories, told in all languages and literatures. A man digs a pit and falls into it himself. He throws a boomerang to hit somebody else, and it hits him. It is the story of Haman, who builds a high gallows on which to hang Mordecai. Then the plot thickens. Instead of Mordecai, Haman is hung on it himself.

But beyond all human forms of the story, it is God's story. "He catches the wise in their craftiness." Men are clever to devise schemes to outwit God, and He catches them in their own ingenious devices.

James Russell Lowell puts this truth about the universe in colloquial dialect, crude but clear:

> *An' you've got to git up airly*
> *Ef you want to take in God.*

One of the fascinating parts of history is the portrayal of men getting up earlier and earlier to "take in God" by more and more ingenious schemes by which to thwart God's word and will. These schemes have boomeranged. How many plots backfire. The newspapers carried a picturesque comment on this truth not long ago in an Associated Press dispatch from Big Stone Gap, Virginia, the sad story of the body of a young woman, "found entangled in a fence which she and her husband had electrified with 110 volts to keep boys out of their tomatoes." Caught in their own craftiness!

A more common form of boomerang in life is the wall of exclusiveness people build around them. These walls say, "Keep out!" and the boomerang is that they keep such people in. They are left in the premature mausoleum they build and die a lonely death in it. For walls have a subtle way of turning into a tomb.

Again, some people are crafty in conduct. They suspend the rules of the moral and spiritual world. Too crafty to be taken in by such things, they are determined to seize life by the throat and choke happiness out of it. But life puts the big squeeze on them. God catches such wise ones by their own schemes of defiance. Happiness is never won by violence. The rules are in a short set of directions called The Beatitudes. God catches them, not by a violent revenge such as that of an Oriental potentate, but by the operation of spiritual laws in life. As one hymn puts this:

And age comes on uncheered by faith and hope.

For how small a portion of life's goodness has anything to do with craftiness! How large a portion has everything to do with love.

Think of the boomerang which comes from man's fantastic craftiness in devising instruments of mass slaughter. That gust of cosmic wind howling through space is the whistling of a boomerang. They that take the sword shall perish with the sword, a catastrophe to be averted only by God's grace, and by man's obedience to God's revelation of His nature and will in Christ.

87. TOP HONORS

The right way for a man to think of us is as Christ's servants, and managers authorized to distribute the secret truths of God. 1 COR. 4:1 (Goodspeed)

How much time we give to the question of what men think of us! Often it seems as though the total takes up half our waking hours. Marie Bashkirtseff confessed to her journal, "I like, more than anything else, to be talked about." Don't we all? Poor Marie! She has done a large service to the human race. She is so without any restraint in painting a picture of herself, that in her journal we can see ourselves, with all our selfishness. And here she confesses her failing for all of us.

We like to be thought about. And when no one is thinking about us, or talking about us, some of us practically cease to live. There is a beautiful scene in Maurice Maeterlinck's *Blue Bird,* where it is told that the grandparents of the children, Tyltyl and Mytyl, come alive in the after world only when someone thinks of them. In a sense not beautiful but ignoble, some people never come alive unless they know they are being thought about and talked about. "Far from the madding crowd's ignoble strife" there is for them nothing but a cemetery. It is a wonderful boon, in view of this human failing, to have the blunt affirmation, "This is the right way for a man to think of us." Paul lived up to that. In many ways he did not care how men thought of him. He said he was not impressive to the eye. He had no golden tongue. He writes that in the eyes of some of the lofty ones in Corinth he was "in disrepute, . . . ill-clad and buffeted and homeless." He did not care at all. But he cared tremendously that men should think of him as Christ's servant and steward! That was what counted, beyond any measure.

Yet what Paul regarded as the highest prize of life, the qualities which mark a true steward, trustworthiness and faithfulness, do not have much glamor for quite a large number of people. They are such homespun qualities, solid and dependable, of course, but some people plead with fate, "Please, something more exciting."

We tend to think the right way for a man to think of us is as a powerful man. Not one to bestride the earth like a Colossus, of course, but at least a man of command who can say go, and he goeth and come, and he cometh. The right way for a man to think of us is as a rich man. Often, we are not so concerned to be a rich man; we like to be thought of as rich. Or we like to be thought of as wise.

Paul never worried about "top honors." He says, flatly, "It matters very little to me what you, or any man, thinks of me—I don't even value my opinion of myself. . . . My only true judge is God himself" (1 Cor. 4:3-4 Phillips). We are trustees of God's secret truth, the truth that if any man is in Christ he is a new creature; the truth that we can be strong for all things through Christ who strengthened us; the truth that faith is the victory that overcomes the world. Do we faithfully administer this trust?

To be a faithful steward, a very trustee of God, of the highest fidelity, was what mattered enormously. When we look down on faithfulness in ministering God's trust as dull and prosaic, we look with blurred eyes. It is as though we were offered the Kohinoor for sale, and we looked over this famous diamond carelessly, and then said, "Nice little imitation. I'll give you five dollars for it."

A critic wrote of a production of *Henry V,* "Shakespeare would have liked it." What praise could compare with that? What praise for a life can compare with this, "God will like it."

88. GOD IN THE COURTROOM

It is the Lord who cross-questions me.   1 COR. 4:4 (Moffatt)

This verse dramatizes vividly the text we must all meet in life. We are in the dock, prisoner at the bar, and God cross-questions us!

The trial scene has been one of the great show pieces of history and of drama and of fiction. The trials, all the way from that of Socrates to those of Charles I and Captain Dreyfus, are followed with intense interest. The trial scene is the hot spot of interest in *The Merchant of Venice,* in *Crime and Punishment,* in *Les Misérables.*

Paul stages a trial scene here, not imaginative fiction, but reality. And a reality in which we are in the courtroom. God cross-examines us. The prisoner takes the stand.

We do not have to put too great a load on the imagination. It has all been spelled out for us. The world's great trial scene is dramatized in the 25th chapter of Matthew. Think of the setting—

When the Son of man comes in his glory, and all the angels with him, then he will sit on his glorious throne. Before him will be gathered all the nations, and he will separate them one from another as a shepherd separates the sheep from the goats.

Then, the Lord cross-questions. "Where were you when I was sick? Give an account of yourself." Again, "Where were you when I was in prison? You never came near the prison!"

So we try to establish an alibi. But that cross-questioning of God which strikes through all our flimsy excuses cannot be side-stepped. It is a pitiful front that is often put up against the divine probe. Leslie Weatherhead tells of a man on his deathbed, and a minister trying to bring some sense of God into his thought. The man complained irritably, "I never had time for that sort of thing." Dr. Weatherhead comments, "He had 3000 Sundays!" Pretense punctured!

This courtroom scene in which God cross-questions us is not put off to the end of life. Every day the questions come. Every day is Judgment Day.

89.   THE VERDICT BEFORE THE TRIAL

Do not pronounce judgment before the time.   1 COR. 4:5
Make no hasty or premature judgments.   (Phillips)

Paul is pressing on the Corinthian church the duty of remembrance that final judgment is in the hands of God. The thing of final importance in the controversy in which he was engaged with some of them is not what he thinks, nor what they think, but the verdict of God, who "brings to light the things now hidden in darkness."

The very words of Paul seem to take wing and move out to cover all judgments. Do not make hasty or premature judgments, before the time when the matter is given a real trial. The words express perfectly the nature of prejudice. "A prejudice," as Ambrose Bierce has explained truthfully, "is an opinion without any visible means of support."

The classic picture of a verdict before the trial is found in that book of profound wisdom, *Alice's Adventures in Wonderland.* The trial of the Knave of Hearts has begun.

"Herald, read the accusation!" said the King. On this the White Rabbit blew three blasts on the trumpet, and then unrolled the parchment scroll, and read. . . . "Consider your verdict," the King said to the jury. "Not yet, not yet!" the Rabbit hastily interrupted. "There's a great deal to come before that!"

But in our practice, so often, we rush to the verdict before any evidence is examined. It is so much easier, and makes no disturbance of the brain. To a tragic extent mankind lives by ideas which are determined by a verdict rendered before any real trial has begun. Dictators such as Hitler and Stalin were the absolute rulers of many millions of people . . . and yet were the absolute slaves of some of the most irrational prejudices that ever warped a human mind. What is called the trial of Christ was no trial but a lynching party. The verdict was already pronounced by the mob and by the officials who were masquerading as judges.

Prejudice, which will not wait for any trial, but rushes ahead of it, is a pestilence that walketh by noonday—and by morning light and midnight. Race prejudice is one of the ugliest and bloodiest things in the world. When it unseats the reason and throttles the power of thinking, race prejudice has started flowing rivers of blood in all the earth. Very often, race prejudice is the last enemy of religion to go down. The depths to which race hatred can go are seen in the strange term which comes from South Africa. The term is "black fruit." That means, in the cant of the ruling class in South Africa, the luscious tangerines raised by the black people. This fruit cannot be shipped or sold in the channels of white trade. It is grown in black soil.

The word "hasty" used by Phillips pictures one source of the evils of prejudice. We get in too much of a hurry to make any examination of evidence. We rush to a verdict as the King of Hearts did. This refusal to take the time or trouble to find out the truth about a person, an affair, or a whole race of people, is a sin that doth so easily beset us. Dr. Samuel Johnson has analyzed this sin with profound insight, in writing of Bishop Burnet's *History of My Own Time*:

I do not believe that Burnet intentionally lies, but he has such prejudice that he took no pains to find out the truth. He is like a man who resolves to regulate his time by a certain watch, but would not inquire whether the watch is right or wrong.

It is easy to say, "Make no premature judgments." We can tell ourselves that every day and go right on making them. Paul has something better to offer. He says, don't judge before the Lord comes. For us this includes, do not judge before the light of God is thrown upon a subject. Then things which are "hidden in darkness" due to our blinded minds are seen in the clear light of God's truth. With the unlighted mind we see a man of dark color. That puts him beyond the pale of our justice or brotherhood. But when the light of God's truth shines on that man, he is seen as one of God's children, and our brother in the family of God. In our hasty verdict we say, "That man is an alien. Look at his queerly shaped head, and listen to his barbaric speech." God corrects that verdict. He says, "your brother in Christ."

90. DO YOU HAVE ANY FAMILY?

For I became your father in Christ Jesus through the gospel.   1 COR.
4:15

This sentence raises a big question, close to the life of an individual Christian, close to the life of a Christian church. It pictures
a unique relationship, a "father in Christ Jesus." The question which
leaps out of these words is, "Is there anyone to whom we have been
the personal conveyor of the gospel?" We would not call that relationship "father in Christ Jesus." Modesty would hold us back. We cannot,
of course, have that particular relationship that Paul had to Timothy, a spiritual influence, plus companionship and fellow worker.

But is there anyone in whom we have had a part in bringing the
new life in Christ to birth? Is there anyone to whom our desire to
see Christ formed in him has been so real that the gift of the gospel
has come through our hands? Or is it all remote and impersonal?
Paul here contrasts the remote quality of influence, a sort of a mechanical quality, with the warmth of one life shaping another, "You
may have thousands to supervise you in Christ, but you have not
more than one father" (1 Cor. 4:15, Moffatt).

Milton laid down a solemn thesis—whether true or not—that as
science advances, poetry inevitably declines. Could a parallel be
drawn to the effect that as churches grow larger and equipment more
extensive, the personal relationship of one through whom the gospel
comes, drops out? It so often does, not through the fault of the size
of the church, and certainly not from effective equipment, but there
comes a remoteness, an aloofness, a sort of sterile impersonality,
which makes the role of a father in Christ more rare. What shall it
profit a church if it have gorgeous stained-glass windows, and a
tower with chimes, and a goodly balance at the First National Bank,
and lose the father in Christ relationship?

That is often done, thank God, by a father or mother after the
flesh. That is one great reason why the church did not die in the first
or second century. Think of the endless line of mothers, such as
Monica and Susanna Wesley; the goodly company of teachers; those
who have filled the high office of friend in its highest service, as the
nurse of the Earl of Shaftesbury, who left a Christian impression
on a life. It has been done by one like Paul who gave so richly of
his own life that the one to whom he gave himself became, truly,
a son in the gospel.

We ought not to forget the word of Horace Mann, "Let the next generation be my client." Let someone in the next generation receive his inheritance in Christ through your hands. The yearning of a heart to fill this great role in the life of a young person finds expression in the imagined word of a teacher who speaks in the poem, "Emily Sparks":

> Where is my Boy, my Boy—
> In what part of the world?
> The boy I loved best in all the school?—
> I, the teacher, the old maid, the virgin in heart,
> Who made them all my children.
> Did I know my boy aright—
> Think of him as spirit aflame—
> Active, ever aspiring?
> O boy, boy, for whom I prayed and prayed
> In many a watchful hour at night,
> Do you remember the letter I wrote you
> Of the beautiful love of Christ?
> My boy, wherever you are,
> Work for your soul's sake,
> That all the clay of you, all the dross of you,
> May yield to the fire of you,
> Till the fire is nothing but light! . . .
> Nothing but light.

91. TALK AND POWER

For the kingdom of God does not consist in talk but in power.   1 COR. 4:20
For the kingdom of God is not a matter of a spate of words but of the power of Christian living.   (Phillips)

Here is Paul, as emphatic as he can make it. And he does well at making things emphatic! No one ever hit a harder blow on the nail.

It is an axiom that talk is no substitute for the deed. That is the very center of our Christian faith, the incarnation, the deed of God in Christ. That axiom is recognized almost everywhere, but men are slow and reluctant to recognize it in religion. One fact that bears on this is that the ceremonies of religion are so satisfying, emotionally and aesthetically, that sometime there is no sense of need to go beyond them. Also, and more important, is the subtle thing about talk.

It acts like a deceptive drug. When one has spoken, particularly when the speech is emphatic or eloquent, there comes the feeling that one has performed a deed about the matter. Talk substitutes itself for action. Sometimes it prevents action. The French novelist, André Gide, once wrote on this matter, "Merely by having talked about this projected book, my will to see it through was weakened."

This is peculiarly the preacher's temptation. And that of anyone who talks much of religious faith. Military generals have suffered from a similar delusion, that an eloquent communiqué is as important as a well-fought battle. There is a continual danger of drowning action by a flood of words. This is the very figure of speech which Phillips uses, "a spate of words," meaning a rising flood, a freshet.

Beyond the danger which lurks in words in spate, there is the lurking danger of hypocrisy, when the rush of words is not matched at all by deeds. Jesus pointed this out again and again. The dishonesty when words are not borne out by deeds in our day has been put with piercing sharpness by J. B. Priestley:

Beliefs that do not directly inspire definite action are merely so much humbug. A man who professes to think one way and then acts in quite a different way is either a fool or a rogue. It is dishonest to condemn slaughter houses and then call for steaks or chops. It is hypocritical to lead what you imagine to be a cultured spiritual life if you are doing it on money wrung out of exploitation and swindling. Victorian novelists pretended to blush and tremble at the very notion of prostitution, and then went cheerfully out on the spree with women of the town. Men were pious church wardens on Sunday evening and commercial pirates and cut-throats on Monday morning. Delicate fine ladies, who turned pale at the sight of a limping poodle, allowed their fellowwomen to work themselves blind and idiotic for them. The manufacturers who often turned the Midlands and Lancashire into a black stinking hell eagerly acquired Pre-Raphaelite pictures of Arthurian knights and dim swooning princesses. There was one code for the drawing room and another code for the foundry and the mill. Men prayed for peace while initiating moves that would inevitably lead to war. They hung colored silks over the iron machinery of society. And what was not cant and humbug was so much ignorance.

Admiration, even in the form of impassioned words, is not enough. You can demonstrate that on any street of fine glittering shops. You can stop at a jeweler's window, look at a diamond necklace, and then go inside and tell him how greatly you admire it. But before he turns the necklace over to you, he will say, coldly, "Show me first your penny." More like it, he will say, "Show me first your $10,000."

There is a striking parallel in the drama. Margaret Webster has written that "the plays of Shakespeare are kept alive only through the medium of the living theatre, of whose inheritance they constitute so rich a part. They were written to be acted, to be seen and heard."

So the only way for the gospels to be kept alive is through the medium of the living persons who make the teachings of Jesus acted, seen, and heard.

The kingdom of God is a matter of *power*, "the power of Christian living." That is the eternal lesson of Calvary. Jesus spoke much of love, in words never to be forgotten. "Never man spoke like this man." But the words became power, measureless power in the *Act* of the cross on Calvary. "And I, if I be lifted up, will draw all men unto me."

92. PROUD OF YOUR CHURCH?

Are you still proud of your Church?   1 COR. 5:2 (Phillips)
Can you put on airs?   (Goodspeed)

There are tears mixed with anger in this question which Paul puts to the people in the church at Corinth who condoned gross immorality. It is not really a question, but a burning ironical reproach. How could anyone be proud of a church which had yielded to the moral stain of its environment?

This reproach is all the stronger when we remember how Paul loved the church. It is because he loves it with such an unmeasurable love that he feels so deeply the shame brought upon it. His high ideal for the church is expressed in deathless form in his picture of what the church of Christ ought to be: "Christ loved the church and gave himself up for her, that he might sanctify her, having cleansed her by the washing of water with the word, that the church might be presented before him in splendor, without spot or wrinkle, or any such thing, that she might be holy and without blemish" (Eph. 5:25–27).

Love could go no higher or farther. Hence the grief that the church had been brought so low. In the figure of speech which Paul uses, the church, instead of being "without spot or wrinkle" had become "soiled wash."

Its shame was what has been the chief cause of the shame of Christian churches through the ages, the divorce between morality and religion. Some in the church at Corinth had sunk below the level commonly found in their environment. In the Church of the Holy Sepulchre at Jerusalem there was, in the Middle Ages, a section called The Chapel of the Derision. It was supposed to be on the spot where Jesus was derided by the Roman soldiers. It is an arresting phrase, The Chapel of the Derision. It startles the imagination. Many a church has been a "chapel of the derision," in that the teachings of Jesus have been really scorned. A church which draws a holy color line is a chapel of the derision of Jesus' teaching of brotherhood. A church which is a mere appendage of a military machine derides the Prince of Peace. Can we be proud of such a church?

Dorothy Sayers has made a list of besetting sins which may afflict churches. Some represent a shameful compromise with a non-Christian culture. Some represent a failure to share the love of Christ for people. She writes that these seven deadly sins of a church are "respectability; childishness; mental timidity; dullness; sentimentality; censoriousness; and depression of spirits."

One result of a combination of these deadly sins is that it does not make a favorable impression on an outsider. The impression which a spineless lack of courage makes is seen in a verdict rendered by Lewis Mumford:

For the little men who guarded Jesus' memory, drained off the precious life blood of his spirit, mumified his body, and on the remains proceeded to erect the Christian church.

Bitter words, and a very unfair reading of history. But they do show the impression that a church of which Christians cannot be proud makes. Of such a church, God cannot be pictured as He is pictured in the glowing words of Hebrews, "Of whom the world is not worthy, therefore God is not ashamed to be called their God" (Heb. 11:16).

Can we be proud of complacency? It is a truly deadly sin in a church. It kills. It kills the spirit which is the very life of a church. That spirit is the unsatisfied heart of a shepherd. "What man of you, having a hundred sheep, if he has lost one of them, does not leave the ninety-nine in the wilderness, and go after the one which is lost, until he finds it?" (Luke 15:4).

Can we be proud of a church that draws a color line which God does not draw or that supports segregation? God is color blind. In Christ there is no east or west, no black or white or yellow or brown or red. But all are one in Christ Jesus. Shakespeare uses an arresting figure of speech about a church. It is "as wide as a church door." These are the last words of Mercutio, the friend of Romeo in Shakespeare's *Romeo and Juliet*. He is wounded in a street fight, and, when he is asked about his wound, he says: " 'Tis not so deep as a well, nor so wide as a church door; but 'tis enough, 'twill serve."

Evidently, a church door was one of the widest things that Shakespeare could think of. What he probably had in mind was the door of a cathedral.

Go in your thought from the church as a physical building to the church as a spiritual fellowship. The door of the church of Christ, through which people are asked to enter, should be a very wide door. How wide is the door of our church?

> *There's a wideness in God's mercy*
> *Like the wideness of the sea.*

Does the width of our invitation match the wideness of God's mercy? It ought to do so. Does our church door freely admit all people, with no distinction of class, wealth, race, and nationality? A very large church, large in membership, wealth, and building, may have a very small door if it is a class church or an exclusive church.

Here are God's measurements for a church door: "Come unto me, *all* ye that labour, and are heavy laden, and I will give you rest" (Matt. 11:28, AV). "Here there cannot be Greek and Jew, circumcised and uncircumcized, barbarian, Scythian, slave, free man, but Christ is all, and in all" (Col. 3:11).

We are to be proud of the church and to strive to make it a church to be proud of, and a church that God can be proud of.

> *The church for you doth wait*
> *Her strength unequal to her task.*
> *Rise up and make her great.*

93. SAINTS JUDGING THE WORLD

Do you not know that the saints will judge the world?   1 COR. 6:2
Don't you know that Christians will one day judge the world? (Phillips)

Our first response to this question is, "How fantastic!" We are liable to go on from there and add, "How idiotic!" We look about the earth and back through history and do not see saints on any throne of power. Louis IX of France became known as St. Louis. But he was an exception, and we do not really know how he achieved New Testament standards of sainthood.

Paul says "the saints will judge the world." The saints have passed judgment on the world, they have sat on judges' benches. Judges' benches have turned into thrones of power. To say this is not to make an excursion into idealism, into what *ought* to be, but to examine history, to see what *has been*.

Keep the New Testament conception of a saint in mind. The name did not call for a halo as standard equipment. The word has been sadly distorted by a common use in our day. Mrs. Nora Hoult, the novelist, has suggested the misfortune of this use. She writes, "It is one of the tragedies of civilization, I think, that anyone seen reading a Bible on the train or in a hotel lobby would be looked on as a saint or a freak, and not, as he might well be, an expert judge of a good story or fine writing." Notice that the word "saint" is equated with the word "freak." A great many people, alas, have that freakish idea!

The saints were not an elite corps. They were those who made up the Christian fellowship. They were "separated people" who had come from the world around them into a "special allegiance" to Christ. There is a real and permanent meaning in that the saint is separated from the dominant forces which rule so many, separated from the frenzy of accumulation, from the dominance of the senses, separated from the eat-drink-and-be-merry which rule so many.

The saints, in that primary sense, do judge the world. They have judged it. Their lives and minds have given a standard for the judgment of the world. The saints have preserved the moral and spiritual standards by which the world is judged. In time, in many things, the world has acknowledged the judgment. The saints judged the Roman world in the custom of exposing unwanted babies so that they died. It was a common custom. They were only nuisances, girl babies, no market value. The saints judged that world and rendered the verdict that such girl babies were not nuisances but daughters of Almighty God. So it was with the carnival of murder, the gladiatorial games in the Coliseum. To the outward eye, it was the Roman Empire judging the games. To the eye of history, and of God, it was the saints judging the barbaric games themselves.

The saints judged the world in the matter of human slavery. It is hard to realize how deadly the grip of the slave trade on England in the eighteenth century. It was as though the slave trade were a giant octopus which swam up the Mersey River to Liverpool and extended its slimy tentacles until it had in its grip the bank, the business houses, even some of the churches. Then the saints, among whom were Wilberforce and Clarkson, judged the world of the slave trade and obliterated it.

The saints brought into clear visibility the standards of God. The true picture of the judgment throne is the parable of the last judgment in the 25th chapter of Matthew, "When the Son of man comes in his glory, and all the angels with him, then he will sit on his glorious throne. Before him will be gathered all nations." Picture? Yes. But the great reality of history. For a central theme of history is the progressive working out of Christ's judgment of the world. The world has been judged by One who walked over only an infinitesimal small fraction of it.

94. SENSE OF SHAME

I say this deliberately to rouse your sense of shame. I COR. 6:5 (Phillips)
I ask it to shame you.   (Goodspeed)

This is a pertinent word to a generation which, unfortunately, is more liable to have a sense of pride than a sense of shame. It is an age which needs to have a sense of shame aroused.

Paul was writing to the warring clans in the church of Corinth. They were going to law against each other in the civil courts, advertising the scandal of fighting in the church. The non-Christian onlookers could say with bitter sarcasm, what was said in deep sincerity of some first-century Christians, "How those Christians love each other!" By their lawsuits they were proclaiming that the love of Christ was not strong enough to keep them from fighting. Paul wanted to rouse their sense of shame.

This is one high service which the gospel can render. It was an effect which Jesus had on people. He had a power to compel people to look at themselves. Peter looks at Jesus, and he sees himself, and says, "Depart from me, for I am a sinful man, O Lord" (Luke 5:8). It is a life-preserving service.

Yet we so often have in our day a patronizing sense of superiority over earlier days because of our scientific advancement and ingenious creations. Consider the *Mayflower*. A cartoon appeared in a newspaper at the time of the arrival in America of the replica of the *Mayflower* after her crossing the Atlantic under sail, showing two aviators beside their planes. One was saying to the other, after reading a paper which he held in his hand, "How'd you like to be on the *Mayflower*, just loafing along at five knots?" These men had driven their planes through the air at two or three hundred miles an hour.

In the question there was an element of amused contempt. The unspoken assumption was that, just because we can travel much faster than the Pilgrims who came over on the *Mayflower*, we have made tremendous advances on them in every respect. But the invisible cargo of the *Mayflower*—the high faith in God, the high ideas and ideals, the iron character—cannot be measured in tonnage or in miles per hour. Many in our day have made idols of speed and size and have confused them with significance. A great many look down on people of former ages because we can fly airplanes and split the atom while they couldn't. It is just as silly as saying that we are a great people because our national debt runs into hundreds of billion dollars, while a short time ago it was only a few paltry millions. We are bigger and naturally better!

There are so many reasons for shame in these days of bewildering mechanical progress. And the gospel will rouse our sense of shame.

For one thing, we can well feel shame over what is often the casual nature of our following of Christ. Thomas R. Ybarra pictures this cynically in his definition of a Christian, that a Christian is a person who feels penitence on a Sunday for what he did on Saturday and is going to do again on Monday.

Eliseo Vivas goes so far as to say that it is a mark of human decency to feel shame for having been born into the twentieth century. We must feel shame for our share in the communal guilt of the murderous twentieth century.

Can we point with pride to that?

We have cause to hang our heads in shame over the fact that so often we do not see the suffering and injustice around us. In the parable of the last judgment those condemned were amazed. They said they didn't know about prisons and sickness and hunger. That was no excuse. It was their business to know. When the American Army at the close of World War II reached one of the Nazi murder camps, the soldiers were appalled at the evidences of wholesale murder. The American commander was indignant at the protestations of the townspeople that they did not know anything about it. He made them march by the gas chambers and the pits filled with bodies. They were made to do what they should have done before. To *see*; not to see the evil, and the suffering in our world, is something to be deeply ashamed of. We need the anointing of the eyes which Christ gives to men, the sharing of his spirit, that our sense of shame may be awakened.

95.   EMANCIPATION PROCLAMATION

I will not be enslaved by anything.   1 COR. 6:12
I am not going to let anything master me.   (Goodspeed)

Here is a heroic declaration of war. It marks the joining of a long,
long battle, renewed year by year, week by week, day by day. There
is no discharge in that war.

It is a task of a continual antislavery society for the rescue from
slavery and the prevention of slavery. The very words suggest humanity as a chain gang. History has been a long, slow history of
breaking man's shackles, those cargoes of agony, the galley ships of
the Mediterranean, the serfs, the slaves. It is not hard to imagine the
forests of Africa ringing with the shrieks of men and women running
from the slavers.

But Paul had in mind in this declaration self-imposed slavery.
He presents a picture of people enslaved by things as well as by
habits of indulgence which strangle a life. A soul can be flattened
out by a passion for things as well as by a craving for physical thrills.
The indulgence of such passion puts a mind and soul on the auction
block. The words resound, "Going, going, gone!"

The enslavement to things is well symbolized by a tragedy that
has happened in mining again and again, a man crushed while
mining for gold. But it does not take a gold mine to cause a cave-in
on a soul. Smaller things can do it. As James Agate has written of a
young woman bred on modern literature, movies, and crooners, "Explore her mind to its inmost crannies and you will find nothing there
but curiosity about the latest hair dyes."

People can be enslaved by tradition, when that word means the
tyranny of doing the same thing forever. Lord Halifax in the eighteenth century said. "Dwell on any thought too long and it will take
you prisoner." People have been taken prisoner by one idea which
has petrified the mind and heart and stopped all growth. They welcome new ideas with the same ardor which inspired Metternich,
who said, "I detest every New Year's Day because it is new." Also
partisanship can be a galling slavery.

If this heroic declaration of war on slavery, "I am not going to let
anything master me," is to be anything more than a declaration of
purpose or a boast or a collapsible wish, a person must have a power
which enhances him. In the long run slavery to things is conquered
only by slavery to a higher power, to God. Paul's word has operating

power for he was captured into slavery to Jesus Christ. He rejoices to call himself "the prisoner of Christ" and "the slave of Christ." It has been truly and vividly said that "the aim of science is to master something, while the aim of religion is to be mastered by Some One." When a man is mastered by Christ he is an empowered person. Then indeed he can say, "I will not be enslaved by anything." In the lives of multitudes, the words of the hymn have become history:

> He breaks the power of cancelled sin
> He sets the prisoner free.

It is close to the truth that in this life we will be the slave of something. We can choose our servitude. When we become the bond servants of Christ, we are equipped with God's power, so that we need not let anything master us.

There is a third step in this emancipation of life. We are not enslaved by anything if we are enslaved by Christ. Paul announnces that glorious third step—"I have made myself a slave to all" (1 Cor. 9:19). In his service we go out to people unafraid, with great words on our lips and in our hearts, "ourselves your servants, for Jesus' sake."

96. GLORIFY GOD

Bring glory to God.   1 cor. 6:20 (Phillips)
Glorify God in your body.

St. Paul and Diogenes had one thing in common. Each went around the world with a lantern. Diogenes was looking for an honest man. Paul's lantern was a searchlight. He went around his world throwing on to the main stage of life and into all its nooks and corners a strong, clear light, "The light of the knowledge of the glory of God in the face of Jesus Christ." He brings every realm of life under the searching examination of the mind of Christ.

In this passage he illuminates sexual life by bringing to bear on it the teaching of Jesus. Paul, here as elsewhere, brings a far, far more powerful motivating force to bear than moralistic exhortation. That force is the grace of God. God has given us deliverance. Man's response must be separation from sin. God is to be glorified by purity of life. To bring the highest relationship into the details of life has been the most powerful force ever applied.

The injunction "bring glory to God" spreads out into the whole of

life. We are not only to glorify God in our body, but to bring glory
to God in the whole of life. If we do not think deeply on this plea,
it seems fantastic to think of bringing glory to God.

> *O Lord, our Lord,*
> *how majestic is thy name in all the earth.*

Who could bring glory to the glory of God? Some of the tragedies
of history have been the prevalence of false ideas of God's glory.
The phrase has been taken as though God's glory consisted of the
massed stone of buildings, gaudy processionals, and all the pomp of
power.

There is one key to the meaning of the glory of God, Jesus Christ.
God's glory is pictured supremely in the words of Jesus, "Now is the
Son of man glorified." Jesus was facing the cross, and in the cross,
that supreme act of self-sacrifice and redeeming love, Christ was
glorified. We bring glory to God when we have the mind of Christ,
when our lives are marked by faith and love. That is the only way
that mortals can bring glory to God.

We can bring to God *the glory of faith*. Martyrs have brought
glory to God by their faith and faithfulness. The person who in a
world of pagan pressures refuses to be conformed, choosing at whatever cost to be transformed by the renewing of his mind unto Christ,
brings glory to God. The lack of belief in God, which gives him no
glory of faith, is vividly pictured in the description of Thomas Carlyle by Henry James, Sr.:

Carlyle is the same old sausage, fizzing and sputtering in his own
grease. . . . He names God frequently, and alludes to the highest
things as though they were realities, but it almost looks as though he
did it only for picturesque effect, so completely does he seem to regard
them as habitually circumscribed and set at naught by the politicians.

When we put God a poor second to politicians or any dark powers,
we bring no glory of faith.

We bring glory to God by sacrificial love. The words of an old
spiritual bid us,

> *Arise, shine and give God the glory.*

We do exactly that when we show outgoing love. William James,
as a young boy, said of a house in Chocorua, in New Hampshire,
"Oh, it's the most delightful house you ever saw. It has fourteen
doors, all opening outwards." A life with doors opening outwards is
likewise a "delightful" life. The people in the gospels to whom Jesus
gave rapturous praise were those who gave with spontaneous un-

measured generosity, the woman who broke a box of precious and costly perfume, and the widow who put in two mites—"her living" —into the alms box.

We can see people giving glory to God in the open doors of their lives, the mothers, such as Lois and Eunice, in the New Testament, shaping lives to do God's will; teachers, who give of themselves beyond the line, and beyond the pay, of duty; helpers of every sort, who do not count their lives dear unto themselves.

An English art critic has said that there were three artists in John S. Sargent, the painter. There were the Sargent who painted for money, the Sargent who painted for fun, and the Sargent who painted for the glory of God. However that may be, there can be three of us, the person who works for money, the one who works for fun, and the one who works for the glory of God, who glorifies God in unselfish living.

97. THE JEHOVAH COMPLEX

I say, not the Lord.   I COR. 7:12
My advice (though this is not a divine command).   (Phillips)
I would say, though not as Christ's command.   (Goodspeed)

This quality of Paul's, his reluctance to claim that every word of his is the word of God, is not often reckoned as one of his major gifts and graces. But a close look will show that it rates high. He shows a modesty that is both amazing and clearheaded. For Paul seems to be saying, "This is just what I think. It is not a divine command. I have no word from God on this matter."

It may not have been a command of God. But Paul's humility in saying that is a truly divine grace. For a large sum of the world's evil and suffering has been caused by people who have reveled in the idea that their every thought was the word and will of God. The Jehovah complex has left a train of devastation wherever it has appeared. Many people confuse themselves with God. When the movie version of *The Ten Commandments* was being filmed, there were many "tryouts for the voice of God." There should have been no lack of volunteers for that role! Many people have tried hard to be the voice of God in their place, their group, their time. They have tried to fence in the mind of God to the dimensions of their own limited understanding. The people who conducted the Inquisition tried to be the voice of God. John Brown claimed that the voice

of God commanded him to commit the savage murders at Osawato-
mie, Kansas.

Harsh, dominating parents have tried to play God and have
claimed for all their stupidities the authority of God. The fathers
pilloried by Edmund Gosse in *Father and Son* and by Samuel Butler
in *The Way of All Flesh* could not say, "This is not a command of
God. It is what I think." Such humility does much to secure the
love and co-operation of a child, but it does not give the pleasures
which some people find in a swelled ego.

What a glorious example Paul gives us to follow, to feel and say:
"I have not been made the special confidant of God on every detail
in the heavens above and the earth beneath! But this is how it seems
to the best thinking I can do."

The voice of God is found in His word in Christ, and in the
action of His spirit in our own hearts.

98. MAKE A VENTURE

Wife, how do you know whether you will save your husband?
Husband, how do you know whether you will save your wife?   I COR.
7:16

This question drops into life like a pebble into a lake—it expands
into ever-widening circles. It is dropped into the discussion of marriage. Paul asks, since God has called us, how do you know you may
not win your partner in marriage to your faith? It expands into the
widest circle, "Since God is at work in the situation, how do you
know a venture for Him may not succeed?" When God is active,
no one can tell what may happen. Do not set limits to God's will
and power. Make a venture into the unknown.

In every circle of experience the plea is the same, don't quit too
soon. Many defeats have come from quitting too soon. The British
expedition to Gallipoli in World War I retired before Turkish bat-
teries which had fired their last shot. Life's great achievements have
been made by men and women who made a venture. After Charles
Lindbergh had flown the Atlantic to Paris, he was brought back to
the United States by a Navy ship. As he watched the seemingly
endless expanse of water, he said, "If I had known how big the
Atlantic was, I would never have tried it." Often too careful scruti-
nizing of the obstacles and adding them up makes the courage ooze
out of our fingertips and keeps us from making a venture.

How do we know? How did William Carey know there was any use trying to bring the gospel to India? How did Wilberforce know that for a few people to fight the mammoth slave trade was anything but a fool's errand. They didn't. But with God in the picture, they made the venture.

The zest of life is in its ventures. We feel the tingle of its risk in Tennyson's "Ulysses":

> For my purpose holds
> To sail beyond the sunset, and the paths
> Of all the western stars, until I die.
> It may be that the gulfs will wash us down
> It may be we shall touch the Happy Isles,
> And see the great Achilles, whom we knew.

It is all a venture. A life limited to its sure things is a dull party. You cannot prove the things that matter most in life. You can prove that Beethoven was born in 1770. You can absolutely prove that. You cannot prove that the Ninth Symphony is great music. Many people prefer the latest wailing noise which comes out of a juke box. You cannot prove the one you love most is lovable. Lloyd's of London will insure almost anything. They will insure the weather on a certain date. They even have a policy insuring against twins. But not even Lloyd's will insure the success or the happiness of a marriage. Like other best things of life, it is a venture, a risk taken in faith. It may be you will touch the Happy Isles.

If we truly respond to Christ's invitation, "Follow me," we take a leap into the unknown. But in that leap of faith is life's highest fulfillment. How do you know? You don't. But you can know God, and that is enough.

99. NEVER MIND

Never mind. 1 COR. 7:21.
Don't let that worry you. (Phillips)

A two-word sentence, the shortest possible! But it is a sentence of tremendous size. Paul gives here a fine study of measurement, trying to save people from mistaken magnitudes. Do not, he says, miss the main point in life. The main thing in life, he says, is not the outside conditions but the inside realities of spirit. No outer condition can separate a man from Christ. Paul asks in effect, "Were you a slave when you became a Christian?" "Never mind." "Don't let that worry you." The important thing is that you belong to Christ. You can serve Christ in any lot.

It was not that Paul was indifferent to slavery. He goes on to say, "If you can gain your freedom, avail yourself of the opportunity" in this very verse. Paul appeals to Philemon to free his slave Onesimus as an act of free will, for the love of Christ. The gospel shows clearly that slavery was not a slight thing. But Paul did not want anything to minimize the first importance of being the new man in Christ Jesus.

It is a great phrase, "Never mind." Do not let the great goal of life be missed by making other things first. Carry this idea of relative magnitudes into other realms of life. Notice that there is a *right* way of using the words, and there is a *wrong* way of using them. We use the phrase all the time. Let us get a correct idea of when to use the words and when not to use them.

There is a bad sense of the words "Never mind." Some people use it of religion. To them, it is not important; it is mainly a matter of words, and they are not important. So they say, "Never mind." They are just as wise as the woman on a ship which had had its rudder broken off in a high sea. She consoled the captain by saying, "Never mind. It was down where nobody could see it. It won't make any difference." To throw over religion makes just as much sense. In both cases, the rudder and religion, it is what steers the ship. So, also, the words are hastily and carelessly used of moral control. Many people who think themselves as "emancipated" from what they call narrow rules of conduct, or "sophisticated," throw over moral control of themselves. They feel, "Never mind, that is not important." They are heading for the collapse of life.

People diminish the great moral and spiritual realities, the mountains of personal life into inconsequential trifles. In the presence of life's highest concerns, they toss off a jaunty "Never mind."

Among Christians, there is often a poor use of the words, when people think of the matter of sustaining their religious life by daily devotions. They feel, "Never mind," as though the religious life would sustain itself. It is just as wise as for a person to pay no attention when his bank balance has reached the vanishing point, and to say of that, "Never mind."

Now look at the good places to use the words.

In the first place, *one great gift of the Christian faith is to be able to say to the worries and anxieties* that mount so in these days, "Never mind." The wearing down of the spirit by the steady beat of anxiety can be overcome by trust. "Cast all your care upon Him for

He careth for you." Not to say it lightly or frivolously, but in seriousness and confidence to look up to the hills of God whence cometh
our help, is to win victory over fear and nervous breakdown.

Secondly, when your friends and neighbors have more of this
world's goods than you have, and things which you could very well
use, learn to say, "Never mind." We can say it, and have no covetousness in our heart and mind, if we take time to realize the real
prize of life. You *have* the gift of God's grace. Jesus puts the right
value on life's possessions. He asked, "What shall it profit a man,
if he shall gain the whole world, and lose his own soul?" If we
remember that life is more than meat, we can say, "Never mind,"
and say with Paul, "I have learned in whatever state I am, to be
content."

Thirdly, if you feel, as most of us do feel at times, that our life
has been a failure in that we have not arrived at a "top" place, and
have no great fame or position, we can say emphatically to ourselves,
"Never mind," or rather let us hear God saying it to us. For Jesus
said that life in the high sense is not to be wasted in worrying over
the question, "Who shall be greatest?"

100. THE TIME IS SHORT

Brethren, the time is short.   I COR. 7:29 (AV)
The appointed time has grown very short.   (Goodspeed)

The "appointed time" here mentioned is, of course, the time till
the end of the age. It was an expectation that marked the thought
and faith of the first-century Christians. It was to be the hour of
deliverance with the "appointed time" so short nothing must prevent
their undivided allegiance to God. In effect He pleads, "Do not let
the fringes of life crowd out the center." The center of a Christian's
life is communion with God and obedience to Him. No other preoccupation, not marriage nor business, should displace it. The plea is
summed up in the words of verse 31 of this chapter, "in the world,
as though they were not absorbed by it" (Goodspeed).

This injunction is always in order. The phrase "the appointed
time" does not mean for us what it meant for Paul and first-century
Christians. But the call for single-minded service to God is just as
urgent. This truth is beautifully put in the petition

O Eternal God, who hast committed unto us the swift and solemn
trust of life, since we know not what a day may bring forth, but only

that the hour for serving Thee is always present: Grant that we may give ourselves with a ready will to make thy way known upon earth, thy saving health among all nations.

A peculiar urgency is given to the words "the time is short," in our day. The time is short, not for any expected second coming of Christ, but for the threatened coming of disaster, the threat to world survival. The time is very short. Undivided allegiance to the ways that make for peace and survival is demanded of us all. No generation of men ever had the lament of Jesus over blind Jerusalem come with such terrible timeliness as ours. It fits with frightening exactness, "Would that even today you know the things that make for peace! But now they are hid from your eyes" (Luke 19:42).

For many people today are sharing intensively the feeling in the old Negro spiritual, "I ain't got long to stay here."

Bring the imagination to bear on these words. It is a dramatic undertaking but terribly close to reality. Think of the little satellites sailing around the earth. Ask what they are saying. All the intent listeners can hear is a "beep, beep, beep." But listen carefully. Its message can be translated into all the languages of earth. It is saying to the men of earth, with piercing sharpness, something like this, "Brethren, the time is short. The atom bomb is a time bomb. You mortals must learn to live together, or you will die together. The big question for you earth dwellers is not 'Will we get to the moon in time to beat some other nation?' but it is 'Will we get to the earth in time to save it from destruction?' Unless you discover a way to peace, the conquest of space may be only a way to death. The power that pushes men to outer space may be the power that pushes them off the earth.

"Also," the satellite goes on, "the earth is more important than the moon. It is possible to save it only by love and brotherhood between men and nations. Other foundation can no man lay for survival than is laid in Christ Jesus."

101.   THE TRANSIENT AND THE PERMANENT

For the form of this world is passing away.   I COR. 7:31

These words do not bring to us the particular form of expectation which they had for Paul. But they do bring to us the same passionate urgency to scrutinize our lives, to distinguish between the claims of the transient and the claims of the eternal. To Paul, the end of the age was soon to come. And, of course, in our own day many are still looking with earnest expectation for the second coming of Christ and the end of the age. It is rarely dated with the exactness of the Millerite craze. When William Miller fixed the date of the second coming at 1843, many people gave away or sold their belongings, provided white ascension robes to be ready on the great day. One man in New Haven built a boat upon the top of East Rock, to be ready to sail away to the skies. One company went to Jerusalem to meet the Lord in the garden of Gethsemane.

Yet, with that specific expectation changed into a different form, the words "the form of this world is passing away" are profoundly true, and bring an urgent compulsion to us. How foolish to make a frantic effort to bring life into slavish adjustment to what is a passing form. As Phillips translates, "The present scheme of things is rapidly passing away" (1 Cor. 7:29). Life's true concern is to get "adjusted" to the permanent and eternal, rather than to the transient.

This comes with sharp pertinence to our generation and culture, when adjustment to the existing ways and codes of the world has become a sort of holy idol. In Paul's day, a popular pagan slogan was, "Great is Diana of the Ephesians." In our day it is "Great is adjustment of the Americans." In some circles anyone showing independent mind and thinking for himself is "unadjusted." The "scheme of things" has been given a false sense of permanence. Dr. Edel, the biographer of Henry James, pictures him as "he strolls across college lawns in the happy belief the world is all an English garden, and time a fine old afternoon." Two world wars and depressions, and now the nuclear age have exploded that happy belief. Even so, there is much bowing down to the existing scheme of things, and if we have no worship beyond that of tinkering talents, we are driven into a uniformity that is a waste land, chilling and killing to the spirit.

In the next sentence, Paul writes, "I want you to be free from anxieties." If the Son shall make you free from the anxiety of getting perfectly adjusted to a transient form of the world, you shall be free indeed.

102. ENDURE ANYTHING

We endure anything rather than put an obstacle in the way of the gospel of Christ.   I COR. 9:12

In thinking of this high declaration of devotion to endure anything rather than be an obstacle to the gospel, recall how terribly hard it is to *endure*. Endurance is much harder than doing. Deeds of derring-do bring an exhilaration, no matter how great the exertion called for. Tennyson's "Ulysses" conveys the excitement:

> Come, my friends,
> 'Tis not too late to seek another world.
> Push off, and sitting well in order smite
> the sounding furrows; for my purpose holds
> to sail beyond the sunset
>
> . . . .
>
> One equal temper of heroic hearts
> Made weak by time and fate, but strong in will
> To strive, to seek, to find, and not to yield.

What could be a more alluring invitation than that? But to endure is hard. To get into the passive voice is hard, to be battered rather than to batter, to be walked upon rather than to walk on someone else. For most of us mortals it is harder to be reviled than to revile. Dr. Henry Sloane Coffin once brought out this truth picturesquely in describing how much harder it is to be a light ship, standing still and taking all the buffeting of the waves, than to be an ocean liner driving through the sea with great power of action.

That was the great achievement of Jesus. He endured. "For the joy that was set before him, *endured* the cross, despising the shame" (Heb. 12:2). One great weakness of many people is that they can't endure anything. Phillips renders the verse, "We . . . have put up with all sorts of things" for the sake of the gospel. Many people are willing to toil terribly, but ask them to endure a slight or an injury, and they are quick to say, "I won't put up with it." The true follower of Christ gives this last full measure of devotion in that he will "put up with all sorts of things" that he may not hinder the spread of the gospel. He is willing to take up a cross and follow him who endured.

103.   THAT I MIGHT WIN

That I might win.   1 COR. 9:19, 9:20, 9:21, 9:22

Five times in the short space of five sentences, these four words appear, like a dominating theme of great music. It is not only the dominating theme of this paragraph, that "I might by all means save some." It is the compelling theme, the high music of his whole life. It is Paul's deepest prayer, the passionate purpose, the driving power of his whole life. No language is too strong to describe it. Not even the abject language of slavery, "I have made myself a slave to all, that I might win the more." Every tributary of his whole personality flowed into this main stream till it had the force of a torrent. Even when he was on trial for his liberty, possibly for his life, all that faded away before his desire to win his judge, Agrippa, to Christ. "I would to God that not only you but also all who hear me this day might become such as I am—except for these chains" (Acts 26:29).

It is tragic for an individual when that great ambition, that great dynamo of power, ceases to act in our lives. To a startling extent it has died down or become enfeebled. There is a crippling feeling abroad. "Let the professionals do it. That is what we pay them for."

Two things follow. First the individual who feels no urge "that I might win" misses a great joy. It is a high moment when one person can take the hand of another and place it in the hand of God. The joy of reaching another is vividly put, in another realm, by Samuel Gridley Howe. He spent uncounted patient hours fishing in the dark stream of blindness, deafness, and dumbness for a little girl, Laura Bridgman. He tells the story, "I worked patiently for three months without a nibble, then there was a tug, and up came the soul of Laura Bridgman." "Up came the soul"—great fishing! It can happen to you!

Secondly, we get the whole matter of evangelism out of its New Testament setting. Many people, the majority in the churches, think of evangelism as a specialty, a matter of mass meetings, and emotionalism. It is dedicating one's friendship and influence to bringing another within range of the Christian appeal. To pursue the subject of fishing (we have good warrant for that for Jesus used it in his first invitation), a parallel that goes to the heart of the matter is described by Edward Weeks, the editor of the *Atlantic Monthly* and a great fisherman. He tells it in his book of memoirs. The wife of a friend of his wrote that her husband had always wanted to fish, but now that he had retired and had time to fish, he was shy and held back because he did not know anything about the mysteries of casting and tackle and flies. Mr. Weeks wrote back, "What Jack needs is an old pair of sneakers, an old pair of trousers, and a bottle of insect repellent. He needs the fun of catching a fish. Let him learn about how not to catch them later."

We all need "the fun of catching a fish," the exhilaration and the zest of "that I might win." The words represent the world outreach of the church, that we might win all nations unto Him. In John Steinbeck's story, *The Red Pony*, an old pioneer speaks regretfully, "Westering has died out of people. Westering isn't a hunger any more. It's all done." God grant that it may always be an undying hunger in His church.

104. "I REALLY FIGHT!"

I do not box as one beating the air.   1 COR. 9:26
I really fight!   (Phillips)

These are vivid sentences, reminding us that the Christian life is a fight, not a siesta. They both draw an arresting contrast between fighting and shadowboxing in the moral and spiritual realm. The three words from Phillips' translation deserves to be engraved on a plaque, to remind the churchgoers that they are in a war, God's holy war. It would give them something to live up to.

Shadowboxing can be a beautiful art. The boxers go through the motions of fighting. It is just an exhibition of skill. There is lacking the blows which resound in Moffatt's translation of Paul's words, "I maul and master my body." In that word "maul" we can almost hear the blows land. But there is no mauling in shadowboxing. Nor is there real fighting in the life of many complacent Christians and some peaceable and restrained congregations. They are just going through the motions, not really fighting. When that happens, there soon won't be any motions.

A picture ludicrous, yet with genuine relevance to hosts of people, is found in the report of a Philadelphia laboratory research on tranquilizers. It revealed the effect of tranquilizers on white rats. When they were shocked by an electric grid, they turned on one another. But after being given tranquilizing pills, they still hopped on the grid when shocked, but no longer fought. Which things, as Paul used to say, are a parable. So many church members are, figuratively speaking, under tranquilizing pills—ideas that take the fight out of them, such as "Take it easy," "Relax," "No use to get excited." So, under the seductive whisperings of the devil, they sink back on the church pew cushions and gently nod.

The lack of real fighting in Christ's cause is marked by the slipshod. People get into the habit of thinking that anything given to Christ, even when it is a mere token, is good enough to get by. Paul hated the slipshod. Jesus despised it. Of course, there is no spiritual value in pugnacity. Mere pugnacity is often mistaken for courage and devotion to the Christian cause. Paul, who declares here, "I really fight," was not pugnacious, as his whole life proved. He was in many riots, but he never started one. For the sake of Christ Paul could restrain himself and be urbane and courteous to a small-time politician such as Agrippa. There is no hostility or pugnacity in his opening words, "I think myself fortunate that it is before you, King Agrippa, I am to make my defense today" (Acts 26:2).

But he did not beat the air. He fought, both in the personal moral battle, and Christ's battle in the world.

It is hard to fight when it would be so much easier to go along quietly with the crowd. John Milton put that with characteristic picturesqueness and force:

To every good and peaceable man it must in nature be a hateful thing to be a displeaser and molester of thousands; much better would it like him to be a messenger of gladness and contentment. But when God commands to take the trumpet and blow a dolorous and jarring blast, it lies not in man's will what he shall say or what he shall conceal.

Paul really fought!

But some alleged warriors in God's army seem to take their directions from Thomas Hardy's long poem, *The Dynasts*. The preface to that drama states that it is "for mental performance only." To them the military command, "take the whole armor of God that you may be able to withstand in the evil day," is "intended for mental performance only."

How desperate is the need for Christians who really fight, in one of the great struggles of our time, for racial justice, instead of mumbling a few stock resolutions about brotherhood! Or in the crucial struggle of our day, thus described by Bergen Evans:

The war between *Homo Sapiens* and *Homo Neanderthaliensis* thought to have been won fifty thousand years ago has broken out with renewed fury and, at the moment, the forces of reason are scattered in dismay, while the jugheads advance in triumph. . . . But courage, comrades.

Harold Bosley puts it, "This generation must either be the best or the last."

The church has had the impressive symbol of the lion. Will a fitting symbol for our time be the rabbit, scampering away at the first gunshot?

"I do not box as one beating the air."

105. DISQUALIFIED

Lest after preaching to others I myself should be disqualified. 1 COR. 9:27

In the last half of verse 27, Paul turns swiftly from the figure of boxing to that of an athletic contest. The picture seems like that of a track meet. One can almost hear the familiar count of today, "Get on your marks, get set, go!" Then suddenly, a contestant or one of the chief figures in the contest is disqualified, ruled off the track. There are two different senses in which this warning applies. Both carry the same truth; there is no immunity in the Christian life. "Let him that thinketh he standeth take heed lest he fall" (1 Cor 10:12, AV).

In one sense, one may be disqualified *in spite of* having taught others. No matter how high the official, nor how notable the achievement, he can end up disqualified. This result can come about in many ways. Mere familiarity with the gospel can do it. The freshness and bloom can be lost through carelessness. The dulling of ethical sensitiveness will disqualify one. A living faith may begin to die.

But a man may be disqualified, not *in spite of* preaching to others, but *because of* preaching to others. A preacher is a forthgiver. He is commissioned to pass on truth to other people. He may get so concerned to do that, that he does not take any of it for himself. There is an old gospel song which says, "If you'd had a blessing shown, pass it on." So the preacher may drop into the habit of passing all the truth on to others. When he discovers a bit of truth, he may say, "What a fine idea for next Sunday," instead of taking it to himself and saying, "God be merciful to me, a sinner." When there is a collection being taken in church, the "safest" place to be is in the pulpit. The collection plate will not reach a person there. So, often, when a searching word of God is being pronounced, the safest place to be may be up in the pulpit. That may be a sanctuary.

For all of us, the counsel of Stephen Spender applies:

> *Never to allow gradually the traffic to smother*
> *With noise and fog the flowering of the spirit*

Nor the word of Christ, "Watch and pray, that ye enter not into temptation" (Matt. 26:41, AV).

106. OUR NIGHT CLUB CULTURE

"The people sat down to eat and drink and rose up to dance."   I COR. 10:7, quoted from Exod. 32:6

These words fit down as closely as a glove over a segment of our American cities, a "Night Club culture." In that culture the chief end of man (and woman) is to glorify the dining table and the dance floor and to enjoy them forever. It is to sit down and eat an outsize meal, including, emphatically, drink, and to rise up and dance. That is the routine of the night club, and the routine of many lives.

The words are found describing a part of the festivities of the Israelites at the grand inaugural of the worship of the golden calf. The night club has always been a festival of the golden calf. It is really a solemn ritual, following the pattern set in the wilderness. "These be your gods, O Israel." So this culture proclaims, "These be your gods, O America." Then Aaron in the wilderness proclaimed a feast. The feast in our corresponding worship of the golden calf is a ritual for the stomach and the feet. The cry is often, "Eat, drink, and be merry, for tomorrow we die."

This Night Club culture is *provincial*. It shuts out the intellectual and spiritual domain of man, its potentialities of exhilaration and achievement. Its high excitement is reduced to the level of feeding time at the zoo. Its most important moments are feeding time and play time.

An arresting description of this Night Club realm is found in a poem, "Bar Room Matins," by Louis MacNeice. It begins:

> *Popcorn peanuts clams and gum;*
> *We whose kingdom has not come*
> *Have mouths like men, but still are dumb.*
>
> *Who only deal in Here and Now*
> *As circumstances may allow;*
> *The sponsored program tells us how.*

Then, of course, our eat-and-drink-and-dance world, this Night Club culture, *cannot fulfill its promises*. The elusive prize of happiness is dangled before the eyes of the customer, but it disappears at each snatch. Happiness is dependent on personality, and that elusive word has been defined by an extensive research as "the extent to which the individual has developed habits and skills which interest and serve others." That is not on the night club program. Happiness has been pictured with fair accuracy by Don Marquis, who said that happiness was like a taxicab, which we don't get if we seek for it, but which will run us down if we stand on the street.

A Night Club culture will never meet the demands of a *world in desperate danger*. Dr. Charles E. Jefferson, shortly after the close of World War I, made a striking application of the old story of Noah after the flood. The text was, "and Noah was drunk." In the face of an opportunity, as the story made clear, of rebuilding a world, making a grand new beginning, with the chance and need of doing that, "Noah was drunk." So, he said, and the succeeding forty years have proved him tragically right, the postwar generation was drunk! So, a Night Club mentality, in the face of today's need for a world threatened with doom, cannot meet that emergency.

107.   THE BLIGHT OF GRUMBLING

Nor grumble.   I COR. 10:10

How easy it is to grumble! How hard it is to keep life on an even keel, and prevent it from going down into the deep ditches of grumbling!

On the surface the habit of grumbling seems a mere flyspeck of a fault, compared to other ills that may afflict a person. But one who has had to live with a chronic grumbler for a year—or a week—will not think so. Looked at long and carefully, grumbling is a major risk of life. It shuts out the real enjoyment and high use of life, just as a blight will kill the flowers of a garden and the fruit of an orchard. Milton's lines apply perfectly to grumbling as a way of life:

> *Comes the blind fury, with the abhorred shears*
> *And slits the thin-spun life.*

Grumbling, when it fastens itself as a habit, has the power to shut out the best things of life. Ronald Knox, of England, has made the pertinent suggestion that Jesus' rebuke to Martha in the home at

Bethany was not so much against those who bustle as against those who *grumble*. In her criticism of Mary, Martha was grumbling. We can still detect in her sharp words the sting of grumbling. And the grumble shut out from her life all that Jesus' presence might have brought into it. She was too busy with the grumble to hear anything else.

For grumbling becomes a person's only language. If, by some remote chance, the full-time grumbler should find anything that is entirely right, he will be a thwarted and frustrated person. Here is a danger spot. Check on the balance between your enthusiasms and irritations. If you have more irritations than you have enthusiasms, you have a very unfavorable balance of trade that will soon land you in spiritual and mental bankruptcy. For when the irritations outnumber greatly the enthusiasms, life goes sour. It is like lifting every day a brimming beaker of last week's milk, left out on the porch. In this passage, in which the plea against grumbling occurs, we are told that in the trek of the Israelites in the desert, some who grumbled were "destroyed by the destroyer." That is still true today, only it is not a fierce man-eating tiger that leaps out of the under-brush on them. It is the habit of grumbling itself that is the destroyer.

It *destroys the Christian life*. There can be no song of thanksgiving on lips that are busily booked up with grumbling, or in a heart that has no heartening, but just a continual heart "murmur" against life. There can be no joy of the Lord without thanksgiving. There can be no real trust in God in a chronic grumbler. Here is a rule of thumb. Whenever you feel a grumble coming on, kill it by putting a thanksgiving over it to smother it. Thanksgiving and trust will lead a person into the Christian mastery of grumbling, "For I have learned, in whatever state I am, therein to be content."

108.   WHO OWNS THE MOON?

For "the earth is the Lord's, and everything in it."   I COR. 10:26

The question "Who owns the moon?" is as fantastic as anything in *Alice's Adventures in Wonderland*. Yet it is not beyond the realm of serious legal discussion and international research. All the questions of possible law and precedents are being pored over. Many military minds in the United States are deeply worried. They expect Russia to get there first and annex the moon. It will be claimed on the basis of discovery, as Columbus claimed America. Then the moon may be established as a military base for the conquest of other planets. The next phase will be selling lots on the moon and making reservations for weekend travel.

That discussion does at least suggest an older question, and a nearer, bigger, and more pressing one, "Who owns the earth?" In this space-obsessed day, it is well to remind ourselves that the earth is more important than the moon. The answer to that question "Who owns the earth?" must be put back into the very center of the world's mind. "The earth is the Lord's, and everything in it." For with outer space becoming a frantic object of concern, there is a vague, disturbing feeling that outer space is beyond God's domain. It is akin to the feeling, clearly indicated in many places in the early chapters of the Bible, that God was tied to a place, and that when the Israelites got far from Mt. Sinai, for instance, they had gone beyond His domain. This feeling today, of course, does not get into articulate expression, but it has made itself felt in many minds. Hence the renewed need for a powerful affirmation of a basic truth of Christian faith, that "the earth is the Lord's, and the fulness thereof" (AV).

There are keen minds which see the need for stressing that the earth and its salvation from obliteration are more important than the moon. Two days after the first Sputnik was put in orbit, *The New York Times* said this editorially, in a powerful manner. The *Times* is not ordinarily regarded as a hotbed of evangelism. This editorial was an evangelistic plea for spiritual forces making possible human survival. The editorial read:

The creature who descended from a tree or crawled out of a cave is now on the eve of incredible journeys. Yet it is not those journeys which chiefly matter. Will we be happier for seeing the other side of the moon or strolling in the meadows of Mars? The greatest adventure of all is not to go to the moon, or explore the rings of Saturn. It is rather to understand the heart and soul of man, and to turn away from wrath and destruction toward creativeness and brotherly love.

The greatest adventure of all is in the realm of Christian love.

109. MAKING A CONVENIENCE OF THE CHURCH

Are you making a convenience of the Church of God?   I COR. 11:22
(Phillips)
Do you despise the church of God?

These questions have not lost their cutting edge in all the centuries
which have passed. In many ways, they are even sharper. They
"sting, and bite and kick me." Here is the church, the body of Christ,
an indispensable agency for the salvation of the world—are you
making a convenience of that? Can human effrontery go any farther?

The RSV translates this question, "Do you despise the church of
God?" The question is the same in both translations, though "despising" the church of God indicates more active antagonism and
contempt than the word "convenience." But anyone who makes a
convenience of the church really despises it, no matter how warmly
he would protest that term.

Paul is giving a sharp rebuke to the Christians who so far missed
the meaning of the Lord's Supper that they made a gluttonous orgy
out of it. They made a convenience out of a sacrament! The question
for us spreads out into the whole realm of a person's attitude to the
church and his relation to it. It strikes to the very center of the
weakness of the church today, its tremendous potential strength, reduced to weakness. Millions of church members make it a convenience rather than a dominting power in life.

If our church lays no great demand on our life, it becomes a pleasant convenience. We give it praise, but not power. A sharp picture
of the difference is found in the biography of a rancher in the rough,
early days of Texas. He was a rough character, called Shanghai
Pierce, who owned 200,000 acres. As a sentimental tribute to his
mother, he built a church as a memorial. Some of his associates
twitted him about it. They asked, "Do you belong to the church,
Shanghai?" His answer was emphatic, "Hell, no! The church belongs to me!" In terms less profane and much more refined, many
people feel the same way. The church belongs to them, it is *their*
church, like their bridge club or golf club, or any group of friends.
They do not belong to the church as to a power that lays a commanding hand on life. It is more of a convenience than a compulsion. To many people it has become a place where it is convenient
to be married, and buried.

Indeed, lower than that, is the "despising" of the church by many people, as shown in the common expression at parting, "See you in church." That is supposed to be a joke, but is always said with the air of contributing a fresh addition to the world's wit, even though it has been said a million times. But it is well to remember that those words, "See you in church," have been the prelude of some of the world's greatest achievements. The little companies of Christians in the days of persecution in Rome said to one another, "See you in church." They did see one another down in the church in the catacombs, where God was shaping a new power in the world. In the heyday of the slave trade in England, William Wilberforce and some of his friends seemed a trivial group, compared to the well-nigh almighty slave trade, which was like a giant octopus, which laid its slimy tentacles on all the institutions of England. But they said, "See you in church." They did. Out of that religious fellowship, God brought the power that played a mighty part in ending the slave trade.

The service of the church to the life of men is glimpsed partially in Ola Winslow's description of the early New England meeting house:

From the side of the pew sermons were light thrown on the mysteries a man could not even state for himself, much less unravel, though they were part of his daily consciousness. Once a week for two hours his thought was lifted above the interminable chores of life, and his destiny linked to something vaster than he could immediately know. His daily performance was tested by a great idea. In the midst of manifold uncertainties he was given a North Star. He needed nothing so much.

The power of the Christian fellowship is found in the fact that a host of the first Christians could never get over the wonder of the love of God, and the church of God. That is our need. We get over the wonder of it. George Cabot Lodge said truly, "When you are accustomed to anything, you are estranged from it."

We "despise" the church when we repudiate the demands of its gospel upon us.

110.   BREAKING THE BOND OF BROTHERHOOD

Do you . . . humiliate those who have nothing?   1 COR. 11:22
*Are you . . . causing acute embarrassment to those who have no other
home?*   (Phillips)

As in many instances in Paul's letters, a great truth grows out of a
sharp rebuke. The big thing which distresses Paul here is the breaking of the bond of brotherhood in Christ. Some people in the Corinth church had made the Lord's Supper the occasion of an exclusive indulgence of gluttonous and drunken excess. They made it
into a complete denial of the purpose and nature of the Lord's Supper. Some could not restrain themselves to wait for the whole company. Some were excluded who had little or no food—perhaps slaves
or servants who could not get there. So they were left out, humiliated
because they were poor.

Our problems are different. There is no contemporary problem of
the orderly and reverent observance of the Lord's Supper. We have
better manners. But we have the same problem at the deepest level
—to prevent the breaking of the bonds of brotherhood by humiliating
some members of that brotherhood. One of the most complete hu-
miliations possible is segregation. As far as true fellowship of Christ's
church is concerned, there are in many places our own "untouch-
ables." We are aghast at the exhibits of what were "slave quarters"
in some ancient churches. But today in some churches there are not
even slave quarters where Negroes may attend. We inflict deeper
humiliation than that. We cause the "acute embarrassment" of "no
admission" to the fellowship of Christ. That makes a pagan temple
out of the church.

A common excuse is "Oh, it's a big problem." Of course it is a big
problem. That is a supreme reason for getting at it with speed and
dedication. But all too often, people follow the advice of Lord Melbourne, the prime minister of Great Britain. He wrote, "Better not
try to do any good, then you'll get into no scrapes." When we have
a greater fear of getting into a scrape over nonsegregation than of
denying our Lord, we do not get into scrapes. But we do get into
a mausoleum for the spiritually dead.

Pestalozzi said, "There are two ways of instructing. Either we go
from words to things, or from things to words." In seeking to avoid
humiliation to any children of God by exclusive fences, we must go
both ways. We must go from the word of God to its resultant acts

of brotherhood, and we must go from concrete acts of justice and love across all barriers of border and breed and birth to the world of the Father of all.

111. DUMB IDOLS

You were led astray to dumb idols.   1 COR. 12:2
You would stray off, as impulse directed, to idols that could not speak.
(Goodspeed)

The story in Acts 17 of St. Paul taking a walk through the market place of Athens takes a strong hold on our imagination. The idols which he saw all along the way take a strong hold on his mind. We get an echo of his deeply moved spirit in his address in the Areopagus, recalling "as I observed the objects of your worship." We can picture him peering at the idols, and reading the inscriptions. Yet the deepest emotion was not curiosity but anger. "His spirit was provoked within him as he saw that the city was full of idols" (Acts 17:16).

Now jump the chasm between Paul's day and ours. Picture St. Paul walking in our market places, in Wall Street and the Great White Way of Broadway, Michigan Avenue in Chicago, Miami Beach, Nob Hill in San Francisco. He would find plenty of idols. We have them. And his spirit would be "stirred within him" as in Athens. A widespread and official belief in theism has not banished the worship of dumb idols from our life.

Nature abhors a vacuum. Something rushes in to occupy the empty space. Where there is a vacuum in the throne room, dumb idols rush in. We engrave the motto "In God we trust," but if it is not graven on our minds and hearts, on our aims and values, idols fill the place. Our time is marked by strange revivals of polytheism. Aldous Huxley has traced cause and effect in his statement, "One result of denial of monotheism is polytheism, the worship of many gods, of man-made idols." Carlyle pointed in the direction of this truth when he wrote that when men give up believing in God, He makes them believe in Cagliostro, the greatest impostor of his day. The higher religions, as Toynbee has pointed out, have been unable to prevent the revival in modern times of old forms of idolatry. They crowd in the vacuum to fill the place of God.

When John Gunther was traveling about the United States, preparing to write his *Inside U.S.A.,* his Number One question to many

officials was, "What do you believe in most?" That is the Number
One question for all men, "Do you believe most in God or in dumb
idols?"

One idol worshiped in Athens in A.D. 50 and in America today
is the same one worshiped with great festival at the foot of Mt.
Sinai centuries before, *the golden calf*. We are disposed to worship
the idol of money as "the power of the box office." A physical image
of the worship was displayed at the palace of industry at the Wem-
bley Exposition at London, many years ago. It was a revolving, in-
vulnerable safe, a glossy, armored ball, which turned around on a
black altar. We see the same worshipful setting in the glittering
automobiles which are installed in our large railroad stations, also
placed on a revolving altar. They are surrounded by many worshipers,
who are indulging in the reverent emotions of covetousness and envy.
Since there has been a slackening of the devoted worship of the
automobile, many people have become skeptics about that particular
idol. They have evolved the agnostic idea of using the auto for trans-
portation rather than for the orthodox purpose of conspicuous con-
sumption.

For hosts of people there are no standards other than popular
appeal and success. There is no business like box office.

Secondly, *parochialism* is an ancient idol, before which millions
of sacrifices have been slain. The modern form is called nationalism.
It is just as dumb and deadly an idol under any name. Its worshipers run into hundreds of millions. Under the worship of the fetish
of national sovereignty, it is the most powerful block to an order of
law which might secure the survival of the world. The sovereignty
of international law over international affairs is a condition of world
salvation. No idol worship must be allowed to ordain disaster.

A third and popular idol of today is *adjustment*. This means
that man must adjust to the reigning codes about him. The mass
of people have been found, by extensive research, to be less tolerant
of nonconformity than leaders of communities. A "well-adjusted"
person is the ideal for he is easier to handle by the political and
economic orthodoxy.

It might seem strange and unduly pious to say that our great need
is "re-consecration." Many will frown at such an old-fashioned word,
as fit only for a prayer meeting. But it gains fitness when we recall
Toynbee's discussion of the "de-consecration" of Western civilization. He writes that the greatest revolution in all Western history
took place in the seventeenth century when religion was abandoned
for science and technology. The subsequent de-consecration of West-

ern civilization created a spiritual vacuum, in which state worship
and the idolization of technology have rushed in.

Do not stray away to idols.

112. THE ABILITY TO DISTINGUISH

To another [is given] the ability to distinguish between spirits.   1 COR.
12:10
The ability to discriminate in spiritual matters.   (Phillips)

This is a high and essential quality of mind, in any realm, the ability to distinguish between things. Paul is writing here of the ability
to weigh and evaluate prophecy. That was a needed ability in the
early church, which was full of ardor and enthusiasm. It was necessary to have thoughtful people to separate the wheat of spiritual truth
from the chaff of mere verbal exuberance. As Clarence Craig writes,
"St. Paul regards the ability to judge true inspiration as being a
work of the spirit, no less truly than the actual revelations." It is
this ability for which Paul pleads elsewhere, "that your love may
abound . . . with . . . all discernment, so that you may approve
what is excellent" (Phil. 1:9–10). For the most dangerous ignorance
in spiritual as in other matters is not illiteracy, but inability to distinguish differences.

That is a great and needed ability in our bewildering world. We
go astray so often by failing to judge clearly between relative values.
There has been through history a contempt for people who do not
know the difference between things which are very different. We
find in Shakespeare the proverb of disdain, of one who doesn't
"know a hawk from a handsaw." A later one is, "He can't tell his
head from his elbow."

So much of our world, science, trade, and education, is built on
the ability to discriminate. It is a high skill to distinguish a real
diamond from imitation paste. It is a high skill to discriminate wool
from shoddy cloth, higher still to determine the permanent from the
ephemeral. If we are to live a mature, effective life, we must develop
the high skill of an appraiser. Jesus was the supreme appraiser of
values. His eye was quick to detect the difference between a jewel
and a paste imitation. He sees a poor widow dropping two small coins
into the alms box. In a high tribute he said, in effect, "This is a true
pearl. This is the real thing. She has given more than them all." An

effusive man rushes up and says, "I will follow you. But suffer me first to do something else." Jesus says, "This is paste."

It is a gift of the spirit to be able to give the right value to things. Without it, we are likely to shop for cheap values. Pray for that gift.

In the realm of which Paul is thinking, to distinguish between spirits, we must cultivate and develop the ability to judge between a sentimental and an ethical religion. Jesus stressed that difference continually, "not those that say 'Lord, Lord,' but those who do the things that I say." The failure to distinguish here is reflected in the remark that in a certain section of the country, no institution had so much reverence from people as did the church, and none had so little influence in the community. We fail so often in our shopping for life's bargains. Over the Merchandise Mart in Chicago, the largest shopping center in the world, there is the claim in large letters, "The best in the world is here." Can the *best* in the whole world be found in any merchandise mart?

A common, and deadly, mistake is confusing goods with spiritual gifts. Disraeli said acutely, "The European talks of progress because by the aid of a few scientific discoveries he has established a society which has mistaken comfort for civilization." The cult of comfort has grown so great in our society that is becomes for many befuddled minds the measure of all things. Many among us are swift to look down on former centuries, because we have modern plumbing, airplanes, and deep freezes, and they did not. That seems to many to show what a great moral nation we are. They neglect to consider other ages' moral and spiritual gifts for the lack of which we are on our way "over the hills to the poor house." Hawthorne put this whole matter unerringly. He wrote down this suggestion for a short story, which, alas, he never wrote:

A man with the right perception of things—a feeling within him of what is true and what is false. It might be symbolized by the talisman with which, in fairly tales, an adventurer is enabled to distinguish enchantments from realities.

There is the true secret—a talisman—which we have in the standards of Jesus—"to distinguish enchantments from realities."

How desperately we need to learn to distinguish "the spirit" in our world of international relations. The distinction so needed is to be seen clearly in the contrast drawn by Thomas H. Huxley back in 1893. He warned his hearers in a lecture that "cultural collapse must surely attend a continued belief in the gladiatorial theory of existence." If society was to endure, he said, "man must learn to distinguish between records of zoological research and guide books to moral conduct." How the more than sixty years since have tragically validated that statement. We are still living under the gladiatorial theory of existence!

The only sure way to distinguish differences is to apply standards. Christ is the measuring rod of individual and social life.

113. THE HEARING EAR

If the whole body were an eye, where would be the hearing?   I COR. 12:17

Well, for the matter of that, where *is* the hearing today?

Paul carries his point here with sharp and irresistible argument. There are all varieties of service, of function, all varieties of people, but one Master and one Spirit. We have a God of infinite variety. If all were head, there would be no feet; if all were eye, no ear. It has been sheer tragedy that the church has gone on so often, through the centuries, as though these words were never written. The followers of Christ have gone on trying to put all God's variety into one mold, one type. As Joseph Parker once complained, "The church has been a great brick maker." It has often worked perversely to press people into the same mold and size.

God is the creator of variety, function, and quality, and the one God of all. That is Paul's message.

There is also here a reminder of the crucial need of hearing. We live in a noisy world. The din has dulled our sense of hearing. Our own internal noise of the commotion of self all too often shuts out the voice of other people and other needs. Yet sensitive hearing renders an indispensable service to the world. There is an undeniable urgency to the call to each one of us, "Lend an ear." It is a great investment paying a high rate of interest.

The art of hearing is playing an increasing role in the work of the psychologist and psychiatrist. One psychiatrist writes of *listening with the third ear*. It has been demonstrated that listening with the first and second ear helps greatly in understanding people and helping them. Skillful listening is a great art and a difficult one. It takes humility, for one thing, and putting another person in the center of the picture. We grow so used to speaking, that active listening demands capacities to which we have not given enough employment. The observation someone has made of prayer belongs in this realm. For one person who says, "Speak, Lord, for thy servant heareth," there are ten who say, "Listen, Lord, for thy servant speaketh." It is hard to get quiet enough and intent enough to hear the still small voice of God. Yet at the threshold of spiritual growth are the words, "Be still, and know that I am God."

We need to listen to people, so that we may discover what they need without their explicitly telling us. Often they will not tell; often they do not even know. True listening is not a passive affair. It is a very active art. We do not read of Jesus ever talking to his disciples on how to speak. He talked much about how to hear. He said, "Take heed how you hear." He heard so many things the others did not seem to hear, or they heard a cry of need just as a bothersome need, as they heard blind Bartimaeus and rebuked him for his cry for help. Jesus had a sensitive ear, attuned to the slightest whisper of need.

There is a large place for the high art of listening to groups of people. For sensitive listening will enable us not only to know what they say, but also why they say it. What they say may be economic or political nonsense. But they may be saying it because of some deep need or suffering or maladjustment.

The question has been raised, "Does America need a hearing aid?" This touches on the need for our nation to listen sharply in a distressed and divided world. Robert Reyfield offers some searching observations about that.

I think that our talking is unsufficiently balanced by listening. I do not think that we listen enough to what other people are trying to say to us about themselves, and I do not think we listen enough to the sound of what we say in the ears of him to whom we say it. We are guided chiefly in deciding what to say by the conceptions we have of what those others ought to like about us if they were just like us. And they aren't. They are different in respects to which we are inattentive. Good talking is an art; good listening is obviously even rarer, and it is rarer because as an art it is more subtle and difficult. But, as it is something that Americans need seriously to cultivate for their own safety, it it worth considering if there are ways to cultivate it.

One of the most arresting cartoons which came out of World War I pictured two statesmen coming out of the closing session of the Paris Peace Conference in 1919. One man put his hand to his ear and said, "I think I hear a baby crying." Not far away there was a baby crying. Draped about him was a ribbon on which was printed, "Class of 1939." Just twenty years ahead. The artist was expressing his fear that in just twenty years the babies of that date would be called up to war. He hit the date exactly! They were called up in 1939. We must be able to hear the still sad music of humanity amid all the noises of future wars, and because we hear, to act.

114. THE SENSE OF SMELL

If the whole body were an ear, where would be the sense of smell?
I COR. 12:17

In the course of Paul's argument for the diversity of services, all under the control of one spirit, based on the analogy of the body, he strikes out questions well worth looking at in their own right. Paul's question, "Where is the sense of hearing?" in this same verse, has already been glanced at. Here, we may ask, what *is* the state of the sense of smell among us? What are the uses of this "lost" sense?

For smell has fallen from its high estate. Compared to other senses, it is in dishonor. People boast of 20–20 vision, but no one takes a bow on being told that he has a 50–50 power of scent, or whatever figures are a good average for a bloodhound. Perhaps the sense of smell is too strongly reminiscent of our relations to the rest of the animal family, our distant relatives.

Yet, considering the ethical issues we face in our time, as individuals and as a society, we may well ask, "Where is the sense of smell?" The ability to smell represents a sensitiveness to wrong. A well-educated nose can tell something wrong by "the smell." There are many people, for instance, who could not give a logically built and persuasive argument against gambling, but who do know emphatically that it has a bad smell. This passion for getting "something for nothing"—it has an odor of decadence about it. There are many financial "short cuts" in our world of business, which, to a person with a keen ethical sensitivity, have a bad aroma about them. It is like a sensitiveness to smoke. One can say, "I don't see or feel any fire, but I can smell something wrong."

Peter Cartwright, the pioneer evangelist, used the word rather accurately in one of his vigorous outbursts. Coming to a river town in Ohio, a sinkhole of iniquity, he paused, sniffed the air, like a war horse sensing the battle from afar, and said, "I smell hell!" He was right. Hell has a rather definite smell at times.

This sense of evil needs to be cultivated. An artist needs a cultivated eye. A musician must have a cultivated ear. A Christian needs a cultivated nose. The two great means of this indispensable training are the words of Jesus—which develop a capacity of warning, a kind of spiritual radar—and the company of the saints.

115. HEAD AND HAND

The eye cannot say to the hand, "I have no need of you," nor again the head to the feet, "I have no need of you." I COR. 12:21

These words cannot be reiterated too often. They make a powerful affirmation that the ideas of the mind or the visions of the eye need the hands and the feet to give them any value. There are times when we are disposed to think that these words have been as completely forgotten as any words in the New Testament. And there are many forgotten words in the New Testament, gone with the wind.

For many self-sufficient heads have said, and many do say, to the hand, "I have no need of you." They feel that the idea itself is enough. A good idea is a thing of beauty and a joy forever, whether the hand does anything about it or not. No use to spoil it by putting it into action. The eye says to the hand, "I have no need of you." A lovely vision is enough.

One great hazard of the Christian gospel and church is the danger of a merely verbal Christianity. There is the persistent delusion that when we have said something fine, we have actually *done* something about it. So there is no use bothering to do anything else. We can kill an idea by smothering it with words. A minister did that gracefully not long ago. He preached on Jesus' warning against laying up treasures on earth and urging his hearers to lay up treasures where moth did not corrupt nor thieves break through and steal. He touched so lightly on the laying up of material treasures, that he sounded as though Jesus were recommending mothproof chests for garments and a safe-deposit box for valuables!

The head and the eye are not enough. Once when one of Napoleon's aids was tracing the proposed campaign, Napoleon stopped him. He said, "Your finger is not a bridge." Exactly. Our words are not a road from here to there. There is heavy constructing to be done, throwing up in the desert a highway for our God, and bridges must be built.

The thinking of the head, of course, is desperately needed in the work of the church. So often people, including some very able businessmen, seem to check their heads in the vestibule, as Moslem worshipers leave their shoes on the porch of a mosque. Take your head inside!

Yet the head and the eye cannot say to the hands and feet, "We have no need of you." They have said it all too often. That is a big part of our plight.

There is one particular realm to which this text applies, that of the life of a parish. The head cannot say to the foot, "I have no need of you," which, being interpreted, means the sermon cannot say to pastoral work, "I have no need of you." A minister may be so enamored of talking that he fails to estimate rightly the need for hand and feet to give carrying power to truth. We need a continual and alert guard against an overintellectualized ministry and gospel, for that all too often means a desiccated gospel, with all the life and fire squeezed out of it. We need protection against a withering disdain for practical work.

Christianity was not launched in the world by a concert audience. It will not be carried on by a concert audience—who come just to hear. It was launched by a fellowship, and will be carried on by fellowship. Effective Christianity is always a conspiracy of eye, mind, hands, and feet.

116. TIED TOGETHER

If one member suffers, all suffer together.   1 COR. 12:26

This is a vivid exposition of the truth that all men, all nations, are tied in one bundle of life. Our world's tragedy is that it has taken nineteen hundred years to see this clearly. And even today millions of people still see it through a glass darkly. The penalty of not seeing it is death. The ancient Teutonic Cimbri used to go into battle with the whole tribe roped together. We have learned that that happens today in two "total wars." If we ever get into a "total peace," it will be when nations are tied together. We have been like retarded children, learning the hard way that "if one member suffers, all suffer."

Interdependence has been the belated discovery of the twentieth century. We are learning in a staggering variety of ways that all live or die together.

It is amazing the way this thesis of the interdependence of the parts of the body has been documented by modern medicine. We have learned about a "focus of infection," that an infection in one

spot in the body can ruin a dozen other spots. Medicine has become
a game something like "Button, Button, Who's Got the Button?"
It is, "Where is the source of the infection?" A nervous breakdown
can come not from nerves but from a tooth. We used to hear, "an
eye for an eye, and a tooth for a tooth." But often today in medicine,
it is "a tooth for an eye." If an eye suffers, the surgeon often takes
out a tooth to cure it. Or he may take out an appendix for an ear-
ache. If one suffers, all suffer.

The same is true of the whole body of humanity. We are all tied
together. A disease may be Spanish influenza, but its effects are felt
in New Zealand. Hydrogen bombs may be put off in Nevada or The
Steppes in Russia, but the fall-out infects the whole earth. An economic depression may start in Detroit and Wall Street, but it brings
inflation to Germany and presents the world with Hitler.

This is painfully true of racial relations. If the Negro suffers in
our country, all suffer. We have not begun to add up the costs of
racial segregation to the whole population, economically, politically,
and religiously.

When learned experts discuss who will win a third World War,
the fitting rejoinder is, "Who won the Bubonic Plague?" or "Who
won the Lisbon earthquake?" For when one suffers, all suffer.

117. "HELPERS"

And God . . . appointed in the church . . . helpers . . . I COR.
12:28

Here, tucked away in Paul's impressive list of God's gifts to the
church, amid high vocations and capacities of many sorts, is the
word "helpers." It looks something like a kitchen maid at a banquet.
The long sentence is a sort of glittering parade with aristocrats going
by, apostles, prophets, teachers, miracle workers, healers, administra-
tors, speakers, all splendidly dressed. And here comes a plebian word
in the plainest of working clothes, "helpers." And yet, when you
stop to think—and do it right now—of the helpers that you have
known, you will see that this role of helper is that of a prince in
disguise. Abou Ben Helper's name leads all the rest. The helpers
were really the "social workers" of the early church, those who
sought to understand and minister to practical human needs. Dorcas,
who made garments, was a helper in textiles.

W. H. Auden writes that the secret of most lives has been that of

"finding the right helper at the right time." That puts the vocation
of being a helper in the right frame. Andrew was the right helper
at the right time for Peter. "He brought him to Jesus" (John 1:42).
In Bunyan's *Pilgrim's Progress,* Evangelist was the right helper at
the right time for Christian. The paralytic who was let down through
the roof of a house so that Jesus might see him and heal him found
four helpers at the right time.

It is a shining word. It is a vocation to which anyone can aspire,
for it comes in so many sizes and dimensions.

> *The splendor falls on castle walls*
> *And snowy summits old in story.*

But more often it falls on unpretentious cottages. The splendor of
being a helper often falls on people who are without homes at all,
such as the poor widow who put her "whole living" into the alms
box, and was given a high citation for being a helper extraordinary.

Thanks be to God, for the "glorious company of helpers" really
belongs in the *Te Deum.* The true helper has a passkey of imagination which admits him to other lives. We often hear the expression,
usually given out as a sigh of wonder, "imagine that." Some people
keep saying it much of the time. It is a life-preserving idea. We
should "imagine that," not as an expression of limp wonder, but as
an active, concentrated, and consecrated dedication of imagination.
Confronted by another person, another group, we should turn the
key of imagination and enter into their experience and realize how
life looks and feels to them. Thus we become helpers. A beautiful
and accurate picture of the service of imagination is found in the
remark of a young boy artist. Someone asked him how he was able
to draw horses and dogs and cats and sheep and pigs. "Well," he
replied, "I just see them on paper and just draw lines around them."
That is a classic in portraying imagination in art. It enables the
helper to live, not one life, but many. It opens the door to a helper's
adventure, the highest kind, "one man's adventures in other man's
lives."

A memorable picture of a helper is found in the biography of Sena-
tor George W. Norris. On one of his visits to his mother, who was
then over eighty years of age, he saw her busily digging up the soil
to plant a tree. He strongly remonstrated with her. "Oh, Mother,"
he said, "why do you work so hard? You will never see it in blos-
som." "No," she admitted, but added brightly, "Someone will." She
belonged to the Ancient and Honorable Order of Helpers!

Being a helper is not assuming the role of busybody. Some folks
seem to think that the free and persistent giving of advice, and

assuming the direction of other people's affairs, is being a blessed helper. All that such "help" accomplishes is to make the busybody a pestilential nuisance. The true helper stays outside till a time and occasion of real need occur, and then he steps in like the grace of God, of which, indeed, he is an agent.

There is a role for the helper in far-reaching international affairs, in the helping to shape the final force which will act effectively for peace. Albert Schweitzer has put this in poetic beauty and realistic truth. He writes:

When in the spring the withered gray of the pastures give place to green, this is due to the millions of young shoots which sprout up freshly from the old roots. In like manner the revival of thought which is essential for our time can only come through a transformation of the opinions and ideals of the many brought about by individuals and universal reflection about the meaning of life and of the world.

118.   NOISY GONG

If I . . . have not love, I am a noisy gong.   1 COR. 13:1

You can just about hear this sentence. Put your ear down to the page and keep still for a moment. You can hear the echo of the percussion instruments, the noisy assault on the ear, the battle of tinware. The contrast which Paul draws in this, the world's greatest poem, between the banging gongs and cymbals, and the quiet voice of love, is so sharp and effective that we easily overlook the lure which the loud gong has for many people. The reason there is so much clanging of gongs in our noisy world of self-assertion is that, to many people, it is just what the doctor ordered. Underneath all pleasant camouflage, they love to hit the gong and crash the cymbals. For these things draw attention to themselves, they startle, they stop people in their track. That, to great hosts of aggressive, self-pushing people, is success in life. Phillips translates with vivid picturesqueness, "If I should stir men like a fanfare of trumpets." What lovely words, "fanfare" and "trumpets"! Many people will eagerly say, "I'll buy that." For they live, not by bread alone, but by "fanfare."

So in the task of persuading people to show the love described in this chapter, do not discount the liking for "noise." Paul disdains a raucous noise. But it is music to many ears. They are like children; the man who plays the cymbals is the king of the orchestra! Our task is to show the delusion of the noisy gong, to show that the high prize of life is love rather than the gong. Love is like playing "Largo" on the violin, rather than clanging a tin pan.

There is danger in the service of the church that a minister or any church leader may be a gong. The saints can tell the difference. Paul says that the saints will judge the world. They also judge the servants of God. What survives in the memory of the church is love, not the echo of a big noise which once filled whole nations with fanfare, but is now as dead as a graveyard. If a person is without love as a dominating power, and is just an ephemeral noise, it will not be a case of "all this and heaven, too," but "all this and nothing at all."

The absence of love between people and groups of people is a deadly thing. It makes a dangerous world. A picture of that is found in Pearl Buck's book of remembrances of her life. In spite of danger and loss which she had suffered from anti-Western mobs, she was always able to accept with genuine sympathy the point of view of the Chinese. She wrote, "As a child so often the Chinese bearers trembling under the weight of too heavy loads carried up from the English ships in port . . . I was troubled because the load was too heavy and the white man did not care that it was . . . and that trouble has followed me all the days of my life."

There are a great many causes for the upheaval in China. But here at least is one—long, loveless years carrying loads too heavy for the backs of men.

"If I have not love . . . I gain nothing."

119.   LOVE IS PATIENT

Love is patient and kind. . . .   1 COR. 13:4

In this glowing list of the aspects of love, a catalogue which reaches the heights of beauty and the insights of psychological realism, patience comes first. It does not come at the end of the parade as a sort of anticlimax. It comes first. And rightly, for patience is the quality in love which makes it last, which gives it permanence. In regard to love of husband and wife, the old rhyme puts it accurately:

> *Love me little, love me long,*
> *Is the burden of my song.*
> *Love that is too hot and strong*
> *Runneth soon to waste.*

When love has not patience, it has no staying power. The high words, "To love and to cherish, in sickness and in health," are merely empty, loud, swelling, balloonlike words, without patience. Elizabeth Barnett Browning puts daily patience as the top climax of love:

> I love thee to the level of every day's
> Most great need, by sun and candlelight.

That is the highest level of all, for "love is patient."

In every variety of love for fellow beings, patience is desperately needed. Thomas Carlyle wrote in a letter, "I have a natural talent for being in a hurry, which is a very bad talent." It is "a very bad talent" in a world such as ours, which is geared to hurry. It is so much easier to love people in general, with the generous help of glittering abstract words, than to love people in particular, with the obstacles of specific characteristics. Carlyle said this memorably, "It is easier to love people when they exist only on paper, or quite flexible and compliant in your imagination, than to love Jack and Kit, who stand there in the body, hungry, untoward, jostling you, barring you with angular elbows, and a stupid will of their own."

That is where patience comes in. If it doesn't come in, love does not come in. This calls for sharp eyesight and an insight into the many disguises of patience. No virtue has more imitations, all of which protect the ego from facing the truth about itself. Laziness, indifference, and cowardice all deck themselves out in the trimmings of patience. These call for a sleepless awareness of all the dark tricks of our minds.

Patience is a supreme need in our international relations. When "patience" is worn "to a frazzle," an exasperated push, or a shot from a trigger-happy youngster, may put, not the fat in the fire, but the world in the fire. George Kennan writes that there are in international problems that have to be lived within stead of being solved. That calls for patience, able to stand a terrific strain. Carrying on a church fruitfully calls for a generous supply of patience. We read that Jesus Christ is the chief cornerstone of a church. But there must be plenty of patience in the foundation. It is so easy to take up one's dishes and go home. Every week men stomp out of the church, and women flounce out. Their self-regard and insistence admit of no patience and of no real love.

There is no easy solution. Patience comes from a love of Christ so strong that it can endure a thousand slings and arrows, great and small. Consider the phrase, "the . . . patience of Jesus Christ" (Rev. 1:9, AV). What patience with his disciples. "O ye of little faith." "Have I been so long among you and ye have not known me?" "Could you not watch one hour?"

Yet having loved his own, he loved them unto the end. For, truly, patience is the last full measure of devotion.

120. DON'T TRY TO BE IMPRESSIVE

Love is not . . . boastful.   I COR. 13:4
Love . . . is neither anxious to impress.   (Phillips)

Of these two translations, that of Phillips is probably nearer to some characteristic moods of our time. Of course, boastfulness is always to be rebuked. A crude boastfulness so fills the mind and spirit that there is no room for passengers or precious freight to be taken on board. Boastfulness rules love out.

Yet, boasting in the literal sense is not done as much as formerly. No matter what our morals may lack, at least our manners are improved. Only retarded minds are given to crude boastfulness. We are more subtle. The "conceited ass" is getting to be obsolete, like the buffalo. Yet there are so many ways of getting the same results as boastfulness brings, without bearing the noticeable stigma of conceit. One of the most prevalent is described here, "being anxious to impress." About that charge we can all bow at the mourner's bench, and pray, "Lord, have mercy on our souls." For the desire to impress with our own importance is a pitfall that lies in wait for all of us. It seems so innocent, and yet can have such devastating results to character. For love goes out of a life, just in proportion as the desire to impress comes in and takes over the controls. Boastfulness and the desire to impress can be a major disaster. Arrogance, impressiveness, rudeness, and irritability are four horsemen of the inner life.

For the desire to impress others with our worth and achievements swings the focus of attention from other people and outward concerns to ourselves. That brings trouble. For with nothing going out from a life in the form of self-forgetful love, attention blows up the ego, causing a bad infection of the self. The "scare" that some people have of not impressing their importance is naïvely put by the author of a novel of the 1950's. The confession is put on the jacket of the novel, "All my life I have been preoccupied with the problem of not permitting myself to settle down into the comfort and convenience of being nobody, which always scares me and still does. That is the reason I have always been interested in two means by which anybody may try to be somebody, writing and acting. I have just written a play, and the best part in it is for me."

The effort to be impressive condemns a person to the most galling slavery imaginable. The necessity to be impressive prevents one from ever fully giving himself up to an emotion or to enjoy anything wholeheartedly or to serving any person or cause with the whole heart. The necessity to see how he is doing must be pulled about with him like a ball and chain. You cannot serve God and your need to be impressive. The outlook on the world to a person who must be impressive is like a wonderful view from a mountaintop, seen by a man with a cinder in his eye. The cinder blots out the view.

Boastfulness in any form blots out the possibility of love. For love is a demanding master. It demands the forgetfulness of one's self. A man who jumps into the ocean to save a drowning child cannot take time to worry about whether he is making a beautiful swan dive or not, and whether he is being noticed. Love casts out the slavery to looking-glass poses. He that loseth his life shall find it.

That same verse goes on to say, "Love does not cherish inflated ideas of its own importance." Inflation of the currency is a dire calamity. Inflation of one's self is one of the worst kinds of inflation. It makes love impossible. And if I have not love, I "achieve precisely nothing."

121.   STATISTICS OF EVIL

Love . . . does not rejoice at wrong.   1 COR. 13:6
Love . . . does not keep account of evil.   (Phillips)

At first glance this statement that love does not rejoice at wrong seems too obvious to mention. It is like saying that love does not carry a dagger or sawed-off shotgun.

But this is where the psychological acumen of Paul comes in. The very mention of rejoicing at wrong points up a subtle danger. Perhaps it is often too much to say that a person "rejoices" at wrong. But there is an inordinate interest in it. Some cynic pictured this liability of human nature when he said that "we can stand the misfortunes of our best friends." We do stand in a slippery place. Let him that thinketh he standeth take heed lest he fall.

There are many reasons for this which a research expert in human nature could pursue for a long time. Love is an achievement, and certainly Christian love is not in full flower a natural endowment. The self gets in our way. The wrongs that others do, by a weird distortion, rebound to our own self-satisfaction. They tend to induce one of the worst twists of our nature, the Little Jack Horner complex. When we hear of the wrongs of others, unless we restrain ourselves by a stronger force, we feel, "what a good boy am I," compared to the one who went wrong.

This danger of becoming what Phillips describes as one who "keeps account of evil" is encouraged by newspapers, at least by the sensational press. It causes people to pray, "Give us this day our daily scandal" or "Give us this day our daily murder." Our appetite for evil is whetted. Some people get to be "buffs" for disaster; they run to each new one with the unerring instinct of a fire engine horse. One woman, far gone in this affliction, said once, "No interesting deaths yesterday."

The malicious gossip does rejoice at wrong. She is all set to ride and spread the alarm through every Middlesex village and farm, with an insidious leer, "Have you heard?" Phillips' translation fits such twisted minds exactly.

Love "does not keep account of evil." You get a picture of the devil's statistician, adding up long columns of every evil in the community and "gloating" over them.

There is an alternative to this statistical avocation, a cure for any rejoicing at wrong. It is not to be deaf, dumb and blind to the evil about us. It is an old strategy—"Overcome evil with good." Let the mind and heart be filled with good so that there is no room for statistics of evil. This strategy is found in verse 6, "Rejoice in the right." Or, as Moffatt translates, "love is gladdened by goodness."

It is, thank God, not difficult to find such people. They have no appetite for decayed food or poisons. As Goodspeed translates, they are "only happy with truth." You can test this easily. There are some people to whom you would not go even with the most astounding scandal imaginable. They do not "rejoice at wrong." But run with such news to others and you will be welcomed with open arms. In fact they'll rush to meet you, licking their chops and drooling for the expected feast.

"Love . . . does not . . . gloat over the wickedness of other people" (Phillips).

122. THINGS WHICH PASS AWAY

"It will pass away"   1 COR. 13:8

Three times in a single sentence these words sound out, like the toll of a funeral bell, "It will pass away." They break in harshly upon the illusion of permanence.

The three things of which it is stated here that they will pass away are among the best-beloved creations of the church and a large part of humanity. Prophecy—a great power. Among other things it is the ability to grasp this sorry scheme of things entire, to see the meaning of forces at work in the world, and to be a power in God's hands in influencing the world. Paul is not minimizing prophecy. In other parts of this letter he gives it a high place. It is insight into God's purposes. But it passes away. Conditions in the world change and prophecy passes away in its relevance to the time. *Tongues* pass away. How people love eloquence! Its cadence is music. But inevitably it is the language of the period, and passes as the period passes. When the order of the age passes away, tongues pass away with it. So it is with knowledge.

These achievements *have passed away*. Knowledge has passed away as a power. Ptolemy, Hippocrates, Aristotle, Galileo, and a hundred other possessors of knowledge have passed away. Knowledge has gone beyond them. In physics, which about 1900 was thought by many to have reached the end of the road of discovery, almost every basic conception has been changed. So with tongues, which Phillips translate broadly as "inspired preaching." How that has passed away, with changing and enlarged conceptions of God's word and will for men! The sermons of Fénelon and Bossuet, of John Knox and Whitefield, of Charles H. Spurgeon, have passed into memory and passed away like the snows of yesteryear. Permanence of anything, except love, is an illusion.

Love remains. Out of all the ancient world, nothing will compare, as a living power in our world, with Christian love. All the towering achievements of our time—these too will pass away in a final bonfire, as though they had never been, unless there are new discoveries in love to meet the terrifying need of our time.

We hear much of a "countdown," that solemn intoning before a deadly bomb or missile is fired—"Four, three, two, one, zero!" It seems often that we are living in a last countdown, "Four, three, two, one, zero!" to the end of the world. As a matter of fact, *we are,* unless we achieve new discoveries of love that make survival possible. Dr. J. Robert Oppenheimer, the atomic scientist, has asked "world strugglers" to love one another as the only hope of the world. All will pass away except love. At the end of an address at the Columbia Bi-centennial Celebration, he said:

This cannot be an easy life. We shall have a rugged time of it to keep our minds open and to keep them deep, to keep our sense of beauty, and our ability to make it, and our occasional ability to see it, in places remote and strange and unfamiliar. But this is, as I see it, the condition of man; and in this condition we can help, because we can love one another.

This love is not a sentimental gesture. It rests on reality. That is affirmed in the words of William James, toward the close of his *Varieties of Religious Experience:*

The visible world is part of a more spiritual universe from which it draws its chief significance; that union or more harmonious relation to that more spiritual universe is our true end; that communion with the spirits thereof is a process in which work is really done and energy flows in and produces spiritual effects, within the phenomenal world.

123. CHILDISH WAYS

When I became a man, I gave up childish ways. I COR. 13:11

The whole enterprise of life is largely concerned with giving up childish ways of thinking and acting. It is concerned with the great goal of becoming mature.

Paul's use of this figure of speech had, of course, primary reference to the coming of the perfect to replace the imperfect. It had reference to the *parousia,* from the Greek word meaning "presence" or "arrival." It meant the future return of Christ in glory, to judge the living and the dead and to bring to an end the present "age" and world order. Then, of course, when that "perfect comes, the imperfect will be done away." This great change is pictured, somewhat imperfectly, by the change from childish ways to maturity.

But beyond that primary reference, there are so many varieties of childish ways which block the growth of our mind and of the betterment of the world, that we may consider one of the great goals of life, individually and socially, to be the giving up of childish ways.

On this subject, anyone can look into his own heart. There is a classic story of an applicant for a place as nursemaid who was asked if she had ever had any experience. Her answer was brisk and confident. "Sure," she said, "I used to be a child myself." There is no better experience, if we can remember it. We should all remember our childish ways to the end that we might outgrow them.

There is this strange thing about Christianity. On the one hand, the perfect symbol of faith, selected by Jesus himself, is the child. Childlikeness is the mark of the Christian mind. "Except ye become as little children." On the other hand one of the deadliest obstacles to the whole Christian enterprise is "childishness." Between the two there is a great gulf fixed.

Look at a short list of these childish ways. Then complete it from your own experience and observation.

One childish trait is that of *being the center of the universe*. It is necessary to survive in babyhood. But carried on into later years it becomes a curse to the overgrown child and to all about him. There are no small babies who hold Copernican theories. The sun, moon, and stars all revolve about them. One psychologist has called this trait of early childhood "magic, hallucinatory omnipotence." When an acute case of this lasts till life's later years, it becomes one of the ugliest things in the world. When the sun refuses to go around the grown-up infant of fifty years, he gets mad, grows red or purple in the face, and yells to the skies that someone has taken his rattle.

Dr. Harry A. Overstreet has diagnosed much of the evils of prolonged childishness. "The most dangerous members of our society are those grown-ups whose powers of influence are adult but whose motives and responses are infantile."

This could be described as the *enclosure of fences* in the child's mind. We all have two circles in our mind, as has been pointed out. One is the "me." The other is the "not me." In childishness there is only one circle, the "me."

Another mark of childishness is *the guest complex*. It is the idea that one is here to be waited upon. The whole attitude to life is that of waiting at a hotel table for a waiter to bring in the dinner. And with an overgrown child, the guest is always right. Such a childish mind never advances to the high role of host.

Complaint is often a mark of childishness, often as constant as that of a "centipede with a corn on every foot."

Toynbee has coined a phrase which describes one trait of childishness, "momentary momentousness." Such a mind finds the thing of the moment colossal.

The childish mind does not know just what drama is. That is, by name. It knows the thing, all right, and becomes adept at it. The childish mind puts itself at the center of every drama. The childish mind is the Hamlet, the Lear, the Othello of every play. The persistance of the self-appearance is well portrayed in the description someone has given of George Moore, the novelist. He wrote that it was "like a succession of pictures, Houses of Parliament with George Moore on the steps, the Coliseum at Rome, with a distant view of George Moore, ruins of George Moore by moonlight."

When the perfect comes, when love comes into life as its dominant rule, then "my childish speech and feeling and thought have no further significance to me" (Phillips).

124. THE CHRISTIAN "TUNE"

If . . . the flute or the harp do not give distinct notes, how will anyone know what is played? 1 COR. 14:7

The answer to Paul's question all too often today is, "They don't." People do not recognize the clear Christian melody coming out of many lives. They do not know what is being played for the very good reason that no sharp, peculiar Christian quality sounds out of many lives.

All through these chapters Paul is contending against practices in the church at Corinth; what comes out of their meetings is often a meaningless jumble of incoherent noise, an unknown tongue. He admits it might be known to God, but to no one else. (Incidentally, the same complaint is fitting in many places today, the gospel is being sounded out in a theological jargon, not much more understandable than a gurgle. Like the Unknown Soldier, it is known only to God, not to the congregation. Even some preachers of the gospel have a vain pride which makes them prefer to have it said that "Dr. Demosthenes is so deep that you can't understand a word" than "The common people heard him gladly.")

The chief weakness of the churches is that there is not enough distinct Christian music coming out of the lives of people. Outsiders cannot tell what is being played. That is the world's loss, and the church's loss. For there is a rare Christian melody when the spirit of Christ takes up the spirit of man and makes the world's undying music. Love takes up the harp of life, and the listening world *does* know what is being played.

But all too often it is hard to tell the difference between a popular tune played rather carelessly in a thousand lives and what ought to be on the instrument of a professedly Christian life, the song of Moses and the Lamb. But when a life filled with the spirit of Christ lets its witness be heard, people do recognize music from another world. In the voice of glad affirmation, the world can hear and say, "Listen, that is not the Hit Parade. That is the Hallelujah Chrous." As trust sounds out of a life, the world knows what is being played; it is the 23rd Psalm. In words of courage in a life the world recognizes the music of "A Mighty Fortress Is Our God."

125.   THE INDISTINCT BUGLE

If the bugle gives an indistinct sound, who will get ready for battle?
1 COR. 14:8

There are millions of men in the United States who know from experience in the army what a terribly distinct sound a bugle can give. That very distinct sound gave rise to what was probably the best-loved song of World War I, "Oh! How I Hate to Get Up in the Morning." The bugle's early morning piercing notes could not be mistaken for "The Afternoon of a Faun" by Debussy, or "The Suwannee River with Variations." Its dogmatism and monotony were impressive, even though its range was small. It said, "Get up."

St. Paul was writing of the proclamation of the gospel. If the preaching is indistinct, who shall get ready for the fray? The answer is the same now as then. It is, put succinctly, "No one."

There are so many ways of being indistinct in formulating and presenting the gospel. But as it is sounded out in the life of some churches, it is hard to tell the difference—reveille or taps. Sometimes the Bugle Blowers do not expect anyone to prepare for war. They are just having a service. If the congregation should begin to count fours and march off in battle formation, they would be dumb with amazement. They might be equally surprised if they should ask at the end of the sermon, "Men and Brethren, what shall we do?"

Sometimes the bugle is indistinct because the gospel message is mumbled in a language foreign to the people. There is a name commonly given to the general run of men, who are without much learning or position of distinction. It is "Joe Doakes." A major question for the church today is, "Can we communicate the gospel to Joe Doakes?" The early church did bring the gospel to Joe Doakes in Greece and Rome. We read the report, "Consider your call, brethren; not many of you were wise according to worldly standards, not many were powerful, not many were of noble birth, but God chose what is foolish in the world to shame the wise" (1 Cor. 1:26) Joe Doakes was there in large numbers. Slaves were in the church, men like Onesimus. This was notable in the Puritan churches. In a list of men martyred during the reign of Mary I, given in Foxe's *Book of Martyrs*, there were not only men like Latimer and Ridley, but men of every occupation, tailors, glaziers, tinkers, carpenters, and many more. But such people are not reached by erudite monographs, somewhat like a Boston draper's description of Bronson Alcott's "Orphic Sayings," "a train of fifteen cars and only one passenger."

Sometimes the bugle is indistinct because there is no sharp message. Father Taylor of the Seaman's Mission in Boston described a lack of message when he said, defending his friend Ralph Waldo Emerson, "He is a good man. He will have to go to heaven, because if he went to hell, the devil would not know what to do with him. But it would take as many of his sermons to convert a man as it would take quarts of skim milk to make him drunk." Indistinct bugles follow the pattern of Steele's essays. He determined to banish all partisan politics, never to raise his voice above a decent drawing-room level, and to confine criticism to the follies rather than to the crimes and sins of society. Fine for an informal essay. But for the bugle, just an indistinct mumble.

For a long time there was a very indistinct bugle on slavery. Today many church bugles have been shamefully indistinct on racial justice and in all too many places less than the needed sharpness on human survival. But a bugle calling to arms, with a clear proclamation of the gospel, how powerful it is! Clement Wood pictures it in lines of gratitude to another poet, Edwin Markham:

> *You were a bugle blown at dawn*
> *Waking your brother in the light.*

126.   USE YOUR MIND

I will pray with the spirit and I will pray with the mind also.   1 COR. 14:15

Paul is warning against an incoherent emotional religion, which "speaking in tongues" meant to so many of the Christians in Corinth. The warning is still in order. He thus states the problem, "For if

I pray in a tongue, my spirit prays but my mind is unfruitful. What am I to do?" Then he answers, "I will pray with the mind also."

The words are a powerful plea for the use of the mind in religion. This does not mean that emotion should be overlooked or disdained. It is God's instrument. What God hath joined together, let not men put asunder. God has joined together in His worship and service, the mind and the emotions. Bring the mind into play in religion. Many of the real losses and tragedies in the history of the Christian religion have come from emotion and brain being put asunder. The union is needed in religion as in art. William Troy has written, "Art is not intellect alone, but without intellect, art is not likely to emerge beyond the plane of perpetual immaturity." That is exactly the plane of religion without brains—perpetual immaturity!

Praying without praying with the mind degenerates into either the empty babble of much speaking, or into an immoral attempt to make an instrumental use of God, a sort of a childish idea of magic, by which one can pry things out of God. A good example of that is that sublime egotist—Marie Bashkirtseff, who wrote in her diary, "I ask that I might know the Duke. Three times already God has listened to me and granted my prayer. The first time was when I asked Him for a croquet set." Praying without the mind, a mind that seeks out what God is and His relations with men and His purposes for them, never gets much above the level of croquet sets.

Paul continues, "I will sing with the mind also." That ought to take care of the whole flood of mushy hymns which have engulfed the churches in the last century, a flood that in the providence of God is receding. Large numbers of people have delighted to "sit and sing themselves away to everlasting"—if not to everlasting bliss, at least to everlasting mental vacancy. There is no real commitment of life in such singing without the mind.

A beautiful expression of the mind in religion is found in that rich spiritual stream, John Woolman's *Journal*. While touring among the scattered groups of Quakers in North Carolina, before the Revolution, he deplored the religion which turned inward exclusively, and did not face such issues as slavery. He wrote, "But here and there a mind was touched, not to a passionate excitement, but to a new way of thinking." John Woolman brought a religion which caused a sensitive spirit to turn and look at his life from a new angle. A "new way of thinking" is a far better response to the gospel than "passionate excitement."

127.   GETTING AN "AMEN!"

If you bless with the spirit, how can any one in the position of an out-
sider say the "Amen" to your thanksgiving when he does not know what
you are saying?   I COR. 14:16

These words bring the wisdom of Paul on the subject, how to get
an "Amen!" It is the height of common sense—you cannot get an
amen from people if they cannot understand what you are talking
about. That would seem obvious and elementary. But evidently it is
not. Many public speakers who tease the ears and minds of the
public have never heard of it.

There are two main senses of getting an amen. One is bad. The
desire to get an emphatic agreement from an audience, a resounding
amen, has been a corrupting force to multitudes of men and women.
To put the winning of heart-warming applause as the chief end of
life, to put in first place what Shakespeare called "to split the ears
of the groundlings," destroys one's ethical integrity. We see it in
political life, in the imitation "leader," who first finds out where
people are going, and then rushes in crying, "Follow me!" We find it
in the public speaker, who is anxious for a reputation, not in the
cannon's mouth but in the audience's roar, who will do anything for
a laugh. (A degenerate form of amen.) In our day, in the entertainment world, all roars are carefully measured.

With a preacher the danger to the mind and soul comes when the
agreement of the audience is the highest good. To get that, the gospel
is shorn of its stern demands and inconvenient questions. When that
is done we have a pulpit where never is heard a discouraging word,
and the sweet-sounding amens are heard every Sunday. Amos,
Micah, John the Baptist, St. Paul, and Jesus would not have won
the amens in such a congregation.

Paul is pleading for a wholehearted response to a whole gospel.
Such true exhilaration of the pulpit brings a positive amen of conviction. Often what Paul is here urging, a clear presentation of the
gospel, is missing. Some preachers go mumbling their way, issuing
murky Delphic oracles, as opaque as a painted window. Such obscure
proclamation of God's truth gets little more positive amen than the
passing of a ten-ton truck. So in this passage Paul reaches his climax,
which should be engraved on the pulpit where the preacher can see
it all the time, "I would rather speak five words with my mind, in

order to instruct others, than ten thousand words in a tongue." Five will put ten thousand to flight.

128. THE IMMATURE MIND

Do not be children in your thinking . . . in thinking be mature.
I COR. 14:20

All too often, the child as a symbol of entrance into the kingdom of God has been taken in a perverse sense. Instead of the qualities of a child, such as dependence and trust—true marks of a Christian —people have taken something vastly different, a *childish* religion. They become just what Paul warned against, "children in your thinking."

The religion Jesus proclaimed suffers a vast transformation when this nursery version appears. It is a form of religion bearing the name of Christianity but embodying many of the worst features of childishness. Paul cries out against this degenerate faith, "In thinking be mature." The Christian life is a fight from beginning to end. One of the decisive battles is that between the child and the man, between childishness and maturity.

One mark of childish thinking is that the child lives so completely in the immediate present. In the bright lexicon of childhood there is no such word as "tomorrow." He wants what he wants now. So it is a mark of immature thinking to let the present blot out the future. The immature mind prefers to take the cash and let the credit go.

In childish thinking inevitably there is an overwhelming concern for personal possessions of things that to a mature view are small. "My rattle" is overwhelmingly more important than "my world." In fact, "my world" does not enter the picture. That is also a mark of many older minds, older but not more mature. A mark even of philosophic minds. Bertrand Russell gives an almost incredible example of this mark of immaturity in the mind of George Santayana. He writes:

A few days before the battle of the Marne when the capture of Paris seemed imminent, he remarked to me, "I think I must go to Paris because my winter underclothes are all there, and I should not like the Germans to get them. I have also left there the manuscript of a book on which I have been working for the last ten years, but I don't mind so much about that."

The world seemed crashing to disaster, but one sweetly solemn thought crowded out all others—winter underclothes!

Childish thinking is wishful thinking. The only reality is "how I want things to be." Ogden Nash has given an impressive picture of this childish mentality, "I wish that all war consisted of was flags flying, and maybe a general getting shot once in a while, and a camp fire and soldiers sitting about it, singing Annie Laurie."

Another feature of childish thinking that every one of us knows all too well from our own experience is blaming all our faults on others. As a character in a contemporary novel explains it, "Society would be all right if it weren't for the other people." "Grow up into Christ"—in measurements and evaluations.

129. THEY FELL ON THEIR FACES

But if all prophesy, and an unbeliever or outsider enters, he is convicted by all, . . . the secrets of his heart are disclosed; and so, falling on his face, he will worship God and declare that God is really among you.
I COR. 14:24-25

It takes quite a demonstration to make a person "fall on his face"! Phillips makes it a bit easier, "fall on his knees." But face or knees, it takes quite a bit of doing .There is no doubt about the fall. Paul writes, "If all prophesy," in word and life, there is a convincing demonstration that God is present in the midst of the fellowship.

Centuries of history have borne out the truth of that. What has brought men to their knees, and has made them fall on their faces in worship, has been the demonstration that God is in the midst of the church, be the group large or small.

Outsiders through the years have asked the question first directed to the early Christians, "By what power or by what name did you do this?" (Acts 4:7). They have come to the conviction that a power out of this world has been at work. It is the persuasion by word and deed that "God is really among you."

That must be the church's secret weapon in all its warfare. It must possess the mind and life that convinces "outsiders"—the very word Paul uses—that God is really present, not by the might of numbers, nor by the power of great cathedrals, but by the spirit of God. There have been many detective stories, but the most exciting and important exercises in detection have been done by "outsiders," seeing if they can find any signs of God's presence and action. It is a sad story when the detectives report, "We find no signs of God being among them." It is a glorious story when they report, "God is really among you."

The same demonstration that God is among His people that was made in the first century of Christianity, is made continually in dedicated lives. One of the most touching reports of such a demonstration has come out of South Africa in its recent years of unchristian "apartheid." A Negro tells an amazing story of his life. Starting in the most abject poverty, he won the chance to go to a teacher's college. Here he met the first white men whose color he forgot, men of God who, as he said, "made Christianity a living reality for me." There, for a time, he fell on his face and worshiped God, convinced that he was really among God's friends.

Margaret Webster writes thus of putting Shakespeare on the stage today, "When living actors play living characters to living audiences the words put on flesh and become incandescent." Lift those words to the highest level. When living actors play the living character of Christ to living audiences, his words put on flesh and become incandescent.

130.   FAITH WITHOUT MEANING

Unless, of course, your faith had no meaning behind it all.   I COR. 15:2
(Phillips)

Faith with no meaning behind it! Surely that is the height of futility! Yet that is a good description of much conventional religion. During World War I a British sergeant was preparing new recruits for church parade. He warned, "When the Padre says the words, 'I believe,' and the rest of it, that is merely cautionary. It doesn't mean there is anything for you to do." There are many people, not in military uniform, for whom the great affirmations of the Christian do not mean anything for them to do. In Paul's words, there is "no meaning behind it all."

Dorothy Sayers has put this lack of great meaning to faith, on the part of many people, into vivid words. She writes of "frank and open pagans whose notions of Christianity are a dreadful jumble of rags and tags of Bible anecdote and clotted mythological nonsense." She writes of the "meek, gentle Jesus, sentimentality with humanistic ethics." The high meaning of the gospel, of God and man and society, is still Greek to them.

There is failure to take into the mind the staggering need for a relevant religion in our world. J. B. Priestley has put that need arrestingly. He writes, "It is good for men to open his mind to deep wonder and awe. . . . Without science we are helpless children. But without a deep religion we are blundering fools . . . reeling in our new and terrible cocksureness into one disaster after another."

Or when there is some idea of the importance of religion in the world, the knowledge is often a jumble. It is about as clear and compelling as the logic of Tweedledee in *Through the Looking-Glass*. He explains it, "If it was so, it might be; and if it were so, it would be; but as it isn't, it ain't. That's logic."

Or, there is no real meaning behind it all. Faith has been kept away a safe distance from life. Such disciples belong to the sect of Lord Melbourne who said that he yielded to none in his respect for religion, provided it did not interfere with a man's private life. They are like Theodore Roosevelt's devotion to peace, as described by G. W. Johnson. He said that Mr. Roosevelt "was always in favor of peace, provided it did not interfere with the fighting."

To prevent this calamity—Paul uses a vigorous word . . . "Hold fast." To hold fast means to take an unyielding grip on faith. That means retention of faith and its continual exercise. It is a far more gripping word than "I'll keep it in mind." For that often means I'll forget it in ten minutes.

131. CHRISTIANITY, AN HISTORICAL RELIGION

For I delivered to you as of first importance what I also received, that Christ died for our sins in accordance with the scriptures, that he was buried, that he was raised on the third day in accordance with the scriptures, and that he appeared to Cephas, then to the twelve. Then he appeared to more than five hundred brethren at one time, most of whom are still alive, though some have fallen asleep. Then he appeared to James, then to all the apostles. Last of all, as to one untimely born, he appeared also to me.   1 COR. 15:3–8

This passage of Paul, along with some others, such as 1 Cor. 11:23–26, proclaims emphatically that the Christian faith is an historical religion. Both the passages in 1 Corinthians begin with the word "received." There was already a tradition of historical fact. There was a core of message, the *Kerygma*, which was the vital center.

It ought to have been evident always that Christianity is an historical religion. But that has been far from the fact. Some of the great battles with heresy have been over the attempts, Gnosticism among others, to cut the ropes which attach Christianity to its foundations in history in the life, teachings, person, death, and resurrection of Jesus. After the attachments to history have been cut, Christianity could sail off into the blue of speculation, like a lost balloon. When our religion loses its local habitation and a name it evaporates into airy nothing.

Where this historical foundation is loosed, as in extreme forms of Calvinism, Jesus as the Revelation and Incarnation of the God of love was rendered into a dim and distant figure, and God into a Stern Lawgiver, caring for His elected saints.

132. THE CLIMAX OF THE RESURRECTION

Last of all, . . . he appeared also to me.   1 COR. 15:8

These words seem like a very definite anticlimax. Paul is giving the tremendous story of the Resurrection. He gives the appearances of the Risen Jesus, beginning with Cephas, then to the twelve, then to five hundred. "Last of all . . . also to me." But it is no anticlimax. The climax of a spiritual truth is always when it reaches a person, an individual, and becomes a living part of him. We can here leave aside the question of Biblical criticism whether Paul put Christ's appearance to him on a level with the other post-Resurrection appearances. Here for Paul was the great experience—"He appeared also to me."

The great liability of Christianity is public approval without private faith. That ruins many things. That was one of the causes of the death of the League of Nations. There was much public approval, protocol, assemblies, and enough gold braid to stretch across Europe. But not enough private faith on the part of nations to keep it alive.

So it is with Easter; not more public approval, but private faith, is needed, personal experience of truth. "Last of all, . . . he appeared also to me."

That personal experience, "Christ liveth in me," is a vital part of the Resurrection story. A young reporter on a newspaper turned in as one of his first assignments a report of a fire. He let his descriptive powers run riot. Half of the story was devoted to telling how he had seen a great light in the sky, and how he managed to get to the fire. The next day he found his long tale had been cut down to two inches, stating there had been a fire, where and when and the amount of damage. The city editor called him into his office and said, in a kindly way, "Always remember that how you got the story is not part of the story."

That may be true in the newspaper world; it is not true in Christian experience. How we got the story is emphatically a part of the story—how the grace of God came to us is part of the story of the grace of God. It was so with Paul. Three times in the book of Acts we have the record of his being on trial. Each time he made the same defense. He told his judge how the story came to him. "I was going down to Jerusalem and something happened. I saw a great light and heard a voice saying, 'Saul, Saul.'" How he got the story of the Risen Christ was a part, a loved part, a wonderful part, of the story. "Last of all he appeared to me also."

133. BARREN GIFTS

The grace he gave me has not proved a barren gift.   I COR. 15:10 (Phillips)

What a tremendous thing to say! "His grace was not a barren gift to me"! How few of us would dare to say it or even think it! How many gifts of God's grace have become barren to those who received it? Jesus drew the perfect picture, that of a man forgiven by his master for a debt amounting to thousands of dollars, rushing out to seize a poor man who owed him comparatively a few cents. So we have seen a person hard, unyielding, and yet forgiven, refusing to forgive another. The words they have said thousand of times, "As we forgive our debtors," are still unknown to them. As far as they are concerned God's grace has been a barren gift.

Life should bloom like a garden. There is a garden more wonderful than any Garden of Eden. Here is God's garden: "The fruit of the Spirit is love, joy, peace, patience, kindness, goodness, faithfulness, gentleness, self-control" (Gal. 5:22–23). To see such a garden in a life is earth's fairest sight.

So often, instead of a garden, there is a sort of desert. Step down the lanes of observation, in the thought of gifts which become barren. One reason for this tragedy is that the attention becomes focused on distinctly minor affairs. One of the patrons of Leonardo da Vinci was Ludovico il Moro. He would frequently take Leonardo away from painting "The Last Supper," and put him to work devising "ingenious mechanisms" for theatricals. Do we not often come pretty nearly doing much the same?

Again, the gift of joyous living so easily becomes a barren gift. We do not keep the poetry which Christ puts into life. Rupert Brooke thus declared his life's dedication. "There are only three things, one is to read poetry; one is to write poetry; the best of all is to live poetry."

To live the poetry of the gospel, surely that is the best of all.

134. THE KEY TO LIFE'S TREASURE

I am what I am.   I COR. 15:10

We often hear these words. But often the inmost thoughts, read by Him to whom no secrets are hid, are more nearly like this: "By my remarkable genius and by my superhuman power, I am what I am." Occasionally God is credited with an assist, but not with much more.

The person who admits such thoughts, even into the darkened chambers of his mind and heart, should remember rule one of the life of the spirit, that humility, not in much-studied words, but so deep that it is unconscious, is the only key which admits to Christian discipleship. Anything worth while is the gift of God. Humility is the key to *learning* anything, and the key to becoming anything worth while.

Also, there is a parallel to these words, a sort of parody on them which deserves attention. It has the clear-eyed observation of a drunk, sitting on a curbstone watching the cars go by. He watches a Cadillac roll by and says, "There but for me, go I." True. The "me" who took life out of control destroyed the potential "I." In that sense life's crucial battle is between the "me" and the possible "I".

135. IF CHRIST HAD NOT BEEN RAISED

If Christ has not been raised, then our preaching is in vain and your faith is in vain.   I COR. 15:14

These words are, among other things, evidence of the central place of the Resurrection in the earliest message, the *Kerygma* of the

Christian church. It was not an ethical culture society which made its way through the Greek and Roman world. There were plenty of those. Good ones too. It was the story of a man who lived, taught, died, and rose again which won converts by the multitudes. The essential message was that of Jesus and the Resurrection.

That basic conviction grows in importance in our day when the main grasp of the truth of the Resurrection and life eternal is slackening among large parts of Christian people.

Take away that faith in Christ rising from the dead—and much remains. Jesus remains, the teacher remains, the Master remains. But the Savior is gone! There is little foundation for faith in a redeemed world. Such a faith must cover more time than Wednesday afternoon, or time itself. There is no hope for a redeemed world if there is nothing that transcends this earth and time itself.

Things often get so bad that only eternity can heal them. If Christ was not raised from the dead, there is no healing. John Masefield has expressed this powerfully in a dramatic scene from his poem, *The Widow in the Bye Street.* A widow is present at the execution of her son. She is moved to pray, and in her prayer for her son, she refers to the hope of eternal life as "a rest for broken things too broke to mend." There was no mending anything on earth for her son. Only the Eternal God can deal with things "too broke to mend."

This is to be held close in the mind to another truth about eternal life. Eternal life means the *quality* of life rather than its length. As one has said, "Easter is not a passport to another world, but a quality of life for this one."

136. THE INEVITABLE TOMORROW

Tomorrow we die. I COR. 15:32

The words here, "eat, drink, and be merry," is one of the world's best-known invitations. It has brought large crowds answering the call. The first two items on the program have almost become professions. Indeed, the gourmet, who devotes his life to eating with all the high seriousness of an anchorite fasting in the desert, plays quite a role among the top brackets. So with the invitation—drink. Cocktails can become a kind of lifework, with its own arts and sciences.

But the third point stumps a great host. Eat, drink—yes. But "be merry"; that has been harder to get going than a broken-down jalopy on a zero morning. All the push buttons in our push-button world will not insure completing the third point of the three-point program, "eat, drink, and be merry." The word that frequently begins as a magic "open sesame," that is, the words "fill 'em up," loses its power. The magic is over.

A foreign critic—perhaps he was a cynic as well—wrote that one vivid memory of America to him was "the appalling efforts of people to entertain themselves." His remark gives evidence that he spent lots of time checking up on the playboys and playgirls. He would have had something to fill out his picture if he had seen more of "the appalling efforts" of men and women and children to keep themselves alive.

The real reason for the collapse of point three, "be merry," is found in what might be called point four—"tomorrow we die." When the dimension of eternity is taken out of life, life shrinks. It is Paul's assurance here that our religion shrinks. "If the dead are not raised" then our faith becomes merely a form of ethical culture. Christ risen from the dead gives depth to life. There is an irreplaceable loss of a power of compulsion if eternal life drops from visibility. Robert A. Millikan, Nobel Prize winner in physics, expressed this connection vividly in his autobiography:

I do not see how there can be any sense of duty or any reason for unselfish conduct which is entirely divorced from the conviction that there is Something and Someone in the universe which gives meaning and significance to life. And no sense of value can possibly inhere in mere lumps of dead matter interacting according to purely mechanical laws.

Society itself pushes the word of eternity out of its life and thought only to court and meet disaster. These words of T. S. Eliot, from "Choruses from the Rock," might be taken with terrible seriousness as an "epitaph for a godless people":

A Cry from the North, from the West and from the South
Whence thousands travel daily to the timekept City;
Where My Word is unspoken,
In the land of lobelias and tennis flannels
The rabbit shall burrow and the thorn revisit,
The nettle shall flourish on the gravel court,
And the wind shall say: "Here were decent godless people:
Their only monument the asphalt road
And a thousand lost golf balls."

137. THEREFORE—

Therefore, my beloved brethren, be steadfast, immovable, always abounding in the work of the Lord, knowing that in the Lord your labor is not in vain. I COR. 15:58

Here is the grand conclusion of the Resurrection, the motive power which it brings to life. You can almost hear it rushing by, like a swollen river in spring when a dam has broken. "The victory through our Lord Jesus Christ"; then, with hardly a stop for breath, *"therefore."* That is apostolic logic. It is God's logic. "Death is swallowed up"—therefore! Bring this power to bear on life. The knowledge that your labor is not vain in the Lord brings endless energy and propulsion.

It answers one of life's questions which sometimes stares us down. This is how William E. Henley framed it:

> O how shall summer's homey breath hold out
> Against the wrackful siege of battering days!

What a description of life—"siege of battering days!" Yet, some days do batter, do they not? It is eternal life realized here and now which conquers the battering. Henley's own, "I am the captain of my soul," can't do it.

It is a gloriously irrational faith. Faith in the Resurrection does not come at the end of a syllogism. It does come at the end of life lived in the power of the Son of God.

Yet the irrational eternal world does find rational guideposts pointing in its direction. Here is a pointing post erected by a great physicist, Dr. Arthur H. Compton. He protests against incredible waste:

> It takes a whole life time to build the character of a noble man. The exercise of the discipline of youth, the pains and pleasures of reality, the loneliness and tranquility of age. These make up the fire through which we must press to bring out the gold in the soul. Having thus been perfected, what shall nature do with him? Annihilate him? What infinite waste!

138.   LAY SOMETHING ASIDE

*On the first day of every week, each of you is to put something aside
and store it up, as he may prosper.*   1 COR. 16:2

Once and for all, St. Paul has announced that the Resurrection and
collection belong together. The news has not yet reached a large
number of retarded minds, but, without giving, there is an unfin-
ished Resurrection. Putting something aside as a habit means getting into a larger world, into God's time and space, where His whole
family lives. One great achievement of putting something aside
every week is that we get impulse into habit. If we just give on the
spot as we happen to be moved or too embarrassed to refuse, we
will come to regard our giving of ten dollars as practically equivalent
to paying the national debt. What we do with our money throws a
strong clear light on what we are.

The surest indication of what kind of a person you are is to be
found among the stubs of your old checkbooks.

A man who has written many biographies made that discovery.
He noted that it was easy to find out what a man said and what he
had done, but when it came to finding out what kind of a man he
really was, the biographer was up a stump. Then he discovered that
the surest way to get the truth was to look at the stubs of old checkbooks. What a man gives money for—that tells the tale.

An old checkbook gossips about us. What does it say about you?

If a man's giving is regular and proportionate, the records of his
financial transactions say: This man really cares. But if his giving is
haphazard or inadequate compared to other expenditures, the checkbook says: This man won't even put God and His work on a level
with the butcher, the baker, and the candlestickmaker, which today
is the electric light company.

In the Dark Ages, when Christianity was making its first impact
on northern Europe, large numbers of the savage tribe of Franks
were immersed. But, they were not quite sure they wanted to give
up their savage battle, so many would go into the water holding
their battle-axes out of the water. They would say, "This hand has
never been baptized," so they could swing it again in slaughter.

We do not carry battle-axes today; they are rather inconvenient.
But we do carry pocketbooks, and often Christian people seem to
lift their wallets on high and, by their meager contributions, proclaim, "This pocketbook has never been baptized."

Regular proportionate giving is the best way of baptizing the pocketbook into the service of God and man.

139. APOSTOLIC GRAMMAR

But I will stay in Ephesus until Pentecost, for a wide door for effective work has opened to me, and there are many adversaries.   1 COR. 16:8–9

What might be well called "apostolic grammar" is often very different from ours. One point of vital difference is the use and placement of the disjunctive conjunction. Among such adversative or disjunctive conjunctions are such words as "but," "however," "consequently."

In the sentence of Paul's, printed above, notice how he uses the word "but." He writes about Ephesus, "There is a wide door for effective work, and lots of adversaries. *But* I will stay on." We so often use the word but in a different place in the sentence and we might say, "True, there is a wide-open door for work, *but* there are many terrible adversaries, so I will pull out." Instead of a fighting flag of battle which shows in Paul's sentence, we can see the white flag of surrender in our sentence. To Paul the word "but" meant a rally. To us it means often a headlong rout.

One of the great acts of life is to put the word "but" in the right place. A perfect illustration of this apostolic use of the word "but" is the gorgeous parade of this word as it marches before us in 2 Cor. 4:8–9:

We are afflicted in every way, *but* not crushed; perplexed, *but* not driven to despair; persecuted, *but* not forsaken; struck down, *but* not destroyed.

Life's crushing defeats overcome by a resolute, "But not crushed."

Thus, by apostolic logic there are three steps to every great decision for service to God and man: First, great opportunities. Secondly, terrific obstacles. Thirdly, let's go!

140. PUT HIM AT HIS EASE

When Timothy comes, see that you put him at his ease among you, for he is doing the work of the Lord, as I am. I COR. 16:10

At first glance, this putting a person at ease seems to be distinctly a minor virtue, only a bit of etiquette, and among many thoughtless people, etiquette has come to be regarded as beneath the notice of a big person. It is too genteel, a trivial ritual of little importance.

Of course, there is much to be condemned in the formalism of small minds, who obey with painful exactitude the canons of social behavior but miss the big issues of life. Thus—

> *To dress, to call, to dine, to break*
> *No canon of the social code,*
> *The little laws that lackeys make*
> *The futile decalog of mode.*
> *How many a soul for these things lives,*
> *With pious passion, grave intent*
> *And never even in dreams has seen*
> *The things that are more excellent!*

But true etiquette is courtesy, and that can be an authentic expression of love. No rule of conduct springs more directly from the motive of love to God and man, than this injunction to the church at Corinth about Timothy, "Put him at his ease."

There are many great things about this act of courtesy. It calls for imagination, the truly divine power of creation. So Paul can say to them, "Timothy is lonesome—he is under suspicion by some of you. You did not invite him. He needs sympathy and friendship. They restore and fortify the soul." So Paul says, "As you stand before Christ, put Timothy at his ease."

Think of the people who have followed that idea during the centuries. They have written a great epic of love. Putting one at his ease has had its victories, nor less than gigantic battles, in the story of the Christian church. One of the deeply moving stories on this truth has to do with the lightning mind of Phillips Brooks. It is found in the autobiography of William S. Rainsford. Young Mr. Rainsford was sent from England at an early age, to take part in an evangelistic movement in the Episcopal Church. The first mass meeting was held in Boston. Young Mr. Rainsford had the main address. As Dr. Rainsford described it much later, it was a total eclipse. He grew so tongue-tied that he had to stop. He sat down with only one hope, that the earth would swallow him up. The earth did not oblige, so he was left, a humiliated failure. Then, he says, he felt a strong hand on his shoulder and heard a kindly voice say, "Mr. Rainsford, I want you to preach for me next Sunday in Trinity Church." That was the voice of Phillips Brooks. It was also the beginning of Dr. Rainsford's wonderful ministry at St. George's Church, New York City. The lightning-swift imagination of Phillips Brooks saved a man for a lifetime of service, by "putting him at his ease."

Some people cannot do it, or will not do it, because they are naturally cold. They act like two-legged polar bears, except that the bears are more playful. Emily Dickinson's father was a notable member of that polar tribe. His son kissed him on the forehead as he lay in his coffin and said, "There father, I have done in death what I never dared to do in life."

It is often said of a man, half in tribute and half in apology, that he does not "suffer fools gladly." A caution is demanded there. Be very careful about the use of that word "fool." It is a deadly word; its careless use is a sin. One drifts easily into the habit of contemptuous disdain for the human race.

But, also, it is deadly because not to bother about people, on the ground that they are fools, makes one harsh and bitter and increases selfishness.

To put a person at ease, in the spirit of sympathy and the spirit of Jesus, calls for the practice of the Golden Rule, "Act, as you would have others do unto you."

This is a fitting text for the coming years in the United States, when the critical aching questions of justice in race relations and segregation in schools will have to be treated. Consider the little Negro child who wishes to claim his inheritance of freedom and opportunities in America. When that young fellow citizen comes, "Put him at ease."

141. *EN GARDE!*

Be on your guard.   I COR. 16:13 (Phillips)

A deadly enemy of religious faith and life is sleep. It is the vacant
mind which allows dangers to creep up unnoticed, and great opportunities to pass by unseized. The New Testament is full of warnings
against the sleepy life. There is the parable of the Wise and Foolish
Virgins, the cautions to watch and pray. The inclusion of the petition "lead us not into temptation" in the Lord's Prayer is evidence of
the seriousness with which Jesus took falling into temptation and
disaster by thoughtlessness.

Of course, the church has had a hard struggle with sleep ever since
Eutychus fell from a rafter in a house where Paul was preaching.
To the Puritans in New England, sleepiness was a sin, and was
sternly reproved by professional awakeners. Ola Winslow thus describes the exorcizing of the devils of sleep in her book, *Meeting-
house Hill:*

To know that "laying downe ye head upon ye arms in a sleeping
posture" during sermon time was taboo, was enough to make the urge
irresistible, as the toll of those guilty of "ye carnal sin of sleepiness,
(extraordinary cases excepted)" will show in almost any congregation.
Similarly, the minor comfort of reaching in one's tobacco pouch pocket,
turning one's back on the minister before the final blessing was pronounced, or rejoicing in the freedom of the street once it was all over
(that is, until two o'clock in the afternoon)—the very thought was an
invitation to trespass.

In passing it should be a good thing for preachers to remember
that there are no longer professional tithing men or awakeners, to
go through the congregation to stir up the drowsy. If there is to be
any awakening at all, it must come from the preacher. He must
reach out and lay a firm hand on the shoulder of the congregation
and say those words, dear to the heart of a policeman, "You might
as well come along quietly." For the preacher is a policeman, trying
to make an arrest.

Consider two reasons for alert watchfulness of things that get past
the unguarded gates of the mind. *One is the danger of taking on
protective coloration from our environment.* It is the capacity for
survival which makes white animals in the Arctic snowdrifts, and
gives to many animals a camouflaged green in the tropics. Without

the alarm check of "watch and pray," we take the protective coloration. The subtle words, "All these things will I give thee, if thou wilt fall down and worship me," drown out other words, or make them seem harsh, "We must obey God rather than man."

Mr. Chesterton has pictured this vividly, and it is not nearly as fanciful as it might seem. He says that at the beginning of the industrial revolution, Satan took the British Middle Class up into a high mountain and pointed out the factories and smokestacks and said, "All these things will I give thee, if thou wilt fall down and worship me." He says "the British Middle Class immediately closed with the offer." When we recall the slaughter of the children in mine and factory, which went on in the early days of the industrial revolution, we know that is exactly what happened!

There are subtle ways of falling down and worshiping Satan. We do it most effectively by taking a commercial view of success. We do it by yielding to alluring compromises with evil practice; we do it by a firm trust in militarism and war.

One other thing which calls for the *en garde* of the wakeful spirit is fear. We read that "love casts out fear." But unhappily the reverse can be true and is true. Aldous Huxley has reminded us in great detail that "fear casts out love." Fear casts out intelligence, casts out goodness. Fear obscures reality and keeps the individual self-centered.

The command for every day is the same. *"En garde!"*

142. THE HIGH ART OF REFRESHING

They refreshed my spirit.   I COR. 16:18

Not all your friends would be readily classed as "refreshments." They may be—and are—people of integrity, straight as a telegraph pole and just about as charming and alluring. Such saints may win many adjectives on their pilgrimage through life. They are given noble adjectives, too, such as "useful," "loyal," and "courageous." Yet one adjective never springs to our lips in this connection, the gorgeous adjective, which St, Paul uses of Stephanas, and Fortunatus, and Achaicus—"refreshing." We would give much to know more about them and in just what ways they were refreshing to Paul. He writes as though it were more than food or drink. They brought refreshing spirits, a much headier drink than any liquid on earth.

What a tribute Paul pays to this trio. Phillips gets great feeling into his translation, "They are a tonic to me." Their very presence brought a bracing invigoration of spirit, so that the whole being tingled with life, even though Paul spent a good deal of his time getting in and out of jails.

This quality of refreshment is hard to analyze just as spring is hard to analyze. It is much better to get down on your knees and thank heaven, fasting, for people who bring refreshment.

Without too much analysis, grapple them to your heart with hoops of steel. Paul had a lot of hoops of that sort, a wonderful collection of refreshing friends. His hoops are on exhibit in the last chapter of his Epistles. The end of the first letter to the church at Corinth, his 16th chapter, is short, but even so, seven refreshing spirits pass by. In the last chapter of Romans about thirty appear. Paul was a great friend, as well as a great apostle.

Some marks of a "refresher" appear. A heart at leisure from itself, so that it does not need its pound of advantage or boastful comment. It is a real thrill to find that this person talking to you is not trying to sell you anything. There is no apprehensive danger that the mask of cordiality will fall and the sales talk begin, just as a corner huckster will do a few tricks, and then from under the counter draw out bottles of snake oil to sell.

Sometimes one's face is no great refreshment. Yet for anyone, a pair of smiling eyes and a few wrinkles around a grin will turn a February face into something suggesting June, and make an enchanting invitation.

John Bunyan was never ordained by any church. But he was ordained by the Holy Spirit of God to be a power for refreshment. He felt that seriousness and gaiety had been joined by God and ought not to be put asunder by man.

T. R. Glover writes about Bunyan as both gay and serious. "Bunyan gave the full expression of his mind, so full of life and humor, so full of experience, gaiety and seriousness at once."

Bunyan himself wrote words which ought to be studied by all solemn souls. In the Second Part of Pilgrim's Progress, Mr. Feeble Mind confesses his ways of thinking, "I shall like no laughing, I shall like no gay attire, I shall like no unprofitable questions, nay, I am so weak a man as to be offended with that which others have a liberty to do."

Feeble Mind was no tonic to anyone. He was the devil's secret service operator, always ready with his dumb wits by utter misrepresentation to discourage the Christian play of life.

It is a high role to which to aspire—He refreshed me. Most of us will not sit on the seats of the mighty. But we can serve God and man mightily on a different level when anyone can say, "He refreshed my spirit."

We read often the beautiful lines of Sara Teasdale:

> *Places I know come back to me like music*
> *Hush me and heal me when I am very tired.*

True. But far more often and a far more wonderful healing is found when the "refresher" comes into view or memory.

NOTES

PAGE	LINE	
13	22–33	Gilbert Highet, *A Clerk of Oxenford: Essays on Literature and Life* (New York: Oxford University Press, 1954).
16	11–26	Richard Burton, "The Modern Saint" (New York: Lothrop, Lee and Shephard).
15	26–32	F. W. H. Myers, "Saint Paul," from *Collected Poems* (London: Macmillan Co., 1921). Used by permission.
17	10–13	Reginald Heber, "From Greenland's Icy Mountains."
18–19	36 ff.	Kate O'Brien, *Romance of English Literature* (New York: Hastings House, 1944).
19	9–13	*Ibid.*
21–22	30 ff.	Berton Braley, from "A Song of Power," in *Poems for a Machine Age,* edited by Horace McNeil (New York: The McGraw-Hill Book Co., Inc., 1941).
24	12–16	Lawrence S. Kubie, *Saturday Review,* Oct., 1956.
	22–27	Ellen Glasgow, *The Woman Within* (New York: Harcourt, Brace & Co., 1954).
26	7–11	George Gaylord Simpson, *Life of the Past* (New Haven: Yale University Press, 1953).
	22–29	W. T. Stace, *Religion and the Modern Mind* (Philadelphia: J. B. Lippincott Co., 1952).
	37–42	Alfred Noyes, *Collected Poems* (Philadelphia: J. B. Lippincott Co., 1947). Used by permission.
33	1–4	Kingsley, "A Farewell."
34	40–41	John Drinkwater, "A Prayer," from *Poems, 1902–1919* (Boston: Houghton Mifflin Company, 1920).
35–36	28 ff.	Phyllis McGinley, "A Little Night Music," in *Harper's Magazine,* Nov., 1957.
37	25–28	Isaac Watts, "When I Survey the Wondrous Cross."
38	9–13	Canon Edward West. Used by permission.

PAGE	LINE	
40	23–33	Dr. Karl Menninger, in *The Churchman*.
41	10–13	Walter Chalmers Smith.
43–44	36 ff.	Parker Morell, *Diamond Jim: The Life and Times of James Buchanan Brady* (New York: Simon & Schuster, 1934).
44	13–21	"Wilderness," from *Cornhuskers* by Carl Sandburg. Copyright, 1918, by Henry Holt and Company, Inc. Copyright, 1946, by Carl Sandburg. Used by permission of the publishers.
45	12–17	Agnes Rogers Allen, "Irresolution," from *Harper's Magazine*, Aug., 1946. Used by permission of the author.
46	24–32	Dorothy L. Sayers, *Creed or Chaos?* (New York: Harcourt, Brace & Co., 1949).
46–47	35 ff.	Stephen Vincent Benét, "Minor Litany," from *The Selected Works of Stephen Vincent Benét* (New York: Rinehart & Company, Inc., copyright, 1940, by Stephen Vincent Benét). Used by permission.
48	19–25	St. John Ervine, *Bernard Shaw* (New York: Morrow and Co., 1956).
54	3–18	Morris Bishop, "The Perforated Spirit," copyright © 1955 The New Yorker Magazine, Inc.
	22–26	Harry Stack Sullivan, *Interpersonal Theory of Psychiatry* (New York: W. W. Norton & Co., Inc., 1953).
56	27–33	Erich Heller, *The Disinherited Mind* (New York: Farrar, Straus and Cudahy, 1957).
57	9–12	*The Merchant of Venice*, Act II, sc. 2.
59	6–9; 11–22	Bertrand Russell, *The Sunday Times*, London, Nov. 10, 1957.
59–60	42 1–3	Louis Untermeyer, *Makers of the Modern World* (New York: Simon & Schuster, 1956).
62	3–8	Arthur Schlesinger, Jr., *Crisis of the Old Order* (Boston: Houghton Mifflin Co., 1957).
63	32–34	Evelyn Hardy, *Thomas Hardy* (New York: St. Martin's Press, 1954).
63–64	38 ff.	Lawrence L. Green, *White Man's Grave* (New York: S. Paul, 1954).
65	6–9	*Letters of William James,* edited by his son, Henry James (Boston: Houghton Mifflin Co., 1920), Vol. I.

PAGE	LINE	
67	22–27	*Dialogues of A. N. Whitehead,* recorded by Lucien Price (Boston: Little, Brown & Co., 1954).
70	21–25	W. Somerset Maugham, *A Writer's Notebook* (New York: Doubleday & Co., 1949).
71	3–5	Christopher Fry, *The Lady's Not for Burning* (New York: Oxford University Press, 1950). Used by permission of the publisher.
73	29–32	Albert Einstein, *Out of My Later Years* (New York: Philosophical Library, 1950).
74	5–8	St. John Ervine, *Bernard Shaw.*
75	31–34	Emily Dickinson, in *Collected Poems of Emily Dickinson,* edited by Martha Dickinson Bianchi (Boston: Little, Brown & Co., 1924).
76	2–5	H. G. Wells, *The Future in America* (New York: Harper & Brothers, 1906).
77	33–37	William L. Miller, in *Christianity and Crisis,* April, 1957.
78	6–9	Ralph Waldo Emerson, oration at Amherst College.
	13–15	Peter Maurin, in *The New Yorker,* article on Dorothy Day, Oct. 4, 1952.
	21–23	Henry van Dyke, *Essays in Application* (New York: Charles Scribner's Sons, 1905).
86	21–30	Logan Pearsall Smith, *All Trivia* (New York: Harcourt, Brace & Co., 1921, 1945).
87	7–12	Carleton S. Coon, *The Story of Man* (New York: Alfred Knopf, 1954).
89	32–36	Edward Gibbon, *Decline and Fall of the Roman Empire.*
91	9–19	J. B. Priestley, *Rain Upon Godshill* (New York: Harper & Brothers, 1939).
95	29–34	Bertrand Russell, address in New York, 1950.
98	14–17	Phillips Brooks, "O Little Town of Bethlehem."
100	3–11	Orville Prescott, in *The New York Times,* May 7, 1951.
	20–24	*Selected Speeches of Booker T. Washington,* edited by E. Davidson Washington (New York: Doubleday, 1932).
102	32–37	Dorothy Canfield Fisher, *The Vermont Tradition* (Boston: Little, Brown & Co., 1953).
103	3–5	*Origen's Works,* English translation by H. Chadwick.

PAGE	LINE	
105	34	John Masefield, "Consecration," in *The Collected Poems* (New York: The Macmillan Company, 1953).
106	7–10	Frank Swinnerton, *Background with Chorus* (London: Hutchinson, 1956).
	17–18	Emily Post, *Etiquette* (New York: Funk & Wagnalls, 1950).
107	34–38	Arthur Schlesinger, Jr., *Crisis of the Old Order*.
110	32–36	Mason Wade, *Margaret Fuller* (New York: Viking Press, 1940).
115	24–37	Phyllis McGinley, "Mid-century Love Letter," from *The Love Letters of Phyllis McGinley* (New York: The Viking Press, 1954). Used by permission of the publisher.
119	9–14	G. G. Coulton, *Mediaeval Panorama* (New York: Meridian Books, 1955).
121	31–42	Lewis Mumford, in *The Saturday Review*.
124	26–28	Bernard Shaw, quote in the Preface to *Androcles and the Lion*.
125	9–18	John Galsworthy, *Addresses in America* (New York: Charles Scribner's Sons, 1919).
127	33–38	*Anne Douglas Sedgwick. A Portrait with Letters*, chosen and edited by Basil de Sélincourt (Boston: Houghton Mifflin Co., 1936).
128	8–12	Leigh Hunt, *Autobiography*.
129	21–24	*Russell Cheney 1881–1945; A Record of His Work*, with notes by F. O. Matthiessen (New York: Oxford University Press, 1947).
129–130	31 ff.	T. R. Glover, in *The Christian World*, London.
131	26–30	Dr. Frederick Grant, in *The Churchman*, Jan. 15, 1952.
133	33–39	José Ortega y Gasset, *The Revolt of the Masses*, 1932.
134	7–12	James A. Michener, in *Holiday Magazine*, Aug., 1952.
	37–38	James Russell Lowell, *The Biglow Papers*, Series I, No. I.
135	5–9	Associated Press dispatch from Big Stone Gap, Va., Aug. 5, 1953.
141	7–24	"Emily Sparks," from *Spoon River Anthology* by Edgar Lee Masters (New York: The Macmillan Company, 1915).

PAGE	LINE	
142	18–36	J. B. Priestley, in *The Saturday Review*, July 27, 1946.
143	1–5	Margaret Webster, *Shakespeare without Tears* (New York: The McGraw-Hill Co., 1942).
144	13–18	Dorothy L. Sayers, *Creed or Chaos?*
	23–25	Lewis Mumford, *The Condition of Man* (New York: Harcourt, Brace & Co., 1944).
148	21–24	Eliseo Vivas, quoted by Bernard Iddings Bell in *Crowd Culture* (New York: Harper & Brothers, 1952).
149	24–26	*Ego: The Autobiography of James Agate* (London: H. Hamilton, 1935).
	33–34	Lewis Browne, *Something Went Wrong* (New York: The Macmillan Co., 1942).
151	25–29	Henry James, Sr., in letter to Emerson, quoted in Van Wyck Brooks, *The Flowering of New England* (New York: E. P. Dutton & Co., 1936).
	37–38	Francis Otto Matthiessen, *The James Family* (New York: Alfred A. Knopf, 1947).
154	8–13	Alfred Tennyson, "Ulysses."
156–157	37 ff.	Prayers for the Church Service League, Massachusetts Council of the Church Service League, Boston, 1930.
160–161	37 ff.	Edward W. Weeks, *The Open Heart* (Boston: Little, Brown & Co., 1955).
162	22–27	John Milton, *The Reason of Church Government*.
	39–42	Bergen Evans, *The Spoor of Spooks* (New York: Alfred A. Knopf, 1954).
164	2–3	Stephen Spender, "I think continually of Those," in *Ruins and Visions* (New York: The Modern Library, 1954). Used by permission of Random House, Inc.
	32–37	Louis MacNeice, "Bar Room Matins," from *Poems 1925–40* (New York: Random House, Inc., 1940).
167	28–34	*The New York Times*, Oct. 6, 1958.
168	25–30	Chris Emmett, *Shanghai Pierce: A Fair Likeness* (Norman, Okla.: University of Oklahoma Press, 1955).
169	20–26	Ola Elizabeth Winslow, *Meetinghouse Hill: 1630–1783* (New York: The Macmillan Company, 1952).

PAGE	LINE	
174	30–33	Newton Arvin, *Hawthorne* (Boston: Little, Brown & Co., 1919).
176	24–34	Robert Reyfield, in *The Saturday Review*, Sept. 26, 1953.
181	36–40	*Fighting Liberal, Autobiography of George W. Norris* (New York: The Macmillan Company, 1945).
182	10–15	*Albert Schweitzer: An Anthology*, edited by Charles R. Joy (New York: Harper & Brothers, 1947).
183	17–21	Pearl S. Buck, *My Several Worlds: A Personal Record* (New York: The John Day Co., 1954).
189	6–11	Dr. J. Robert Oppenheimer, in an address at the Columbia University Bicentennial Celebration, 1955, as reported in *The New York Times*.
	15–19	William James, *The Varieties of Religious Experience* (London: Longmans, Green & Co., 1929).
190	26–28	Harry A. Overstreet, *The Mature Mind* (New York: W. W. Norton & Co., Inc., 1949).
194	10–12	William Troy, in *Forms of Modern Fiction*, edited by William V. O'Connor (Minneapolis: University of Minnesota Press, 1948).
	35–37	John Woolman, *Journal and Other Writings* (New York: E. P. Dutton & Co., Inc., Everyman Edition).
196	32–37	Bertrand Russell, *Portraits from Memory* (New York: Simon & Schuster, Inc., 1957).
198	15–16	Margaret Webster, *Shakespeare without Tears*.
	33–37	Dorothy L. Sayers, *Creed or Chaos?*
199	3–6	J. B. Priestley, *Rain Upon Godshill*.
204	21–26	Robert A. Millikan, *Autobiography* (New York: Prentice-Hall Co., 1950).
	31–39	T. S. Eliot, "The Rock," copyright, 1934, by Harcourt, Brace & Co., used by permission of the publisher.
210	15–23	Ola Elizabeth Winslow, *Meetinghouse Hill: 1630–1783*.
212	30–32	T. R. Glover, *Poets and Puritans* (London: Methuen & Co., 1923).